Press Relations Practice

by the same author

Copywriting and its Presentation

Public Relations in World Marketing

both published by Crosby Lockwood & Son Ltd

Press Relations Practice

by Frank Jefkins
MAA, MIPR, MinstM, MAIE

INTERTEXT BOOKS, LONDON

Published by
International Textbook Company Ltd
Intertext House, Parkgate Road, London, S.W.1.

First published 1968
SBN 7002 0076 2

Printed in Great Britain by
Butler & Tanner Ltd, Frome and London

Preface

This is a book which someone should have written many years ago; and although I have assembled what I believe to be the best ways of practising press relations, this would not have been possible if real masters of the craft had not left their mark during preceding decades. As examples of this I have quoted some of the work produced by Freddie Gillman at BOAC several years ago, releases in which not a word is wasted.

But the trouble is that press relations is an activity which looks to be so easy it does not have to be learned, yet the standard of the average press release is abysmal and that is being rather polite. Too many writers of press releases have forgotten how hard it was learning to walk and talk. In similar fashion they fail to accept that the practice of press relations has to be learned too, and this is not helped by the mistaken belief held by press officers and employers alike that any journalist automatically makes a good press officer. The majority of press releases scornfully spiked by editors every day are written by ex-journalists who know little about press relations and even less about public relations. This book is therefore something of a challenge, and if any reader does think he knows it all I would recommend him to compare his work with the releases reproduced here from Eric Buston & Associates Ltd of Bristol.

Many people have very kindly sent me specimens and case histories for inclusion in this book, and I am extremely grateful for their help. Acknowledgements are included in the text where applicable. But it is very difficult to find any really excellent examples, and I have gone through hundreds of press releases which I have collected from many sources. I have even asked editors to send me good specimens. Quite honestly, if a national contest were held for press releases I doubt if there would be many award winners. The standard of British press release writing is far, far below that of, say, advertisement copywriting, direct mail creation or house journal editing. But then the experts claim that the subject cannot be taught. It can and it must if PR is to meet the challenge of the 70's, when I am convinced there is going to be a tremendous demand for every kind of PR service and precious few trained and skilled practitioners to meet the demand.

Not too much has been said in this book about education and training because at this moment the IPR is in the throes of re-organising its examination structure. Nor have I referred to the NUJ, although the NUJ is very active in the field of PR and very much alive to the needs of recruitment into PR and training for PR. But the IPR and the NUJ (and also the AA, IPA and Institute of Marketing) have much to contribute to the raising of press relations standards.

Although I have been closely associated with publishing, and have written a good deal, I came into PR not from staff journalism but from advertising and freelance journalism. In fact I had the sort of Publicity Manager jobs which require press relations as well as advertising skills. I had to write advertisement copy and press releases—and know the difference!—although in those junior days we called press relations editorial publicity.

Consequently, I am in the fairly unusual position of being able to see PR from most points of view, and I have attempted to present some of these contrary and sometimes violently varying viewpoints in chapters 17 and 18. I have also projected some thoughts on the future of industrial advertising and the trade and technical press, the occasions when advertising can be a waste of money and PR an investment, and the need for and problems restricting the use of research techniques as aids in the planning and testing of PR operations. Some of these thoughts may be provocative but they are not intended to be conclusive. PR is where advertising was 30 years ago—where I came in!—and PR is at the present time a very imperfect business requiring a great deal of open-ended thinking.

Nevertheless, press relations remains the bread and butter of much of everyday PR. If we don't know how to lay our bricks we shan't be able to build our house. Therefore, the theme of this book is that press relations seeks no favours but will be favoured if it helps editors and others to gain appreciative readers and audiences. In so doing it provides a service which can be an important facet in the marketing scheme of any type of organisation—public, voluntary, industrial or commercial—which must make itself, its services or its products clearly understood if it is to operate efficiently, successfully or profitably.

Croydon, July 1968

To my wife Frances,
son John and
daughter Valerie

Contents

1 Press Relations and Public Relations 1

2 The Press Officer: Responsibilities and Recruitment 5

3 The Press Officer and the Press Office 12

4 Planning a Press Relations Campaign 24

5 Presentation of the Press Release 37

6 How to Write a Press Release 53

7 Some Press Releases Analysed 58

8 Pictures and Captions 85

9 Communication Media 96

10 Organising Press Events 109

11 Information Services—Their PR Value 134

12 Product Publicity 142

13 Exclusive Signed Feature Articles 154

14 Exhibitors and Exhibitions 164

15 Exports and Overseas Press Relations 181

16 Some Problems of Press Relations 194

17 The Image and Marketing 210

18 Research and the Recording of Results 219

Appendix 1 : IPR Code of Professional Conduct 236

Appendix 2 : Bibliography 237

Index 239

I

Press Relations and Public Relations

The initials *PR* are so commonly used that it has become easy to confuse press relations practice with its parent public relations, especially when so many people from company directors to editors either see no difference between the two, or believe that press relations practice is the beginning and the end of public relations. It may sometimes be the end, in the sense of the end product, but it is certainly not the beginning.

Public relations concerns the relations which any sort of organisation may have with any groups of people. These groups are called *publics*. In PR we do not address ourselves to the public, or the general public, but to particular defined publics. Unlike consumer advertising, consumer PR is not addressed to the mass buying public but to different sub-sections of it such as, put at its simplest, men, women and children.

Or to take the example of an industrial company, publics can extend from the residents of the town in which the organisation exists to the ultimate users of the product, who could perhaps be on the other side of the world. This may sound a slight exaggeration but it is often true that the products of a factory making capital goods such as cranes, railway locomotives or transformers are not sold in the town of manufacture and consequently the activities of the company may be unknown to most of the townspeople. Such ignorance means a lack of community relations, which among other things could make staff recruitment unnecessarily more difficult. It also means that the management badly needs to look to its public relations generally.

But between these two extremes of community and consumer there are many different publics—often quite different for each individual organisation—with their own characteristic points of view and they can include employees, members, ratepayers, visitors, suppliers, sub-contractors, shareholders and many other categories according to the nature of the organisation.

In the paragraph above we used the word *organisation* as a convenient word to mean any organised unit such as a company, local authority, hospital, university, charity, voluntary society, public authority, or government department.

PR consists of relations with people. The telephone switchboard operator, the delivery van driver, the personnel manager and all the heads of departments are responsible for giving the organisation a good or a bad name. Often, we gain our first good or bad impression—or *image*—of an organisation from the person who answers the telephone, opens the door, receives our enquiry at the desk, or writes to us. One of the most fundamental PR tasks in many organisations is teaching staff how to be of service in every personal contact they make. Indeed, in some big American corporations this is becoming a specialised PR function now known as *public affairs*. But we all know how admirably customer relations have been achieved in the airline business where the air hostess is such an excellent example of good public relations!

In some organisations there is an implicit philosophy which engenders good relationships with everyone with whom there is contact. Manners maketh man is a very true PR concept. Marks and Spencer have built a fine business on the basis of excellent staff and customer relations. This is real PR. Bad PR exists when a company is the butt of innumerable complaints like Eastern Airlines some years ago whose passengers went so far as to set up a series of We Hate Eastern Airlines Clubs! This is the ideal point at which to observe that one cannot polish a bad image. The image can be radically improved only because the organisation has itself been radically changed for the better. Eastern Airlines had to do this.

The Press Officer

The goodwill of various publics can be established and maintained only provided a conscious effort is made to create channels of communication and in this it is just as important that the organisation understands external attitudes towards it as it is for the organisation to create and sustain a clear impression of its policy, products or services. Public relations activities may include any or all of the following communication media:

The spoken word—documentary film—radio—television—house journal—sponsored books—newspapers and magazines—print—visual aids—exhibitions—models.

These media may be used singly or jointly, as when a film and a scale model may be used on an exhibition stand from which educational literature is distributed, while press releases and pictures are available in the press room. From this example we begin to see that the specialist activity of press relations emerges. Press relations is concerned with the supplying of news and information in the desired form at the right time to media such as press, radio, television and newsreel.

In achieving the overall aim of public relations a very important role is played by the press officer, whose function is to set up an ideal working arrangement with the major communication media which publish news and information on the strength of its authenticity and value to readers, listeners and viewers. Good press relations are therefore responsible ones of mutual trust. The press officer is the liaison between communication media and his organisation and the author of material for publication.

But it is also important that the press officer should not consider himself to be a self-sufficient PR service, and that he should see himself contributing to a team effort. For example, even though they may not be integrated and treated as a consolidated effort, PR is carried out well or badly by many people within one and the same organisation, as we have already seen above. And while organisations as yet making but limited use of PR may do so through the employment of a press officer, in many other organisations the press officer will be a valuable member of the team. In organisations which are constantly "in the news", the press officer has a vital role to play; in fact, his role will be so important that his office and home addresses and telephone numbers will be published in books of reference such as the *World's Press News Directory of Newspaper and Magazine Personnel and Data*, and he will be truly "on tap" at any time of the day or night.

The press officer must therefore occupy a position of sufficient authority to warrant the trust and respect of both management and the press. In particular, this means that he must enjoy the unstinted confidence of the press and not be regarded as little more than a watchdog with no reliable knowledge or genuine authority to speak for his organisation. When the press attributes a story to a "spokesman" the press officer should be that spokesman. But obviously he cannot act in this capacity unless management is prepared to tell him all the facts, and delegate to him the right and power to speak on management's behalf.

When it is realised that in the USA famous press officers like Ivy Lee were operating very efficiently in exactly this manner as long ago as 1906, there is obviously something remarkably wrong—almost feudal—in Britain where public relations, and the efforts of press officers in particular, still earn snide remarks from some well-known names in the press and on TV. These otherwise entertaining and intelligent celebrities of communication media should really know better, the more so since without the painstaking research and fact-finding of conscientious press officers they would sometimes be very short of material! Press relations will have won their rightful place in Britain only when the press officer has earned and won acceptance as a helpmate rather than a hindrance. That is an immense challenge. It is of course met daily by many press officers who do have the fullest confidence of editors, but this is a growing business and inevitably standards vary and criticism is more common than it need be.

The purpose of the chapters that follow is to provide a practical guide to the functions and techniques of press relations which, if diligently followed, will greatly improve the work of many press officers—some of whom may have been quite unaware of their failings—and will help to remedy the dismal situation in which much of the criticism directed at press relations is all too justly earned.

2

The Press Officer: Responsibilities and Recruitment

The press officer's job is not to write and distribute material as directed and authorised by his employer. He is not a tame scribe. If employers of press relations services merely want to say what they like when they like they should use a direct mail agency which will prepare and post such material provided it is neither unethical nor illegal. It is the press officer's place to reason why, and that is one of his most testing responsibilities. Although the press officer is employed by the purveyor of news he can only follow that employment successfully on his employer's behalf if he recognises that he must behave responsibly to communication media. The press officer is a professional, not a hired hack writer.

This is something which few advertising agency people can either understand or stomach, perhaps because they work in much more prescribed circles or even because it is their experience that having booked advertisement space they can sometimes lean heavily on the advertisement manager and induce him to obtain a write-up out of his editor. This does happen, of course, and the most flagrant instances are the articles which accompany large-space advertisements for new cars. Consequently, few people take these reports seriously—that is, as impartial editorial—because they are invariably too good to be true! Being neither genuine editorial nor sincere press relations, they are looked upon as just another part of the advertisement.

Impartiality has its penalties however. When the film critic on a South Coast evening newspaper chose to write honest film reviews he was refused press passes by the local cinema owners! That film reviewer is now the famous television critic on a national newspaper.

The same kind of support for advertisers appears in the newspaper supplements dreamed up by ingenious advertisement managers. Again, they really have nothing to do with PR, and sometimes they are of little advertising value, but the press officer may be asked to write a piece for the feature. Genuine press relations efforts are publishable on their merits, not because advertisement space has been purchased. In fact, the best PR story is generally one which appears nowhere near an advertisement for the same thing!

Ten Responsibilities of a Press Officer

What, then, are the responsibilities of the press officer? How can he steer clear of all these pitfalls of what others mistakenly expect of him? How can he establish a clear image of what he himself stands for? Let us provide some answers by means of a 10-point check list.

The competent press officer should:

1. Establish internal lines of communication so that he has ready access to sources of information within his organisation.
2. Collate information and pictures for future use, building a comprehensive fact and picture library.
3. Issue material in a form acceptable to various media so that his organisation is made known and understood, its achievements are appreciated and its reputation is deservedly enhanced.
4. Maintain a press service so that all enquiries from media are dealt with quickly, efficiently and honestly.
5. Be impartial to the extent that media will trust him to supply ungarnished facts.
6. Be able to judge the news value of information supplied to him, and be prepared to reject a story which is not suitable for release.
7. Be constantly aware of the danger of issuing false or misleading information, even though it may be supplied by an apparently reliable source.
8. Feed back information, such as external attitudes or news about rival organisations, so that his service provides a two-way liaison.
9. Be so organised that he can provide a fully competent press relations service, on a 24-hour basis if necessary.
10. Record the results of his efforts and report accordingly to his superiors.

To some readers these ten responsibilities—the ten commandments of press relations—may come as a bracing surprise. Certainly, a good many cynics in both the advertising and the press world do not expect a press officer to be so meticulous or fastidious. But scruples are the strength of press relations and these responsibilities are taken very seriously by those who adhere to the Code of Professional Conduct of the Institute of Public Relations, not purely for moral reasons but out of economic necessity. It is only when such responsibilities are accepted that the press officer can operate effectively and deserve the respect which is accorded to any other professional practitioner. Or put another way, it pays the press officer to be honest, and this must be recognised by those who employ his services.

To whom is the Press Officer Responsible?

This is a difficult question to answer because press relations practice is seldom clearly defined as an organisational function. Strictly speaking, the press officer should be responsible either directly or through the PRO to top management. In actual practice this may not be so.

In a voluntary body he is likely to be a member of a small team of permanent officials headed by a general secretary or director, while in a local authority he will be responsible to the town clerk. In industry, as already mentioned, his status and supervision can vary tremendously. He may be the only PR man and his chief may be a promotional executive handling marketing, sales or advertising. Again, he may be a specialist assistant to the PRO whose status will depend on the extent to which the board is PR-orientated.

The above paragraph assumes that press relations are conducted by a full-time press officer, but this is not always the case and this book is intended for others as well who may have to deal with the press, having no journalistic experience or inside knowledge of publishing house operations and requirements. Marketing, sales, advertising, personnel, works and shop managers may well have to deal with the press from time to time.

It is, unfortunately, true that a good many press releases are issued by people completely unskilled in this work and often utterly unaware that any special skill is required. Since the number of organisations issuing press releases is large, whereas the number employing press officers is comparatively small, it is not really surprising that so many press releases received by editors are unpublishable. Only a proportion of the blame for poor press releases can therefore be directed at professional press officers.

From these remarks it will be seen that press relations are dabbled in by a large number of people, with or without ability, knowledge and experience. For successful press relations, however, a competent trained press officer is necessary.

How are Press Officers Recruited?

We come now to the most pertinent question of all. The answer is directly related to the quality of press relations practice. What are the present methods of recruiting press officers?

They are so many and so diverse, as to be almost absurd, and there is serious need for a more direct entry to press relations with provision for trainee facilities, day release for training, and possibly some form of specialist qualification as distinct from the all-round qualification of the IPR. But at present we find press officers recruited from the following fields:

Newspaper and magazine journalism—Advertisement copywriting—Freelance writing—Technical authorship—Graduates—Transfers from other jobs in the same organisation—Trainees.

The latter category is almost non-existent in any real sense of the word. There are some instances of trainee PR executives who include press relations in their training. But as yet there is very little attempt to recruit trainee press officers from among graduates as happens in the advertising world. It is a very unsatisfactory state of affairs, but undoubtedly one of the most potent reasons for the absence of trainees is the lack of employer appreciation of the need for training. It is all too easy to assume that someone who has worked on any sort of newspaper or magazine is automatically qualified to be a press officer. As the reader of the following chapters will discover, this simply is not the case.

Do Journalists make good Press Officers?

This may sound a silly question, but it is not. Far too often management, needing to appoint a press officer yet knowing little about the subject, will take a short cut and appoint a journalist assuming that *any* journalistic experience is sufficient qualification for a good press officer. This assumption is seldom valid.

Some of our leading PR practitioners were, of course, very fine journalists. Newspaper experience is not only writing experience, but includes familiarity with the wider aspects of life, the way in which the world earns a living, and the manner in which we are governed. It may also include managing a publication with all its business and labour relations implications. Not every journalist, however, enjoys such broad or senior experience, and it may be that the ex-journalist press officer who produces poor press releases was formerly engaged in a minor journalistic sphere where he gained but limited understanding of journalism itself. There are numerous grades of journalistic experience and it is therefore rather a big mistake to take for granted that *any* journalistic experience is sufficient qualification for a good press officer, even a junior one. It is worth repeating, then, that an employer can easily make this mistake, and our business sometimes suffers from the frequency with which this misunderstanding has occurred.

A journalist working on a paper presents his copy in a very different way from that required of an accomplished press officer. The staff journalist is often working to meet a deadline and tends to type imperfectly on small pieces of paper; rarely does he have either time or need to produce a beautifully typed manuscript. His job is to complete an assignment, and he does not have to market his stories. Nor does he have to please more than one editor. A conscientious press officer, however, is aware that his release has to compete with scores of others and that he must take the extra trouble necessary to produce a release which sells itself through its clarity of heading and content, neat setting out and legible presentation.

It is consequently fairer to say that the abilities and character likely to produce a first-class journalist will equally make a first-class press officer, but that is very different from saying that ex-journalists make good press officers.

From these remarks we can see that a good many people other than journalists are capable of excelling as press officers provided that they can match up to the requirements listed in the next section.

What makes a good Press Officer?

The simple answer to this question is that anyone who can write concise, precise English; is a thorough, methodical and imaginative organiser; likes, understands and gets on with people; has wide interests and experiences; is in every way an intelligent, adaptable, broadminded person with an infinite fund of curiosity; is always willing to recognise his own limitations yet maintains a zest for learning; who above all has a tenacious, persistent nature so that he never gives up, never allows himself to be fobbed off, nor falls victim to disappointment but is always enthusiastic without being boastful about what he hopes to achieve; anyone who fits that job specification will make a first-class press officer. This is very different from the typical advertising agency idea of someone who is merely able to "con" the press: he has to be a person of distinct attributes and integrity. This job specification may surprise some readers and suggest that the press officer has to be a "miracle man", but then we are aiming at perfection, not black magic.

From the above paragraph it will be apparent that journalistic experience is not absolutely necessary for a man—or a woman—to succeed in this occupation. But write well he must, and he may have gained his skill as a freelance writer, possibly as an advertisement copywriter, perhaps as a technical author and very likely as a University graduate who has been compelled to write on a variety of topics in very demanding and competitive circumstances.

News Sense

There is, of course, one attribute that a trained journalist does have which is indispensable to a press officer, and that is "news sense". In the past journalists have been favoured recruits to PR because they alone have been expected to possess news sense, but if others can acquire this ability to detect what is certain to interest other people they will be well equipped for the job. Looked at more closely, what is this "news sense"? Isn't it exactly the same as the marketing man's ability to produce and sell goods that will satisfy a need?

News sense is not so much creating news as recognising what aspects of a piece of information, or what manner of presentation of this information, will most succeed in interesting the readers of a certain section of the press. It is really a piece of elementary motivation research!

For example, a company may obtain an export contract for the supply of a given quantity or value of goods. This item may rate a couple of lines in a business column or magazine. Similar stories are published, practically listed, daily. Often, the two or three lines printed have been subbed down from dull, wordy releases of practically no news value.

The press officer with a nose for news will delve deeper for a real story. Call this creating news if you like, but he cannot invent what is not there to be discovered. If someone has the wit and the will to look into a contract and find out, say, that this was the first time such a contract had been awarded to a British company, and then go on to find out how this British company—his company or client—had in fact beaten foreign competition then we are approaching a story of "hard" news importance. This story need not be just an item for the business section but possibly worth space on the front page, a story of interest to radio and TV, the COI and the External Services of the BBC at Bush House. But it all began with a dull-seeming two-line admission by an unimaginative export manager who could not really be expected to have a "news sense".

The Press Officer of the Future

At present, in Britain, we are on the threshold of PR as a business function, and particularly as one which can aid nearly every stage of the marketing exercise whereas advertising is but one stage, and the demand for press officers and other specialists will be such that they will have to be trained specifically for the job. New recruits are likely to come from many walks of life and among the younger entrants to press relations the graduate may well be the only applicant likely to have the qualities listed above. This immediately suggests a higher status for the press officer, and the author believes that this is necessary and just.

Future prospects for employment in press relations seem to lie not so much with one-time journalists as with men and women—this can be very much a woman's calling—who are prepared to learn what is required by the editors of hundreds of entirely different journals. The press officer who can satisfy critical editorial needs cannot help but succeed because his work will be welcomed by editors.

This must be of some encouragement to the majority of PR students, trainees and new entrants to the business who have never worked in journalism; to all those who have to include press relations as part of their job as publicity managers, personnel officers, works managers, election agents, entertainments managers, and in some cases proprietors of businesses which they are developing single-handedly and cannot as yet afford specialist assistance. All organisations have to communicate with their publics, and where no press officer is as yet engaged *someone* has to understand something at least of the techniques of press relations.

This is not to say that *anyone* will make a press officer—his myriad qualities have been emphasised already—but there are many people who nevertheless do have to deal with the press and can learn much of the necessary basic techniques. Works managers and local branch managers are people who can often augment the work of the company PRO if they have a sensible understanding of the journalist's point of view and the way in which news is gathered, evaluated, edited and published to a deadline. Any organisation which operates from scattered premises and locations should ensure that in each place there is a responsible spokesman who is appreciative of press relations.

3

The Press Officer and the Press Office

An example of good press relations, and appreciation of a rare sort, occurred on June 14th 1967 when Her Majesty the Queen thanked the press for enabling the royal children's education to proceed without undue press publicity. Said the then Press Secretary to the Queen, Commander Sir Richard Colville, speaking to members of the Press Association:

"*I can tell you that the Queen and Prince Philip are grateful for the co-operation of the Press which has so far enabled their children to be brought up sensibly and for their education to proceed smoothly.*

"*Moreover, they are always willing to consider giving facilities for the exceptional occasions when it would be in the public interest.*"

With this introduction to the role of the press officer let us now consider the necessary qualifications and abilities of a press officer, remembering that no matter what the columnists and TV satirists say he is not an exponent of black magic nor a hidden persuader.

The press are sometimes cynically disposed towards PRO's and press officers because they mistake them for press agents. Press agentry, is concerned with publicity seeking not so pure and simple. The whole aim is to get pictures and stories into print by one means or another that will publicise the press agent's client, and clients are usually personalities such as entertainers, tycoons, politicians and the like—people who have to be in the news to exist. Press agents are sometimes more frankly called publicity agents. Their work is akin to advertising in effect, but the method of operation is often dubious.

The difference between press relations and press agentry is clear when the principle is accepted that the press officer aims to issue material which is first and foremost news of reader interest. Publicity must accrue from this basic value, but the news will be issued with proper regard for the integrity of the press. Editors will be encouraged to feel that they can rely on the press officer for news and not that he is twisting their arms to secure puffs.

This difference is reasonably well understood when the source of the news is an official information service, and now that news distribution is becoming a very important branch of marketing this commercial aspect can be more help than hindrance.

Advertised goods and services are openly advocated whereas personalities rely upon publicity gained by whatever means may be within the ingenuity, power and purse of the press agent.

Advertising takes the risk of publicly making claims, and it is nowadays so hedged about by both legislation and voluntary control that most advertising is highly trustworthy and reputable. It has to be, and companies stake reputations worth millions of pounds on their advertised claims.

Desirable Qualities of a Press Officer

Now let us be analytical and consider the four most desirable and important abilities of a press officer. These are the ability to:

1. Obtain facts
2. Write Journalistically
3. Market Stories
4. Time distribution of Stories.

1. *Ability to Obtain Facts.* He must be able to interview people, prepare a questionnaire, or carry out either field or desk research to get the information for his news stories. In this he must be politely persistent. One can find out anything if one tries hard enough, but the ability to investigate calls for more than inquisitiveness. It requires wide experience and catholic tastes for with these attributes points of sympathetic human contact are possible. No-one wants to talk to another who appears narrow, selfish, ignorant and unsympathetic. The press officer cannot afford to be a cynic, for a cynic suffers from an immature personality.

But above all, in his search for facts, he must be conscious of the value of these facts from the point of view of the ultimate reader. An employer or client may wish to present facts which are important to him: the press officer must assert his unquestionable right to demand and to issue only the facts which are publishable and readable. If such facts are withheld, the press officer is bound to declare there is no story that he can release. If he is asked to decorate the facts more favourably, it is his place to dissent. And if he suspects that the information is not all that it seems, it is his duty to check the facts before editors take his material on trust and publish to their disadvantage.

Without integrity any person engaged in PR work must fail, and this applies particularly to the press officer whose stock in trade must be trust. No matter how cynically certain sections of the press may regard the press officer he must nevertheless be above suspicion. Unless his employer understands this position the press officer will be unable to perform his functions. All this may sound very purist, but would a surgeon permit the patient to direct an operation?

There is no doubt that at the present time there are PRO's, PR consultants, press officers and others holding associated positions who, through fear of dismissal, permit misguided users of their services to abuse them. But the man who fears dismissal deserves his fate because such fear, in reality, can be derived only from his inability to do his job properly. By this is meant that to enjoy the status of integrity the press officer must argue from a position of strength given him by his superior experience, training, qualifications and not least of all his proven ability to deliver the goods on his own initiative.

When a PR consultant excuses poor work on the grounds that "the client insists" that a story be written in such a way, or that it must be embargoed, or that elaborate press packs must be put in an exhibition press room, that consultant is incompetent to the point of wasting his client's money. That such a dim state of affairs is all too common only goes to show the lowly state of our business and the ineptitude of certain practitioners who will, apparently, do anything for money. *In PR the customer is seldom right.* The PR man should be paid to be right.

2. *Ability to Write Journalistically.* As we shall discuss this in more practical detail in the chapter on how to write press releases, the subject will be but briefly touched on here. A poet or novelist might make a poor press officer. We are not writing to impress or entertain. Our words must interest and inform, briefly and clearly. Every word must count but superlatives have no place since we cannot put words of praise in editors' mouths. A press release contains no comment. We have to write as we might expect a journalist to write, given the same facts, and we cannot express his opinions for him. Thus in a press release, we do not write of a "famous" company.

Journalistic writing is the opposite to essay writing. There is no introduction, development and conclusion. Instead, in a news story, the gist of the story is told in the first paragraph, and then expanded in the paragraphs which follow. This can be seen at once in any newspaper. When novelists try to quote an imaginary news story they invariably fall into the trap of writing their news stories as they write their books, and these so-called newspaper reports are quite unrealistic.

3. *Ability to Market Stories.* Once he has a story the press officer must know where to place it, and who is most likely to publish it. This is very much a "selling" operation even though the stories are submitted free of charge. But more than this, he must not only send releases to the editors most likely to be interested in them but he must avoid annoying other editors by sending them stories which he should know are of no interest to them. The marketing of press releases requires a thorough knowledge of media, and the acquisition of this knowledge is a painstaking business. The press officer who writes a story and then does a blanket mailing of all the journals covering that subject is an amateur compared to the man who knows his media and selects the right publications for each story.

Sometimes clients ask PR consultants what mailing lists are used for their stories. A good press officer does not keep "lists" because there is no permanent set of publications that is suitable for every story issued by a particular organisation. This point must be emphasised since it is seldom appreciated. The constant study of media is therefore imperative because changes are so frequent. The market for any given story must be known and understood.

Reference to the building up of addressing plate libraries, from which addresses can be selected, follows in the section on the press office, and Chapter Nine is devoted to communication media.

It must be emphasised that media selection is not a question of "contacts" but of knowledge. A press officer may have five thousand or more addresses in his plate library according to the nature of the organisation. He cannot possibly know all these press people personally, but he should have seen most of their publications at some time, and either know something about the style and make-up of these journals or have the necessary information in his office. There is plenty of published information.

In other words, the press officer has to be his own literary agent.

4. *Ability to Time Distribution of Stories.* This ability derives chiefly from knowing how publications are produced, printed and distributed. The printing process is the most important of the three: is it letterpress, photogravure, or lithographic including web-offset? Printing is a complex subject, but an elementary knowledge of it is essential to anyone engaged in PR. If the press officer understands the process by which

various journals are published he will know how to time the release of his stories.

He will know that a morning national is printed at night, the first edition for the provinces coming off the presses about 10 p.m. and the London edition about 4 a.m. Only something dramatic like a front-page murder story will interest an editor after 10 p.m. and even a "hard" news story from a PR source is unlikely to be of much use to such an editor after tea-time.

A woman's weekly printed by photogravure may go the printer six weeks before publication, and its planning, writing and illustration will have been done over a period three to six months before publication. On the other hand, a monthly letterpress journal needs material before the middle of the previous month, while a weekly magazine printed by the letterpress or web-offset process may want material as early as the previous Friday or Monday if published on a Wednesday or Thursday respectively.

A provincial weekly newspaper sold on Friday is often made-up on Tuesday, set and proofed on Wednesday, printed and delivered on Thursday, which means that copy is required on Monday at the latest. Thus, stories to the provincial press should be posted on Thursday or Friday, or hand-delivered on Monday (perhaps following a telephone call to say the story is on its way).

Here is an example of how a story was published in a local paper. Certain work was to be done to the parish church, but by the time it had been completed and photographed the story would have been too late for that week's issue, and stale news for the next. A photograph of the exterior was taken on the Thursday. The story was written up from the job specification and approval obtained of the draft, and the picture, caption and release was delivered to the newspaper office on the Monday morning. By the time the story appeared in print on the following Thursday the work had been completed as reported.

But writing before the event can have its snares, and there is the famous example of the Crawfie story in *Woman's Own*, written weeks ahead because this magazine is printed gravure, which described the Queen riding in her carriage down the course at Ascot when in fact there was heavy rain on that day and the royal ride was abandoned! Unfortunately, the issues were already printed, and the story had to go out as it stood in millions of copies.

The Press Office

The department run by the press officer is known as the press office, and journalists making enquiries are as likely to ask the telephone operator for the "press office" as the "press officer". Consequently it should be organised and equipped so that it can operate efficiently and with expert understanding of how the press works and what it wants. It should have good inter-communication or direct-line facilities so that the press officer can communicate quickly within his own organisation. He should be served by a first-class secretary who knows exactly what to do in his absence, and in a large organisation there will be assistant press officers. In some organisations with scattered locations it may be necessary to have press officers in the field who can be instantly contacted. Ideally, the press office will possess modern equipment such as electric typewriters, Telex, and tape recorders, a first-class duplicator, a folding machine, a collating machine and a postal franking machine. Special reference to addressing plates will be made later in this section.

Two things are essential to the successful running of a press office—firstly, access to information internally; and secondly, access to information externally.

Access to Information Internally

This is often very difficult to establish, and the newly appointed staff press officer will have to exercise patience, persistence and a great deal of tact if he is to succeed in creating workable lines of communication. The reason for this is simple, intriguing and very human. People either take newsworthy material for granted, or—especially if they are junior executives—they are worried about giving away company secrets and advantages to their competitors.

Ideally, the press officer should be at the receiving end of information which wide-awake PR-conscious people throughout the company are passing on to him. This wonderful state of affairs is not impossible, and actually occurs in organisations where the staff have been educated by an enlightened management, and this can be done through staff journals, training schemes and staff conferences. It can happen in companies where the staff are themselves kept well informed about company policy and activities, and where there is a PR department with press officers who visit and make themselves known and understood to the staff throughout the organisation wherever they may be, at home or abroad.

The press officer has to cultivate people at all levels in the organisation so that he has friendly access to informants. He must be able to correspond with, telephone or call on *anyone* in the organisation from the chairman to the caretaker. This is his privilege.

He does not wait for information to come to him: he has to be organised and accepted so that he can go out and get it.

Becoming accepted means that he must do a PR job for himself. He must make himself known throughout the organisation, and the results of his work must be seen and appreciated. Copies of press releases and press cuttings should be distributed to branch managers, works managers and others, and on factory notice boards copies of selected press cuttings should be displayed to show how well the organisation is reported in the press. People like to know that they are in the news, or at least that their organisation and what it does or makes is publicly reported.

The press officer has the distinct and pleasant advantage of becoming a popular personality, but he does have to be careful to avoid creating jealousies by appearing to steal the limelight. His role is that of stage manager, not the star of the show. He may write the speeches but he will not give them. Often he will ghost-write articles signed by his superiors. He may write much of the house journal despite the credits given to apparent contributors who may have supplied only incoherent notes. The press officer has to be a ubiquitous invisible man at times, the enthusiastic organiser hidden in the wings, the one who gets little praise for the miracles but all the blame when the smallest thing goes wrong.

Editing the staff journal can be an asset to the press officer because it provides constant contact with members of the staff everywhere, and if it is the kind of organisation which has factories or offices in scattered locations a system of communication can be established by the appointment of local correspondents. Thus, the press officer can operate through a network of informants.

But equally, the press officer who works in a smaller compass will still need to make himself known to possible sources of information. For example, a seaside resort publicity manager needs material for press stories, and it pays him to keep the local press well informed about his activities so that those engaged in the local holiday industry will appreciate his activities on their behalf and support him with useful facts and news items. The work of his committee and department should therefore be regularly reported in the local press.

Access to Information Externally

The information required here consists of the journals and the journalists who will be interested in receiving his press releases, pictures and articles. It depends on the nature of the organisation and its newsworthiness whether this information will be retained on a card index system or with a more elaborate addressing plate library.

Plates are best if used often enough to warrant the expense of making them. They make possible very speedy addressing of envelopes which is a monotonous and laborious job if every envelope has to be individually addressed on the typewriter. Equipment is available ranging from modest hand-operated addressing machines to large automatically operated systems.

In setting up an addressing system two things should be remembered. First, the chosen categories should be easy to locate when required. It is hopeless to have the addresses but never know how they have been filed, and all plates should be numbered for accurate re-filing after use. Secondly, the addresses must be kept up to date by watching for changes as reported in the trade press, or as indicated in the press officer's day-to-day work, while a periodic check against, say, *British Rate and Data*, is imperative. Changes of address and title are frequent, while some journals cease publication and others are launched.

If plates are held for correspondents and other staff writers, plate changes are likely to be frequent because journalists tend to change jobs quite often. This sounds like a lot of work but a live address library is the gold mine of an efficient press office. It is extremely hard to keep an address library fully up to date, but the attempt must be constantly made. Editors will, of course, expect the press officer to be infallible about addresses.

Included in this library should be the addresses of freelance writers who write on subjects relative to the organisation, and this category can be built up by making contact with contributors to journals and authors of books. This can be a very valuable (although sometimes overlooked) section of the press, and these writers will appreciate the efforts of the press officer who keeps them informed and so helps them to earn a living. Some press officers are impatient of freelance writers, but this is a foolish attitude because many editors call in these freelance writers to produce special supplements, features, give-away booklets and to deal with special sides to publishing such as readers' letters and reader enquiry services. The astute press officer will use every communication resource open to him. There are, for example, several organisations such as Joan Storey and Roger Smithells which supply regular features to journals and all these must be included in the address library.

Starting up an Addressing Plate Library

Since there are so many thousands of newspapers and magazines how are their titles and addresses to be found when setting up an address library? The information is published in a number of directories which are all useful for slightly different purposes, and the press officer should have a complete library of these books, making sure to buy each new edition as it comes out. We have already mentioned *BRAD* which is published monthly for the benefit of the advertising business, but a monthly subscription may be too heavy and rather unnecessary for the press officer, although an occasional copy is valuable for checking purposes. The following annuals are recommended:

The Newspaper Press Directory. This is a massive book giving information about journals published throughout the world, which even lists house journals. Its chief value is that it describes the readership of each journal or, in the case of local newspapers, it describes their area of distribution.

Willings Press Guide. While details of readership are not given, titles are listed in alphabetical order and are easily found if individual envelopes are being types as may occur with a special mailing for which cards or plates do not yet exist. This book includes some additional titles of overseas journals not to be found in other directories.

Advertiser's Annual. Although the addresses are predominately those of advertisement and not editorial departments, this annual often includes journals not to be found elsewhere, and its classification headings provide useful categories on which to base an address library. This annual is also valuable as a source of ancillary services and suppliers useful to the press officer.

World's Press News Directory of Newspaper and Magazine Personnel and Data. Every press officer must be grateful for this slim grey annual which expands its range of information every year. It is indispensable. For example, it gives the names of editors, feature page editors and special correspondents on all the larger newspapers and magazines published in the UK. It lists the special correspondents in categories such as agriculture, motoring, science, aviation, industry and so on. Similar information is given about radio and TV, news agencies, photographic agencies, and information bureaux—government, official and commercial. There is also a section on hotels suitable for press occasions.

In addition, the press officer should acquire the various official booklets which are issued from time to time by the Board of Trade and the Central Office of Information which list the facilities provided by these official means of communication with the overseas press, radio and TV. These are listed at the end of Chapter 14.

If the press officer has to mail stories to the overseas press he can obtain quite good information from the directories listed above, but more complete directories are published in the larger countries although these can be expensive to buy.

Press Cutting Services

It is important to know the results of press relations work, and since it would be impracticable to subscribe to every journal to which stories are submitted the services of a press cutting agency are necessary. In London and certain other parts of the UK there are agencies which will supply cuttings at a fee for so many cuttings per subject. Some agencies also charge a search fee irrespective of whether cuttings are actually found.

These agencies receive a certain amount of criticism because they seldom succeed in finding more than about 50 per cent of the cuttings which exist. There are many reasons for this failure, but they are not entirely the fault of the agencies. For example, a story might appear in only one edition of a newspaper. Moreover, cutting agencies do not necessarily search every publication issued in the country. There are also stories which refer to the organisation or product without actually naming it, and such items are likely to escape the press cutting staff. On the whole, the fees charged by these agencies are not high. The most satisfactory service results when a broad subject heading can be given to the agency rather than just the name of an organisation. Press cuttings as a means of recording results are fully discussed in Chapter 18.

The Do's and Don'ts of Good Press Relations

To conclude this chapter here are twelve points well worth remembering as a guide to good press relations.

1. *Understand the Press.* Don't expect editors and reporters to be out to trick you, but remember that publishing is a highly competitive business. Be realistic. If you try to hide facts you are asking for trouble. The press can be ruthless. Don't favour one paper more than another, and don't give unfair exclusives. Let every paper have the same chance with the same story and pictures. And don't give different pictures to competing journals in the same category.

2. *Tell the Truth.* Don't issue half a story, or try to gild a story in

your organisation's favour. Press people will usually respect confidences. Put newsmen in the picture as much as you can.

3. *Be Always Accessible.* Make sure the press can reach you at any time. When you leave the office leave a trail, say where you are going. Put your address on your press release. Give your private telephone number as well as your office number. Respond quickly to requests for information, written or phoned.

4. *Be Prepared.* If a story is likely to break, check policy and have the facts ready. Know what you are talking about. This can be very valuable if you have to refute false statements or misunderstandings.

5. *Regard Press People as Fellow Practitioners.* Respect their calling and invite them to respect yours. Remember, you can only argue from a position of strength. Don't try to teach them their job. Don't try to tell them what is news. Be patient with the cynical reporter who sneers at PR. Go out of your way to tip him off about a possible story. Press officers and journalists should work as a team.

6. *Show Visiting Pressmen Round.* Turn calls into memorable visits. Take visiting pressmen behind the scenes. Open their eyes. Let them meet people. Make them feel welcome. Make them feel they can drop in whenever it pleases them.

7. *Provide Facilities.* Make it easy for reporters to get their stories away. Find them a quiet room, a desk and a chair, a typewriter and a telephone, a company car if necessary. Don't begrudge them any assistance. Observe every courtesy, hospitality and respect due to a guest.

8. *Maintain a Friendly Relationship.* Keep friends with the press, but do not exploit friendship. Think of occasions when you can be nice to press people. Don't try to buy their favours with too many drinks or lunches. Try to remember names. Keep a personal book of names. You will meet hundreds of journalists and remembering all their names is not easy.

9. *Don't Get a Reputation for Stopping Stories.* Sometimes you won't want them to print a story, but always try to have a replacement story if you can. Remember, the reporter is expected to come back to the office with a story.

10. *Don't Expect a Story because your Organisation Advertises.* Keep the two separate. Don't get involved in advertising. Avoid the blackmail of write-ups *if* you advertise, and vice versa. Your work must be publishable on its own merits.

11. *Be Careful over Corrections.* Errors do occur. Take them up, the editor may be genuinely unaware of the true facts. But do not antag-

onise editors. No editor likes to publish an apology or correction. Errors can sometimes be made good in another story another time.

12. *Remember Dead Lines, Copy Dates, Publishing Days.* Don't waste reporters' time with stories too late to catch the right edition. Watch out for Saturday stories. Sunday papers carry little news and by Monday a Saturday story is cold. Don't give evening papers a story at five o'clock. Remember that monthlies need stories six weeks ahead, and that gravure-printed magazines work months ahead. If space has been promised for a feature article make sure you supply the MSS by the agreed copy date.

The twelve points offered above provide a workmanlike basis for good day-to-day press relations. The basic philosophy is good relations in all directions, within and without one's organisation. Nothing is perfect. The press officer will work most efficiently when he has no illusions about all sides of the world in which he has to operate. He has to deal with people and people are irrational, exasperating and human just like himself.

N.B. There are special services such as PRADS of 31, Vauxhall Bridge Road, Victoria, and Morgans PR/Systems (Romeike & Curtice Group), Hale House, 290–296, Green Lane, London, N13, who offer press release production and distribution services based on accurately kept mailing libraries. These services can be especially valuable to the consultancy with a variety of clients whose stories may interest thousands of publications at different times so that there is a constant danger of plates becoming out-of-date. Moreover, these firms are equipped to process mailings economically.

4

Planning a Press Relations Campaign

How do you plan a press relations campaign? What does it cost? Is it planned in isolation as a separate activity or can it be planned in concert with the overall marketing scheme? What results are likely and can any sort of target be set? Are the costs likely to be justified by the results? Can we therefore include press relations in the marketing budget in a tangible way?

These are practical questions, and there is no need for them to be followed by an awkward silence.

In PR we do not operate in a vacuum of intangibility, for while it is true that goodwill is an intangible asset of small book value the press relations aspect of PR is much more precise. We propose to issue newsworthy information which, as part of a marketing plan, must produce either a negative or a positive response. That response has a value. It can show antipathy to an organisation, product or service, and be a form of market research which warns the marketing man how he must next act. Or it can show sympathy, interest, enthusiasm, demand and so encourage the marketing man to go ahead with his promotional plans.

Press Relations and Marketing

In these ways press relations can serve as a marketing reconnaissance. But that is not all: press relations can also supplement a promotional campaign and enhance the value of all the sales, advertising and merchandising efforts, while as will be shown in a separate chapter, press relations can also enhance the value of participation in an exhibition.

Now we are dealing with marketing realities as distinct from the mere issuing of information. A press officer is not just an information bureau clerk for while that may be a useful PR service, an aid to marketing like a showroom or display centre—purely advisory—that is a sophistication to be dealt with later. Here we are talking about grass roots press relations, an activity as vital to a marketing programme as the salesmen in the field, the advertisements in the press, or the labels on the product. Press relations has a place—doesn't just deserve a place—but emphatically takes a place in the marketing mix. It is a weapon in the publicity armoury, and must be accounted for and its results checked like those of all other resources at the marketing manager's disposal. From this we see that few if any marketing managers can afford not to employ a staff or consultancy press officer and this appointment is essential, not a doubtful fad to adopt as the whim ordains.

The best way to substantiate these claims is to describe the execution of press relations tactics in viable marketing terms. Suppose we have a product which we know to be efficacious but which invites the scepticism of those unfamiliar with its performance. Many famous products were once in this predicament, to quote only the motor car which had to be preceded by a man bearing a red flag. Because of this barrier of prejudice, conventional advertising would serve little purpose.

To advertise such a product may produce little response because readers may not believe the claimed performance to be possible. To overcome this incredulity the volume of advertising might have to be inordinately expensive. It is precisely in these circumstances that press relations techniques can help the marketing man.

By means of a press reception and demonstration, or a press visit to the factory or to an installation, associated with press releases and feature articles, not forgetting radio and TV, educational information can be published which will permit the product to be reported and discussed freely by knowledgeable people. This sort of coverage will be independent—as independent as a book review compared with a book advertisement—and the risk will have to be taken that some writers may be adversely critical. Nevertheless, being new, the product or service will have genuine news value and it will provoke reader interest. This reader interest is likely to be more receptive because the facts will be presented by the editorial columns of the journal, and the journal's integrity and value depends on this information being fair and reliable.

Editorial coverage of this kind can produce several hundred enquiries from one story. In fact, new products have been launched entirely by this method. These enquiries (and many journals provide reader service cards and coupons to stimulate enquiries) can be a form of research for the marketing man, indicating the extent and type of market interest. His future advertising plans may be shaped more accurately by the results of the initial editorial publicity and the interest it arouses.

Planning in Detail

From this general introduction to some of the tasks which press relations can perform let us look more closely at the actual planning of a press relations campaign. It is all very well saying you can write, distribute and publish this story and achieve that interest and response. But where does the press officer start, how does he know which tactic to adopt? Obviously, he does not just sit in the press office hoping some editor will ring up for a story. He must be a self-starter.

First of all he begins with the basic principle that if he has any information which will help an editor maintain or increase sales and readership, the press officer can find a good home for it to the advantage of his organisation. Unless we start here we need not bother. It is important to emphasise this because employers of press officers may be tempted to say, "We are going to advertise our product in these papers and we shall expect you to get free editorial mentions in the same editions." That is a nonsense. That is puffery at its worst. It may be what a number of marketing, sales, advertising and other business men may want from press relations, but it is not what they are likely to get, and the press officer may have to begin by disillusioning these people of such misconceptions about his work.

Generally speaking, press relations are likely to follow one of the following courses:

1. Preparatory advance educational information.
2. Information supplementary to an advertising campaign.
3. A continuous news service.

Let us, as an example, apply these to a commercial airline. The first kind of programme—advance information—might lead up to the operation of a new route or a new aircraft. The second might be conducted during the advertising of the new route or aircraft. The third would apply to the daily mixture of news about the airline's general operations which is aimed at all the publics whose continuous understanding and goodwill is important to the airline.

With a little imagination the reader can apply these three types of programme to the organisations he knows best, noting that a press relations programme need not be associated in any way with any existing short-term promotional scheme. It is possible for a press relations programme to operate irrespective of whether there is any special promotional activity, as in the case of a local authority anxious to keep its rate-payers fully informed about its activities. On the other hand, a charitable organisation concerned with a continuous press service through most of the year would require support to supplement, say, its Christmas card and Christmas appeal campaigns.

We have said that the press officer must be convinced that he has news to communicate. Now, we see that he has to decide how he is to contribute to the overall operation of his organisation, whatever kind it may be, commercial, voluntary or public.

A Typical Campaign

Let us assume, then, that the marketing manager of a company manufacturing convenience foods (that is foods which require no preparation and merely have to be heated ready for the table) has gone through all the preliminary research, laboratory, dietary, recipe, costing, packaging, naming, pricing and distribution stages and has now reached the point when a product is ready to go into production for supply to a calculated market. The marketing manager now wishes to support both his sales force and his retail distributors with a combined advertising campaign and a press relations programme. Let us further assume that the advertising will include the retail trade press, commercial TV, women's weeklies and a premium offer backed by in-store displays. The aim is to achieve repeat sales of an all-the-year-round popular food. There are many products like this to mention only instant coffee, frozen peas and tubes of mustard.

The press officer—and it does not matter whether he is on the manufacturer's staff or whether he is employed by a PR consultant—is asked to present his plans. How does he go about this?

He has a new product: that is news. The advertising schedules will indicate the publics: food retailers; the mass consumer public and housewives in particular, but possibly children, husbands, those who live alone or those like campers, yachtsmen, tourists who carry handily packed foods; and caterers who may buy in bulk. It is very likely that the press officer can extend the information and appeal to customers other than those comprising the broad market. (It might not pay to advertise in yachting papers whereas a specially slanted press story could be very useful to editors of such specialist journals.)

The press officer can proceed to plan his programme along the following lines:

1. What is new, different, special, interesting about the product?

2. Who is likely to be interested—who are the publics?

3. How can he reach these publics—what media or techniques should he employ?

4. What will all this cost?

5. What will the programme achieve?

If the press officer plans along these lines he sets out to answer the questions posed in the opening paragraph of this chapter.

For the purpose of this exercise let us say that the product is a prepared main meat dish wrapped in foil and has merely to be heated and served with a vegetable such as peas which may have been either canned or frozen. At its simplest, it can be eaten this way but other or additional vegetables and gravy could be added. It is tasty enough to serve once a week.

The product is ideal for the working housewife, but also saves a lot of time for any busy woman who does not wish to be tied to the kitchen. Anyone can serve such a meal, and it will store for months, so possible customers are legion from girls in bed-sitters, bachelors, and old people to holidaymakers in caravans, boats and tents. There are distinct commercial possibilities ranging from canteens to cafés. And it's far more sophisticated than a can of baked beans.

All these publics can be reached through the countless people who write, talk and demonstrate on the subject of food. All of these can be reached by the following scheme.

1. A press reception and sampling session at a hotel to which would be invited journalists who write about home and catering topics in women's magazines and the women's pages of newspapers, plus journalists from the food retailing and catering trade press, and their counterparts from radio and TV. Some of the more specialist papers can also be invited—those dealing with outdoor pursuits—and there are a great many freelance journalists who write on this kind of topic. The advantage of a press reception is that the product can be tasted and tested, and examples of its use and usefulness can be demonstrated. You cannot achieve this physical testimony with a press release or even do it so well with a posted sample which may or may not be put to the test.

2. Press release follow-ups will be necessary, with recipes and ideas to stimulate the interest of journalists.

3. Printed recipe leaflets will be valuable too.

4. Photographs of the product served with various vegetables must be available from the start.

5. It is likely that co-operative efforts can be achieved with the press officers for associated products such as frozen vegetables.

Counting the Cost

Once again we will base the exercise on an assumption, this time that we are mounting a short-term press relations programme to support a product launch. We shall, however, need to spread coverage over about three months since we are dealing with both daily and weekly newspapers, printed quickly by letterpress and weekly and monthly journals which, if printed by gravure, may go to press several weeks before publication.

The most expensive item is the press reception. Taking a figure of £3 a head to cover the hotel and catering, sampling, and press kit expenses, and expecting, say, 30 guests, we can arrive at a cost of £90. The bar expenses need not be heavy if there is an active programme with a welcoming drink on arrival and a bar and buffet at the close, the reception taking place during the late morning. Other expenses may be the hire of demonstrators, and possibly costumes to add gaiety. If it is run by a staff press officer his costs are probably not included but if the event is run by an outside consultant there is likely to be a time-based fee of around £100. We are concerned therefore with a total cost of between £150 and £250 according to whether the event is organised internally or externally, the difference being the allocation of staff costs.

Other costs will include press releases, envelopes, photographs, captions, recipe leaflets and postage. All in all, allowing for recipe leaflets printed in colour, there could be a materials cost of £300 to £500.

The total budget could be between £750 and £1000, bearing in mind that this is a national effort and in addition to the press attending the London reception press material and samples will have to be distributed to newspapers and magazines in the provinces, not forgetting the national press of Scotland. However, this is but an outline of the distribution of the stories.

And so we arrive at the achievement, measured beside that of the sales force, the distributors and the advertising. In a joint marketing enterprise the results are seldom divisible, but with the aid of such a press relations programme the results are likely to be more marked. Writers and broadcasters will have told their audiences about the new food, how it tastes, the convenience it offers. The advertising will be more meaningful. Housewives will be informed, diners will recognise the item on the menu, holidaymakers and tourists will remember to pack the ready-made meal, and the idea of trusting an absent cook will be accepted. Advertising will have its impact, securing repeat sales, directing to the point of purchase, doing its hustling job but press relations will have done the human job of overcoming hostility to a strange idea, presenting the testimony of trusted editorial, spreading knowledge of its versatile application, and establishing the confidence that must stand behind the purchase of a successful product.

In other words, modern marketing is an integrated force of which press relations is a valuable part. To succeed in marketing a new product it is necessary to employ all communicators and all communication techniques. Press relations is one of them. Not to use press relations in such a campaign could be likened to trying to make a television receiver work despite the lack of a vital component.

Measuring Results

However, to say that the results of press relations are seldom divisible may not satisfy those who have to justify budgets. While it is true that many of the results of press relations are intangible—just as those of any other aspect of marketing including advertising can be intangible—and it is the total result that matters, there are certain results which are directly attributable to the special techniques of press relations. They will be more readily recognised in some campaigns than in others, as will be seen in the examples given in the next few pages, and more will be said on this subject in Chapter 18 which deals more analytically with research and results.

These achievements will include press cuttings which can be evaluated against the readership of the various journals—*not* against the equivalent cost of the same volume of advertisement space!—and there will be the enquiries and requests for recipe leaflets, samples or whatever may be offered. These cuttings will show, for example, how far interest has penetrated beyond the mass consumer readership of the advertising schedule media, to the canteen caterers, caravanners, campers and so on. Trade press coverage of the advertising campaign will have interested distributors and helped the sales force. Stories in the catering press will have helped café proprietors with their meal-planning. General coverage in the popular press will have helped to achieve quick acceptance of the product, whether for eating at home or eating out. Press relations can be seen to do a worthwhile job because when people become familiar with a product—or a new idea in food—in their everyday reading they will respond more receptively to advertising. The advertising does not first have to demolish the possible barriers of ignorance, apathy and hostility.

And there are other positive results. News of the successful launch is likely to provide story material for city editors, and this will encourage stock market confidence in the company. News about the successful new product will make good reading in the local press in the vicinity of the factory, and good community relations is always worth fostering for many reasons, not forgetting staff relations and staff recruitment.

The point of all this is that press relations carries the information, message, news, idea, what you will, to an infinitely wider audience than is usually possible or economical with advertising. And even though it is true that a carefully managed advertising campaign will convey the message, quickly and persuasively, to the majority of likely buyers it is also true that the effective demand which every manufacturer seeks will be gained even more economically if press relations techniques have also been employed to establish the knowledge and confidence which stimulates reader and viewer acceptance and response.

Liaison with other Departments

It is important that the marketing manager sees that there is proper liaison between the press relations efforts and the production programming and retail distribution. For example, new products or new models make news and the press officer can often obtain publication of pictures and stories. But if these new lines are not available in the shops potential buyers, stockists, wholesalers and the manufacturer's own sales force will all be frustrated and the press coverage will be both an embarrassment and a waste. Yet this happens repeatedly, especially when PR consultants are engaged and those responsible for supplying the consultant with information do not first check that the goods are in fact in supply, or will be when the items are published.

When sending such releases to the consumer press it is essential for the press officer to be armed with a list of London stockists, and better still if he can have some provincial ones as well such as a well-known chain of stores. This is to help the reader service departments of journals. The writers of some features (e.g. the Shopping Bag feature in the *Evening News* and items produced by the Joan Storey Organisation) are extremely careful to avoid upsetting readers because goods described are not available. Many such features do not name the product but do name the supplier, so the press officer must be ready with such distribution information before he releases a product story.

This is not always as easy as it seems. Some companies sell only through wholesalers, others may have very mixed ranges of products, and so neither may be able to check deliveries and guarantee available stocks in any given shop. The most they can say is that certain big stores like Gamages, Selfridges or Lewis's are agents or stockists. The problem can be overcome by swift co-operation between the press officer and the sales manager. If the likely appearance of, say, a story in a provincial evening newspaper can be relayed to area distributors a stock of the product can be placed in a shop whose address can then be passed on to the newspaper in readiness for passing on to enquirers after the story has appeared. This stock may come from a wholesaler, but it may have to come from a salesman's buffer stock. Very properly, some feature writers will not refer to specific products unless named stockists are supplied because it would be foolish for them to make recommendations which readers cannot take up. This shows how carefully executed press relations work must be, and how closely it needs to be linked to the marketing operation.

SOME EXAMPLES OF PRESS CAMPAIGNS

Now let us consider some actual examples which indicate both the advantages of preliminary PR launchings using press relations techniques, and the contribution they can make to marketing strategy.

A Property Maintenance Service

The company concerned was nationally famous. Research and development had discovered a new scientific process for eliminating a very troublesome condition found in many older houses. The company could market this additional service through its existing network of branch offices. It was a foreign process which had Ministry support in the country of origin. Success had been achieved in extraordinary circumstances, dealing with the problem in historic buildings where it was even more serious than in Victorian dwellings in Britain.

But on the face of it the system sounded absurdly impracticable, while a different one employing similar basic principles had resulted in the promoters going bankrupt a few years previously. Advertising was both premature and unlikely to be convincing, especially as there was a Government leaflet condemning the first method which had left behind a trail of unfortunate experiences. Nevertheless, the company was convinced of the efficiency of the system which they were permitted to market under licence from the foreign inventor who was himself successfully applying it in his own country.

Press relations techniques were applied very successfully in conjunction with a series of experimental applications on public and domestic buildings including a cathedral where the condition was known to be beyond control by conventional methods. A press reception was held in London with technical demonstrations, and despite some scepticism (including an out-and-out "don't believe it" response by the scientific correspondent of the *Financial Times*), the system was accepted and reported very largely because the company had such a good image that journalists were unable to believe that such a reputable company could foist a fraudulent proposition on the public. This act of faith spoke highly for the company's public relations, and press relations in particular.

The result was that over the next few months pictures, reports and technical articles appeared, including ones written in depth by the company's own technicians, in journals such as *Architect and Building News*. Reprints of these articles, and photographs taken of trials, were used at technical seminars for professional property advisers such as architects, building society officials, property owners, estate agents and surveyors.

The system became known, understood and accepted, and during this educational period men were trained to specify and install. Today the company has a complete division specialising in this work alone, and for some years now the service has been widely advertised in the national press. Without the initial press relations and follow-up PR programme very briefly sketched here, this service to owners of older property might never have become available in Britain.

A Toiletry Product

This product was the brainchild of the editor of a woman's weekly magazine, and the need for such a product was indicated by the number of readers' letters which posed the same problem of personal hygiene. The editor approached a medical expert for advice, and found that a hospital doctor had evolved a product to relieve the problem among his female patients. The editor saw the commercial possibilities, and approached a manufacturer.

The product was duly manufactured, but it was a difficult item to discreetly describe in public advertisements. So this editor devoted a whole page article in her multi-million circulation weekly to the introduction of the product, samples being offered. On the basis of this introduction the manufacturers were encouraged to go ahead and obtain retail distribution through Boots and other pharmaceutical retailers.

A New Kind of Insurance

A company, not itself engaged in insurance, decided that a form of insurance would be a valuable service to offer in conjunction with other services. But it was an entirely new subject for insurance, and people had to be convinced that it was necessary, and that included brokers. Once again, advertising was out of the question on economic grounds because enough could not be undertaken to be effective. The company was prepared to spend a couple of years educating the market.

There was an initial press reception; special articles were published in appropriate journals read by both brokers and likely policy holders; and the subject was even discussed in a BBC radio programme which offered financial advice to listeners. It was a slow haul, but the company has since extended the insurance cover to an associated field which was considered to be an even bigger risk, and this was surely evidence that the original scheme had won acceptance, largely through a painstaking educational campaign employing press relations techniques to support field salesmen.

Services to Local Authorities

A company was convinced that it could extend its sales through the numerous local authorities throughout the UK and Europe. It had products and services of interest to many different departments. But the opposition was intense because local government officers preferred to use direct labour, even though this might be unskilled, even casual. Moreover, some authorities were unwilling to admit that they themselves were able to provide only very limited services since they lacked not only skilled labour but the special equipment and the variety of techniques which were available from the commercial company. There was also a public service attitude that it was wrong to employ a commerical company anyway. Nevertheless, there were a minority of local authorities which did use the company's products and services, and they were enthusiastic about them.

A very interesting PR campaign was mounted with press relations playing its usual valuable role. The press officer visited local authorities in South London, Essex, Yorkshire and Scotland where it was possible to photograph the company's teams carrying out different types of work on behalf of local authorities, and feature articles—officially approved—were published in magazines such as the *Municipal Journal*, *Municipal Engineer*, *Municipal Review*, *Highways Engineer* and *Scottish Public Services*. Reprints of these articles were used as literature at technical one-day schools attended by between 80 and 120 local government officers in venues such as London, Brighton, Nottingham, Edinburgh and Belfast. Some resistance was still met because the products sold by this company did not conform with the recommendations laid down in the *Municipal Year Book* which was regarded as a Bible when considering tenders. Unfortunately the information in that admirable annual was some twenty years out of date (by commercial if not local authority standards!), and the editor accepted an offer to have the relevant section re-written by a scientist who was competent to define the latest and most effective materials and techniques.

The company also loaned its own equipment and staff for the making of a film-strip which local authorities use for staff training purposes. The result of all this was that eventually the company found it paid to insert advertisements in the local authority press, and today there must be few if any local authorities which do not use at least one of the company's many formulations or services, and this has been extended to apply to countries all over the world.

A Do-it-Yourself Product

But there is no guarantee that press relations will pull off a miracle. If the product is not right a press relations campaign will oblige the product to suffer a scrupulous scrutiny, and this can be as devastating as it can be salutary.

Not long ago a do-it-yourself product for the home was launched at a time when a less sophisticated version had gained a modest success. There was a well-attended press reception at which a practical demonstration was given. The product was generously written up by a press willing to believe that it was all the manufacturers claimed for it. However, whatever its qualities the product also possessed the flaw that it was rather too complicated even for do-it-yourself fans, and gradually the press turned against it. A big advertising and merchandising campaign was launched, but sales flopped. Neither press relations nor advertising can promote a poor product.

A Home Aid Device

A well-known company produced a novel device to utilise spare production capacity. There was no intention of marketing the product in a big way, and the entire promotion began with an imaginative press officer who recognised that the device had so many applications in homes, offices, factories, hospitals, public places and so on that there was scope for a series of press releases each describing a special application. These stories were each mailed to groups of journals.

It was a novel, attractive, inexpensive product which made a good item in many a feature. Its use also coincided with certain Government requirements which appeared in a new Act relating to office premises, and the product also received the accolade of Council of Industrial Design approval. The company was surprised by the demand which resulted from extremely wide editorial coverage, and the product has since become a regular line, catalogued, advertised and widely distributed. The original promotion was entirely by means of a very inexpensive press relations exercise calling for careful media selection and the adaptation of the story to suit the media. The only initial advertising consisted of a few announcements in the trade press, a carton and a dispenser pack. Here was a case of a product which was news of real reader value, helped by the fact that it was also pictorially attractive and interesting.

5

Presentation of the Press Release

There are two important aspects to the production of a successful press release. One is the way it is presented and the other is the way it is written. Although the presentation is largely a matter of stencil-cutting and duplicating what has been written by hand or on a typewriter the author should have the final appearance in mind at the creative stage. He will then discipline himself to apply techniques which are logical, and therefore essential, if a publishable press release is to be produced. He will restrict capital letters to proper names and eliminate full points from abbreviations for practical and not pedantic reasons. He will also know that what may be good secretarial practice is not necessarily good press relations practice, and he will be able to instruct secretarial staff in what, to them, may well be strange typing techniques and styling.

Therefore, in this chapter the basic presentation is analysed and discussed very carefully. A first-class press officer will be meticulous over these details. How a press release should and can be written will be dealt with in the next chapter.

The purpose of good, correct presentation is threefold: 1. to achieve legibility; 2. to make the release attractive to read; and 3. to minimise editorial work so that the release is capable of publication as it stands. The less a story is cut or re-written the less likelihood there is of its meaning being changed. But having said that it must be admitted that while a trade magazine may print the story exactly as submitted by the press officer the national newspaper will invariably do a re-write job to suit its own style and may well use the press release merely as a piece of information on which to base a story resulting from further investigation. In both cases, however, it is essential that the press officer shall issue his information in a thoroughly professional manner, and this really boils down to presenting the facts as an editor would like to receive them.

These three requirements therefore imply a knowledge of human psychology and an appreciation of editorial needs. Unfortunately so many press releases, even some produced by eminent organisations and individuals, fail to meet these three elementary requirements. The presentation of a press release is just as much a piece of marketing as the packing of a shirt in a plastic bag and a nice box. Nobody wants to pore over a difficult-to-read, unidentified, grubby-looking press release produced by a careless typist using a battered typewriter and an aged duplicator. The sad answer is that at least 50 per cent of the press officers in the UK are unaware that it is possible to duplicate a release *impeccably*. The contrast between good and bad presentation is being emphasised today by those who enjoy the advantages of the electric typewriter.

Essential Elements of Presentation

The presentation can be divided into the following ten elements:

1. The basic sheet.
2. Length, ending and authorship.
3. Headlines, subheads and paragraphs.
4. Style and punctuation.
5. Embargoes and dating.
6. Picture availability.
7. Typing the stencil.
8. Running off.
9. Assembling.
10. Envelopes.

1. *The Basic Sheet*

Sheet Size. For press work, the tendency has been to use quarto paper (10 × 8 inches) in the main, but in recent years the continental A4 paper size ($11\frac{3}{4} \times 8\frac{1}{4}$ inches) has been introduced. An advantage of this larger size sheet is that it makes it very easy to restrict the majority of news stories to the ideal of one piece of paper, a distinct advantage from the point of view of a busy editor. It is always psychologically easier to induce someone to read what is presented to them on one side of one piece of paper.

The Printed Heading. A press release which is merely duplicated straight on to plain paper without a printed heading looks dull and amateurish. A printed press release heading, like any letter-heading, should quickly establish the identity of the sender. When a reputation has been won for good, interesting and accurate press stories instant recognition by means of a distinctive heading will be a desirable asset since the editor of even a small trade paper may receive as many as fifty different press releases of varying length in a single morning's post.

The headings one sees vary tremendously in design, some being very colourful and striking, perhaps using the house symbol and house colour, but the best are fairly simple and do not occupy too much space. They are not meant to be advertisements, yet some resemble sales letter note-paper. The wording should clearly state the name, address, telephone number and Telex number (if there is one) for further information, and a night or home telephone number can be helpful.

A PR consultancy has the problem of declaring the identities of both itself and its client, but from the editor's point of view it is the *client's* identity which matters even though further information is to be had from a consultant. It is therefore wrong, if common, for the consultant's name to predominate, and it is better if a separate heading is designed and printed for each client. This, for some strange reason, is rarely done and yet it seems the obvious thing to do. There is no reason why the individual headings cannot be printed in the house style of the consultancy so that there is a family likeness between a series of headings for individual clients. Thus it is possible to give prominence to the client while clearly identifying the consultant as the source of information.

Peter Ransley, editor of *Plastics and Rubber Weekly*, when asked to name press release heading designs he liked, told the author, "*I think I prefer as uncluttered top of the sheet as possible so as to leave plenty of room for sub-editor's marks.*" He went on to mention the heading used by Eric Buston & Associates Ltd of Bristol.

There are two interesting things about the Eric Buston heading. First, it is printed in green, a rare colour among press release headings which are more often printed in either red or blue. Second, and this is both unusual and effective, all that is printed at the *top* is the small but bold declaration NEWS RELEASE between a pair of bold rules, and all the information about the consultancy is given modestly but clearly at the foot. The effect is to give emphasis to the story, and since the story is reproduced in black it contrasts very legibly with the neat, informative but unobtrusive green print. Moreover, since the subject of the news release will be clear from the headline and the openings words, this style of press release heading is self-identifying so far as the client is concerned. The Eric Buston heading is a very thoughtfully designed yet thoroughly businesslike one.

2. *Length, Ending and Authorship*

The question of length occurs many times in this book. The more concise and precise the release is the more readable and acceptable is it likely to be. Nevertheless, with very technical products it may be proper to cover the subject in sufficient depth to make the story worth publishing. Discretion must be applied according to the topic and the media.

However, in this chapter we are concerned with length from the point of view of presentation, and length can sometimes be determined at the typing stage because if a second sheet is going to be required to carry a continuation of only a few lines it is usually possible to cut the story in order to keep it on one piece of paper.

Again, there is the question of extra work and extra costs. A PR department or press office in industry is seldom over-staffed and a few words running over on to a second sheet means an extra stencil to cut, an extra stencil to run off on the duplicator and a third extra job in stapling the two sheets together.

Similarly, the PR consultant who charges his clients for the consumption of unnecessary reams of paper, as can happen over a period of a year, is not acting very responsibly if paper is wasted, so length of releases can be a matter of strict account management. In a consultancy it is essential to be cost conscious. There are only two people who can pay for wasted paper, the client or the consultant.

Finally, there is the question of editorial time and editorial needs. Editors receive so many hundreds of press releases every week that they simply do not have the time to wade through pages of verbosity. The news agencies, which generally put out on their wire services stories of no more than 80 words, despair at the daily arrival of long-winded press releases which condemn themselves on sight.

Thus, when the facts are presented as briefly as possible, and the story can be read almost at a glance, there is seldom any need to go beyond the ample space provided by an A4 sheet.

The *Ending* of the release and its *Authorship* are related to the length, and particularly to the more detailed release which does run to more than one sheet.

All press releases should close with the name of the writer. This is important when the story has originated from a consultancy, less necessary when it has come from an organisation whose press officer is named on the printed heading. But closing the story with the author's name is also a very clear way of finishing, because use of the author's name makes it obvious that nothing more follows. It is a more sensible way of establishing the end of the story than printing *Ends* which, like other expressions such as *Over*, is better suited to non-visual messages. Giving the writer's name is also a good way of establishing personal contact and personal responsibility for the facts. A press officer will be encouraged to take care that he puts his name only to stories which do him credit!

3. *Headlines, Subheads and Paragraphs*

Here we have three elements of a press release on which there seems to be hardly any agreed standard practice, yet when ordinary editorial needs are considered there can surely be no question about the *required* practice if good press relations are to be maintained. Let us examine each one in turn.

Headlines. Although it is tempting to invent clever, alliterative headlines, don't! No-one will use them. Each editor likes to write his own, unless he is lazy or there is no better alternative to yours. The purpose of the press release headline is to quickly *identify* the story. The headline, which is not to be confused with the printed heading already discussed, has a practical purpose to perform, but it may never be printed if only because editors do not want to print the same headlines as their rivals. Sometimes employers and clients try to insist that the press officer should word the headline in some dramatic or persuasive manner, but the press officer must dissuade them from doing this. If a news story begins with a headline like that of an advertisement the editor may well be put off so that he thinks—before he has read it—that the story will be equally full of superlatives and nothing more than a "puff". The headline can therefore create the right impression that what follows is a genuine, factual, news story.

However, there is always the exception that breaks the rule. While the foregoing is sound standard practice there can be occasions when the story of a seemingly dull or difficult subject can be given a lift and marketed by a bright and possibly humorous treatment such as MORE PARLIAMENTARY PIGEONS LOSE THEIR SEATS which was the headline to one of Peter Bateman's stories about the treatment of pigeon-infested ledges on the Houses of Parliament. Such headlines are part of Peter Bateman's inimitable literary style, rather than an attempt to concoct clever headlines. His stories continue in the same light-hearted style! A gimmicky headline followed by a straight, informative news item is out-of-place, more likely to irritate than amuse. Bateman's treatment helps to make a sometimes unpleasant story about vermin perfectly publishable in the popular press, and to achieve this end his kind of headline is justified.

Subheads. Again, it is tempting to insert subheadings to add interest to a story, but they may be a nuisance to the editor who either does not use them, or likes to put them in where they suit him, often as part of the typographical artistry of the page, relieving the monotony of grey type with bold black subheadings. So it is best not to use subheads, except in a very long release which has clearcut sections dealing with separate items such as a number of different models, brands or products. Even then, it may be better to write individual releases on each subject rather than bury the various items in an omnibus story. Commonsense must prevail to some extent. In all these matters the press officer has to remember that his story will be going to many editors who will each have distinctive styles of presentation, and therefore it is wise to present the basic story as baldly but as clearly as possible, leaving each editor to set it out as he pleases.

Paragraphs. The use of paragraphs and their presentation is imperfectly understood by some press officers, but the lesson can be learned very quickly by studying the columns of daily newspapers. Modern journalism calls for short paragraphs. They help people to read quickly, and to absorb the message clearly. Short paragraphs can be deliberately used to keep the interest flowing.

The setting out of paragraphs is not limited to their length, however. Most newspapers and magazines indent all paragraphs except the first, and press releases should adhere to this style.

If a press release is not produced in this way the editor or his staff have the extra task of adding printer's signs which mean indent. One of the purposes of these recommendations, let us repeat, is to help the press officer to issue press releases which are not only attractive and readable but have the virtue of saving the editor unnecessary work. A news story with unindented paragraphs is a nuisance in that it requires just that extra bit of subbing, merely because the press officer is unprofessional or because his secretary insists on using a style which is foreign to publishing, although smart for business correspondence.

4. *Style and Punctuation*

Capital Letters. Capital letters belong to titling or to proper names. Indiscriminate use of capital letters can be the bane of an editor's life. A company or product name should never be written *entirely* in capitals, nor should initial capitals be used for nouns as they are in German.

Thus, in a sentence, WOODWORM is wrong, so is Woodworm, but Woodworm Control Ltd is correct. Or, to take another example, the following is wrong.

"*The new range of Central Heating equipment made by ABC Ltd includes Solid Fuel, Gas-fired and Oil-fired Boilers.*" It should be like this:

"*The new range of central heating equipment made by ABC Ltd includes solid fuel, gas-fired and oil-fired boilers.*"

Far too many press releases are written in the first of these two styles, and it is plain to see the extent of editorial correction which is necessary. To sprinkle a press release with needless capitals is to suggest to the editor that the press officer is incompetent and, more than that, that he seldom reads a newspaper or magazine!

Technical people are apt to refer to Cocoa, Radar, Timber, Steel, business people to Directors, Boards, Annual General Meetings and Dividends, but these capital letters are wrongly used and must not be used in a press release.

Nor should emphasis be given by typing passages in capitals. All emphasis should be left to the editor since, as we shall see in the next chapter, it is not the place of the press officer to comment or invite testimony. If the editor chooses to use emphatic devices such as capitals, large type, bold type, italics or even underlinings, that is entirely up to him. It has nothing to do with the author of the press release who must content himself with supplying factual material free of bias. Otherwise the press release becomes an advertisement. This distinction is sometimes, and understandably, difficult to appreciate by advertising people when they are employing press relations services.

Underlining and Quotation Marks. No underlining should appear anywhere in a press release, not even in the headline, because whereas to the writer underlining means a rule or line set there for emphasis, to the printer an underlining is an instruction to set in italic type. Consequently, an editor may underline the words he wants set in italics, but it is no business of the press officer to stipulate which words should be set in italics, except in the case of foreign words or Latin names in scientific matter.

Similarly, quotation marks can generally be avoided, and it is better to neither quote nor underline the names of ships, songs, books, films, plays, houses, and so on, leaving it to the editor to decide whether to put in quotation marks or to italicise. The time to use quotation marks is when actual speech is being quoted, or when material from another source is being quoted, always remembering that it is necessary to place quotation marks at the beginning of each paragraph and to conclude the entire speech or quotation with quotation marks. Otherwise it is not absolutely clear where the quotation starts and finishes.

Numerals and Symbols. A paragraph should never begin with a numeral, and if the sentence cannot be recast satisfactorily the numeral should be spelt out. Except in special cases, numbers from one to nine should be spelt out, after which numerals such as 59 and 101 should be used until the numbers become so unwieldy that it is clearer to spell out many thousands and certainly millions. Five millions or £5 million is more readily understood than 5,000,000 or £5,000,000. The actual numerals should be given in dates, June 1st and not June First, and 1970, not one thousand nine hundred and seventy, and definitely not nineteen seventy. Similarly, we write the 20th century as we do the 19th hole. The press officer has to be extremely careful that accurate and easily understood figures are given in press releases. An error can be disastrous once it is printed, and little can be done by way of correction. If the story has been widely distributed the error may be perpetuated for weeks, months, even years. There is a very real risk that someone, a typist or typesetter, may omit or add a nought. If figures can be spelled out in unmistakable words many unfortunate errors can be avoided but of course there are some technical subjects where it is common practice to use figures no matter how complex and the press officer has to obey this requirement.

The same safeguard applies to measurements and signs where there is any risk of mistake as when the inch sign (″) could reproduce indistinctly and be taken for the foot sign (′). It is therefore sensible in press releases to write 2 feet and not 2′, and 2 inches and not 2″. Equally, it is advisable to avoid the signs and write 90 degrees and 100 per cent.

While on this subject, it is all too easy to be slapdash about the use of figures, signs and punctuation, and inconsistencies like the use of 1½″, one and a half inches, and one-and-a-half inches in the same story must be eliminated. Such inconsistencies are surprisingly frequent in the same press release! Editors are confronted with ½ lbs and half pounds, 100 mile and hundred mile, 4-wheel and four wheel so that once more he has to waste time on making more corrections. In the short space of a few hundred words the press officer should be capable of repeating numerical facts in the same way.

A sign which is badly abused is the ampersand (&) which should never appear in a sentence unless it is part of the normal way of spelling a company name. At best, it is a lazy device, sometimes resorted to by those who write quickly in longhand. The ampersand has its uses where space is scarce, that is in headlines and tabulated matter such as lists, catalogues and accounts.

Full Points or Full Stops. Full points should not be used between initial abbreviations such as BSc, BBC, MCC and so on. If they were inserted, viz: B.Sc., B.B.C., M.C.C., the effect would be a spotty mess. Needless editorial work can again be eliminated by the omission of these points in the first place. A study of the press will show that the Financial Times index is abbreviated as the FT index, the Greater London Council as the GLC, the United States Army as the US Army and Member of Parliament as MP. This absence of full points in abbreviations is common to all types of publication, and although exceptions can be found the appearance of the text is always improved when the full points are omitted. Many publications will not print letters after people's names, and while it is acceptable to give an author his degrees and professional qualifications in the *title* of an article it is unlikely that they will be printed if included in the *body* of a press release.

Full points remain a vital form of punctuation, and the so-called letter-writing style which omits all punctuation must not be used when typing a press release.

Punctuation Generally. The clarity of a news story can depend upon use of punctuation, and commas, colons, semi-colons, dashes and brackets are the signposts of written communication. The pedantic use of punctuation can impede reading, but the lack of essential punctuation can cause misunderstanding. Sometimes punctuation is omitted through carelessness, and stencils must be scrutinised to see that parentheses are completely punctuated, and if a dash is introduced that there is a corresponding one at the end of the aside and before the sentence is completed. The apostrophe is often omitted, and so is the interrogation mark. It goes without saying really that the press officer cannot do his job properly without a first-class secretary, not just a typist. Editors can be very scornful of the indifferent punctuation to be found in far too many press releases.

5. *Embargoes and Dating*

The date when a story may be published, the use of dates in stories, and the date when the release is issued are three things of great consequence to the recipient of press releases.

Embargoes. An embargo is an instruction to the press that the story is not to be published before a certain date and perhaps even a certain time on that date. There are many genuine occasions when an embargo is vital, and this is often so in financial PR or when stories are being issued in different parts of the world where disparity in times could cause embarrassment if publication took place literally at the same time. The announcement of price changes or the publication of a speech are typical examples where it can be very helpful if an editor can have the news well in advance provided he respects the privilege and does not "jump the gun" or print the speech before it has been delivered!

But having admitted the necessity for embargoes, it must be emphasised that embargoes should be used sparingly and sensibly with the object of helping editors to have material in good time to permit the earliest possible publication. A privileged editor will be grateful, and that is good press relations, but it is very wrong to use embargoes indiscriminately, and even lazily because the press officer cannot be bothered to time or stagger mailings so that an embargo is unnecessary. Long embargoes are bad and hardly ever justified. They usually have the effect of killing interest in the story.

For the great majority of press releases no embargo is required, and where it is not apparent that an embargo is seriously needed its use is liable to annoy an editor who may feel entitled to ignore it. In fact, where an embargo is unexpected and irrelevant it may even get overlooked!

Most stories should therefore be for immediate release, and if that is so it is pointless to print *for immediate release* across the top, unless it comes from one of those rare organisations which seldom issue a story without a stringent embargo. One suspects that some of the releases from commercial sources which bear dramatic embargoes or permissions for instant publication are produced by somewhat amateurish writers who are trying to capture some of the supposed glamour of a hectic Fleet Street newsroom.

Dates. If a date is important to the story it should be included in the narrative, and the month should read first and be spelt out in full, thus: November 12th 1970. If this sequence of month and date is used a sentence can begin with the month, while within the story the correct emphasis is placed upon the month which is generally more significant and memorable than the day of the month. This significance is further borne out by the fact that press reports often refer to months only, or even to "this month" or "last month".

If the release describes a stand at an exhibition, the headline should state all the relevant details about name of exhibition, venue, *dates*, hall and stand number. In London alone there are two or three exhibitions taking place every week and editors cannot be expected to know when and where every exhibition is being held. Yet, perhaps surprisingly, it is common to see press releases which refer quite vaguely to "the

NEWS RELEASE

BALLOON ASCENT AT LISTERS CENTENARY GALA DAY

Jambo, the silver and orange balloon, which once travelled across East Africa, will be the centre of attraction at the R.A. Lister & Co. Ltd. Centenary Gala Day in Dursley on Saturday, June 17th.

During the afternoon Jambo will be making a number of captive flights up to a height of 100 ft. and the climax of the celebrations will be the balloon's ascent from the recreation field.

The owner of the field in which the balloon lands that evening will be presented with a Lister teakwood garden seat as a memento of the Centenary.

Jambo's most important race was during an international balloon sport week at Murren, Switzerland, in a balloon contest flying over the Alps. The balloon stands 55 ft. tall, is 38 ft. in diameter, can carry up to five people and holds 27,000 cu.ft. of gas.

The balloon pilot is 29-year-old Malcolm Brighton, a trained aeronautical engineer, who this year completed a 55-mile flight across the English Channel.

The full programme of entertainment on Gala Day commences with an impressive procession tracing the 100 years of Listers in Dursley. The procession commences at Bull Pitch at 2.30 p.m. making its way through the town as far as Woodfield, Cam.

Some of the attractions are a donkey derby, fun fair, army motor cycle display, flower show, dancing, ox-roast, and sporting events and the day will be rounded off by a firework display.

The Chairman of the Centenary Celebration Committee, Mr. James Lister, said that admission to the Gala would be free and the Company extended an invitation to everyone in the area to join in the celebrations.

- ends -

FROM Brian Cooper
Eric Buston & Associates Ltd

PRESS AND PUBLIC RELATIONS CONSULTANTS
TOWER HOUSE FAIRFAX STREET BRISTOL 1
TEL BRISTOL 27666 Nights and Weekends 625301 or 621405

May 1967
BTC/PK

Figure 1. A well laid out press release on a simple but effective printed sheet (actual size $11\frac{3}{4}'' \times 8\frac{1}{2}''$). This is the sheet referred to on page 39 of the text.

LANCER BOSS AT THE PORTS & TERMINALS EXHIBITION

From their range of more than sixty trucks, the Lancer Boss Group are exhibiting five on Stand 26/27 and another four at the Black Rock demonstration area. Although the emphasis of the Group's products is on container handling, those exhibited are capable of covering every conceivable type of application where lift trucks are useable.

The giant Lancer 2500 Series, the largest sideloader in the world, is demonstrating its ability to load, transport and stack 20ft containers three high if necessary - the most efficient and flexible container handling system in the world today. Another giant is the Boss D Series, the largest front lift truck in Europe, offering an alternative container handling system. Both these types of truck are already in use in the United Kingdom, Scandinavia and Holland.

The Lancer 4/88, the most advanced sideloader yet designed, and developed from the 400 Series of which there are more in the world than any other type, is also being demonstrated. Its many features include the ability to lift 75% of its 4-ton load at maximum outreach without the use of stabiliser jacks, thus providing unlimited side-shift.

Among the Boss front lift trucks are the latest smallest additions to the range, the M and P Series. all available with diesel, petrol, electric or L.P. gas propulsion. The Boss P.E. 4 being demonstrated has a capacity of 4,000 lb at 24 inch load centre and is equipped with 'Supertronic' S.C.R. control gear, allowing effortlessly smooth acceleration and deceleration as well as superfine 'inching' control for delicate and difficult handling operations.

contd.....

LANCER BOSS GROUP · LEIGHTON BUZZARD · BEDFORDSHIRE · TEL: L. B. 2031

Figure 2. A selection of press releases chosen to show a range of well designed headings; all are printed in colour.

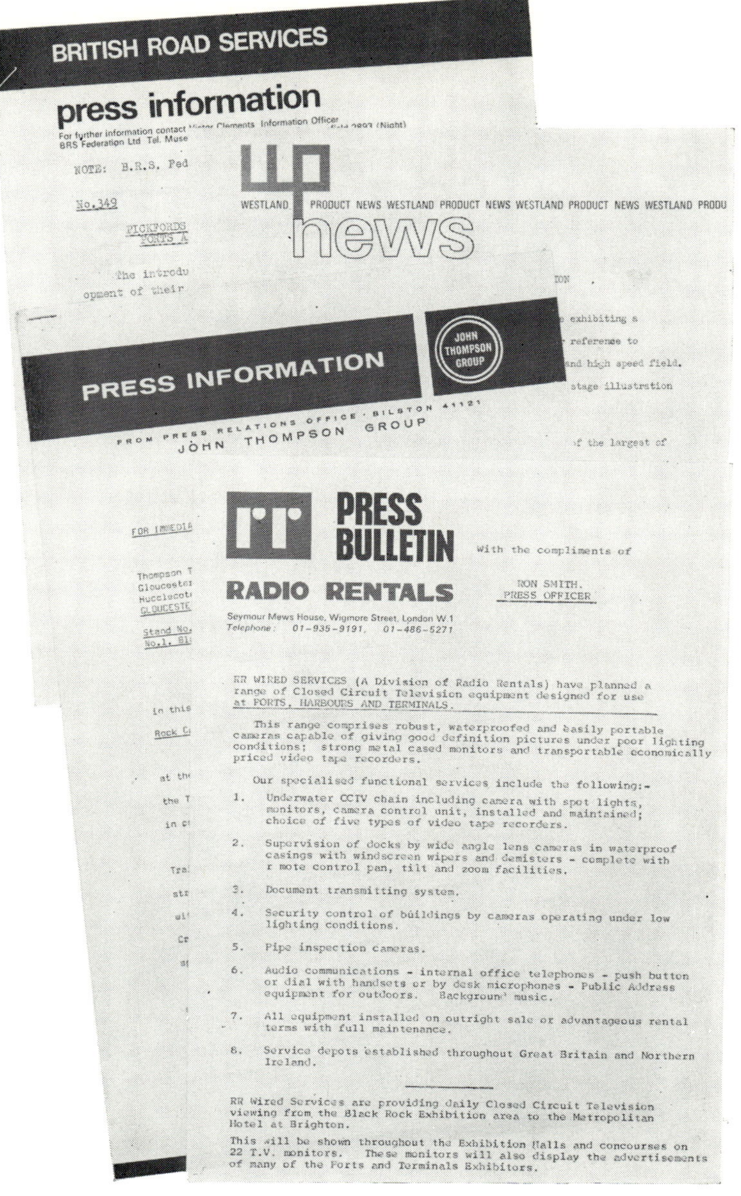

BRITISH ROAD SERVICES

press information

NOTE: B.R.S. Fed

No.349

WESTLAND PRODUCT NEWS WESTLAND PRODUCT NEWS WESTLAND PRODUCT NEWS WESTLAND PRODU

news

PRESS INFORMATION

JOHN THOMPSON GROUP

FROM PRESS RELATIONS OFFICE · BILSTON 41121

JOHN THOMPSON GROUP

PRESS BULLETIN

With the compliments of

RADIO RENTALS

RON SMITH.
PRESS OFFICER

Seymour Mews House, Wigmore Street, London W.1
Telephone: 01-935-9191, 01-486-5271

RR WIRED SERVICES (A Division of Radio Rentals) have planned a range of Closed Circuit Television equipment designed for use at PORTS, HARBOURS AND TERMINALS.

This range comprises robust, waterproofed and easily portable cameras capable of giving good definition pictures under poor lighting conditions; strong metal cased monitors and transportable economically priced video tape recorders.

Our specialised functional services include the following:-

1. Underwater CCTV chain including camera with spot lights, monitors, camera control unit, installed and maintained; choice of five types of video tape recorders.
2. Supervision of docks by wide angle lens cameras in waterproof casings with windscreen wipers and demisters - complete with r mote control pan, tilt and zoom facilities.
3. Document transmitting system.
4. Security control of buildings by cameras operating under low lighting conditions.
5. Pipe inspection cameras.
6. Audio communications - internal office telephones - push button or dial with handsets or by desk microphones - Public Address equipment for outdoors. Background music.
7. All equipment installed on outright sale or advantageous rental terms with full maintenance.
8. Service depots established throughout Great Britain and Northern Ireland.

RR Wired Services are providing daily Closed Circuit Television viewing from the Black Rock Exhibition area to the Metropolitan Hotel at Brighton.

This will be shown throughout the Exhibition Halls and concourses on 22 T.V. monitors. These monitors will also display the advertisements of many of the Ports and Terminals Exhibitors.

Figure 3. A further selection of press releases. All headings are in colour.

Furniture Exhibition", simply because the author has not recognised that although it is the only exhibition in which he is interested it is only one of many about which editors receive press releases, especially editors of journals covering subjects other than furniture.

It should not be necessary for an editor to have to ring the press officer and ask "when did it happen?" Moreover, dated stories should be issued promptly so that their news value is not lost, and this implies knowing the last date or even time for copy for different types of publication. It may be that it is too late to write, stencil and post or hand deliver a press release and that the story must be despatched by telephone, telex, UNS, PA or Reuters. In the next chapter we shall examine a BOAC press release of this nature.

Dating Releases. Apart from dates which are part of the information supplied, releases themselves should be dated. Some press officers insert the date at the beginning of the first page, others at the foot of the story. It is also useful practice to number all stories, and this is helpful for record purposes so that the sequence of stories is made known. A consultant will also find it convenient to use his job number so that he has a convenient system for identifying releases in client reports when invoicing, and to combine the job number with the date in a coding at the foot of the large page. However, this is not necessarily explicit to an editor unless the month is spelled out thus: XYZ1001/OCTOBER 12th 1970. There are, therefore, at least three methods of dating releases: (i) at the beginning, as with dating a letter; (ii) at the foot of the story and after the author's name; or (iii) combined with a coding system which is useful for other purposes. Whichever method is chosen, dating is important to prevent out-of-date information being published, as can happen with magazines which file press releases for future use.

6. *Picture Availability*

It may not be feasible to send a photograph with every press release issued. With large mailings the cost of prints is not only prohibitive but wasteful. There may be a choice of picture if, for instance, the story is about several different products or models, and again it would be wasteful to mail a complete set of pictures to every editor on the mailing list. But the availability of pictures can be stated on the release, and since this is not publishable information these details should be set apart from the body of the story, that is, below the author's name. (Alternatively, the pictures can be identified and described on an accompanying order form.)

7. *Typing the Stencil*

A news release cannot be legibly reproduced unless the typing of the stencil is perfect. Should this really have to be said? There is simply no excuse for faint grey releases which are hard to read, or for over-typing, or for black blobs resulting from clumsily made corrections. Yet poorly produced releases are more common than they should be. The stencil should be cut by a first-class secretary who understands *why* perfection is necessary. She should have a machine good enough for stencil cutting. Damaged rollers must be replaced, too sharp letters filed down, and the machine maintained in perfect working order. Cutting press release stencils is not a job for an inexperienced junior.

Judging by the large number of releases which the author has collected or otherwise had the opportunity of seeing, those issued by consultancies tend to be better produced than those issued by organisations with their own internal PR departments. This may be because organisations produce a lot of duplicated material for internal use, and they are less careful about the standard of production. A consultancy, on the other hand, is more inclined to take professional pride, and is also aware that copies sent to clients place the consultancy on constant trial. Much depends on the supervision, and that means on the extent to which the press officer is *aware* of what can and should be produced.

But it is not just a matter of taking pride in one's work for its own sake. A badly duplicated release is hard to read, so why should an editor bother to read it? Knowing that editors receive such large numbers of releases every day it is surely only sensible of the press officer to make sure that everything he sends out is a pleasure to read. This depends on good stencil cutting in the first place, but it is the press officer's responsibility to approve the stencil before it goes on the machine. (Litho-printed releases have fewer problems.)

When typing the stencil *Spacing*, *Margins* and *Continuations* must also conform to editorial needs.

Spacing. All manuscript work should be double or one-and-a-half spaced in proportion to the size of the type on the typewriter.

Machines with very large type faces should not be used for press release work since they will spread the story over more pages than, say, Elite type. Nor should a typewriter with italic type or all capitals be used. When a lot of text has to be read it is easier to read serif type, and this is even truer when reading duplicated material however well it may be reproduced. While electric typewriters produce excellent results it is best to choose one with serif type that is neither too large nor too light. A press release produced from a typewriter with bold

Elite serif type can be set out with one-and-a-half spacing and will look thoroughly legible while meeting the object of spacing which is to permit the editor space to make amendments and instruct the printer.

Margins. Margins are necessary for the same editorial purpose as spacing between the lines. A right-hand as well as a left-hand margin is needed in a press release, although this is not usual with general manuscript work for articles and books. Both margins should not be less than $1\frac{1}{2}$ inches wide.

Continuations. When the press release consists of more than one sheet this should be clearly indicated at the foot of the page, and all succeeding pages should be numbered. If this is done more elaborate continuation references are redundant, but some people do put the title of the piece at the top of each page to make absolutely certain that scattered pages can be reassembled safely. This is really a matter of personal style and preference, but since a press release is supplied as a complete story, the pages stapled together if there are two or more, there is no point in writing *More* at the foot. Use of the word *More* is convenient when a MS is being produced in a number of loose sheets, as may happen in a newspaper office or with a book.

8. *Running Off*

One Side of the Paper. All manuscript work must be typed or duplicated on one side of the paper only, and anything on the reverse side will be ignored. Editors and publishers always work from material on one side of the paper only; when type is being set the sheets of copy are held on the typesetting machine in such a way that it would be awkward for the operator if there was copy on the reverse side too.

Reproduction. There are excellent machines on the market such as Gestetner and Roneo, and stencil machines are preferable to spirit duplicators for this class of work, while lithographic office printing machines are sometimes used. The stencil duplicator provides a good balance between speedy preparation and legible result. But, again, this is a job which requires an expert operator, and good results are unlikely to be obtained if the machine is used—and probably misused!—by various people in the office. One specialist operator is essential.

Copies must be thoroughly legible. This is just as much a matter of machining and watching results as it is one of good stencil-cutting. Corrections should be undetectable. If the operator finds that copies are coming off poorly, and they cannot be improved by mechanical adjustment, a new stencil must be cut. The same thing applies when stencils are re-used but fail to give the desired quality of reproduction.

The machine should be kept in perfect working order, and it should be serviced immediately the slightest fault occurs otherwise the machine may break down just when it is urgently wanted. A fault should never be allowed to get worse: it must be put right at once. Duplicating machines are rugged and reliable but they have to work extremely hard in a press office. Faults are generally caused by abuse at the hands of unskilled operators. Advantage should therefore be taken of the offers by duplicator manufacturers to train operators.

9. *Assembling*

As we have already said, the ideal news story is one that is confined to one sheet of paper—and an A4 sheet is quite large—but there are times when a story does run to two or three pages. It is surprising how many different ways there are of joining sheets together! The paper clip is dangerous and can come adrift in a pile of editorial material on the editor's desk. Some fastenings are physically dangerous! The most suitable is the small wire staple, provided it is properly depressed and not left humped. When folding the release for insertion in the envelope the stapled end should be enclosed within the folds, otherwise there is risk that the metal will rip the envelope during its passage through the post.

It is also important to fold cleanly to avoid unnecessary bulk which can spring open a poorly sealed envelope. If mailings are frequent a folding machine is a good investment, and there are several makes on the market which handle work of various complexities.

This is possibly a good point at which to warn the press officer that secretaries are not always aware of the rough handling which postal packages have to suffer. Letters are stuffed into letter boxes and then into mail bags; the mail bags are manhandled in vans, on railway stations and in sorting offices; and for delivery the letters are bundled in bits of coarse string. Unless items for the post are securely packed and sealed they will stand little chance of surviving the hazards of the postal services. The onus is on the sender to protect whatever he mails.

10. *Envelopes*

The release should be folded as few times as possible so that it is as presentable as possible on arrival. There is no point in folding a foolscap or A4 sheet so that it will squeeze into a small business envelope. An A4 release needs to be folded only twice to fit a DL size envelope. A bulkier release, or a feature article, is best folded only once and posted in a 9 × 6 inches envelope, although if a quantity is to be posted this will incur a higher postal rate as this size is larger than a Post Office preferred size.

However, when accompanying a half-plate photograph (the size of print least likely to get damaged in the post by the string which postmen tie round bundles of letters for any one address) the release has to be folded once each way for insertion in an 8 × 5½ inches envelope. A single sheet press release is preferable with photographs so that there is no danger of damage from the metal staple.

When large photographs are being posted it pays to use card-backed envelopes, but on the whole these are too expensive for mailings of large numbers of releases accompanied by pictures. Cut card can be purchased in order to stiffen 8 × 5½ inches or 9 × 6 inches envelopes. If the card is inserted next to the addressed side of the envelope (an advantage not to be had with card-backed envelopes) there is no risk of the picture being damaged by postal franking or date stamping.

Some of these recommendations may seem fussy but it is the press officer who takes his job seriously and goes to some trouble to please the editor, and be of service to him, who will produce press releases which will be welcomed and published. The results will speak for themselves, and it is not really very difficult to do the job professionally. Incidentally, it will be noticed that none of these recommendations is aimed at pleasing employers or clients!

It is a simple matter to draw up a brief version of these recommendations and to see that every member of the press office staff has a copy to learn by heart, and stick on the wall if need be.

In this chapter the author has not hesitated to slaughter some of the sacred cows of press relations, some of which are included in older and out-dated sources of advice on this subject. Typical sacred cows are embargoes, and the use of expressions such as "for immediate release" and "ends". There is no need to clutter up press releases with this mumbo-jumbo. Most of these terms were derived from journalistic practices which were perfectly all right in their original place—as when a series of stories from a wire service needed to be clearly separated—but these habits of the newspaper office are not necessarily applicable to individually produced press releases.

One of the silliest and most thoughtless mistakes made by some press officers is to add a note at the end of the story requesting a cutting if the story is printed! Many editors are generous about sending cuttings, or better still actual copies of the journal (although more often than not these specimen copies are sent by the advertisement manager!), but it is rather tactless to ask editors for favours. An exception, however, may be when the story is sent overseas and it is doubtful whether a press cutting will come through a press cutting agency. But some editors will not take kindly to a request for cuttings, certainly not the kind who think they are doing the organisation a favour by printing the story in the first place. When despatching press releases a copy of the story and, if possible, a copy of the mailing list should be sent to the press cutting agency.

6

How to Write a Press Release

The first thing to make absolutely clear is that a press release is just as much a specialised literary form as an essay, poem, short story, novel, text-book, letter, report, article or a piece of advertisement copy. Each requires its particular writing skill. A press release is not a short article, nor is it a kind of advertisement. It is not sufficient to copy out the wording of a sales leaflet and call that a press release, something which is done so frequently by the uninitiated that it is not surprising that editors wax profanely about some of the press releases they receive.

Press release writing is a literary form quite unlike any other, and it has to be learned and practised. It is different because it has to inform in such a way that the information is seen by editors to be worth passing on to their readers. That implies a *double* communication, to and from the editor, so that a press release is not even a news story such as a reporter might produce. It is no use adding a polite note: *Dear Editor, this is very important, do please publish it!* The editor must be able to discern its qualities for himself, and these qualities are based on the relevance and importance of the story to the editor's readers.

A method of writing press releases is offered here which aims to train the press officer to set out his facts in an orderly and intelligent fashion. But it should not be considered to be a short-cut, that is a way of avoiding painstaking effort, as all creative work must be. It merely gives a guiding framework for logical exposition of facts. When one has written in this way for a time the discipline should become automatic, rather like dressing in the morning. One does not first put on one's hat, then a tie and after that a vest, and yet many press releases are written in exactly that sort of illogical manner.

In press release writing it has been rather taken for granted that a writer who has had journalistic experience can adequately write press releases without any further training. Nothing could be further from the truth. A carpenter does not automatically make an expert wood carver, and even the experienced journalist needs further training to write good press releases.

Now we are at once confronted by a singular problem. Seldom can we write an individual story for each separate publication, and so our press release has to try to be broadly pleasing and valuable to a number of editors, even though we may be helped by the fact that they are all editors of a special kind of journal such as women's magazines or provincial evenings.

Our piece of writing occupies a position roughly mid-way between copywriting and reporting, but judging by what editors receive a good many of the authors have no knowledge or experience of either and naturally have no ability to write something so subtle as the sort of composition described here.

During a visit to a London news agency the author was told that two huge bins of rejected press releases were disposed of daily. The reason for this colossal wastage of paper, effort and money was that news agencies like to distribute stories of about 80 words and need press releases of little more than 100 words. Yet hundreds of press officers are guilty of sending utterly useless press releases to news agencies, sometimes even to the wrong news agencies. These agencies should not be added willy-nilly to a mailing. For instance, a product publicity story is hardly ever likely to be of interest to the Press Association, and certainly not to the Associated Press—if the difference is understood that one supplies the British home press and the other the American.

An insight into how editors do actually regard incoming press releases was given by Peter Ransley, editor of *Plastics and Rubber Weekly*, when he addressed members of the Industrial Marketing Association, in London, on February 7th 1967. He spoke on "What editors expect from public relations—and what they get". He showed what he got by presenting the pile of press releases received in one day, a Friday. Said Mr. Ransley:

"*This is one day's post. I haven't selected lurid examples from my black museum of press releases.*

"*Before I come to the vitriol let me say this. Without* PR *it would be very difficult to run the weekly I edit.* PR *must be one of the main sources of material for any trade or technical weekly and I'm duly grateful for it.*

"*However, for ten minutes, I propose to be rather ungrateful.*

"*I analysed this (pile) over the weekend. I must confess I was a bit shattered.*

One gets so inured to the process of transferring unacceptable material from the post into the wastepaper basket that one forgets how much of it there is. It's not that it's badly written, although some of it is *badly written; the over-riding fault to me is the low level of the news content, and the rather stale flavour of the news when it is there.*

"My analysis is a very rough one, but it will give you a general idea.

"There are 69 items in this pile.

"25 per cent are rejected immediately, either because they have really minimal news value or they deal with subjects outside my field.

"35 per cent have some possible news content but are marred by obvious errors. Most of these will probably be rejected.

"36 per cent have some possible news content—generally a higher level than the last category—and have no absolutely obvious errors of presentation. A fair proportion of these are classified as possibles and go on to the next stage.

"4 per cent—just 4 per cent—are news stories which I would classify as important.

"You can see the importance of presentation. Some stories will always be rejected because they don't fit the market. Some will always be accepted because they're important. With the bulk of stories—71 per cent in this example—professional presentation can mean the difference between print and the waste-paper basket."

And there we have an indictment from an editor that nearly three quarters of the press releases he receives are not publishable because they are not sufficiently newsworthy. He went on to comment on some of the rejected press releases. In many cases the facts were so buried in turgid, illogically presented prose that it was difficult to detect the news value. In other words, the majority of the press releases brought along to the meeting by this speaker did not measure up to the strict requirements of the author's formula, and that means that either these stories should never have been sent out in such a rough draft state, or there was no story there in the first place. They were certainly not fit to post, and whether they were actually approved by employer or client is beside the point.

However, it would be unjust not to stress the quality of the 20 per cent or perhaps even 25 per cent of excellent press releases which are written by masters of the craft of press release writing. No doubt they will smile when they see the method advocated here, for it is really only an assembly of commonsense, and is no magic formula but the method which truly proficient press officers have been using for the past 30 years. Later, there will be an example from the press section of the Air Ministry, dated June 21st 1937, which bears this out.

This, and BOAC releases of more than 20 years ago, were given to the author by Freddie Gillman, a real "old-hand" at writing newsworthy press releases, with the following very apt remarks:

"I have for long had a bee in my bonnet about press releases. As so much of PR *is involved in communications of one kind and another, I am convinced that a press release should be impeccable—or as impeccable as possible. I receive a dozen or more releases from one* PR *source and another every week and frankly I am appalled by many of them.*

"Far, far too many of these releases include little information likely to interest any newspaper and far, far too many of them, if they have any news at all in them, give it in the body of a lengthy release and not in the first paragraph where it should be. I had one the other day which was three pages long, single-spaced, and it referred to an insignificant event that occurred ten days before the release was issued! Can you beat it? Not long ago I asked the chief news editor of one of the world's biggest news agencies if he found PRO*'s releases of any value. He told me that at least 75 per cent of them went straight into the waste-paper basket because he and his colleagues knew from experience that it was a sheer waste of time even to look at them!"*

Freddie Gillman is a past-president of the Institute of Public Relations and was, before his retirement, chief press and information officer to the British Overseas Airways Corporation. He remains a very active PR man.

One final point before the formula is considered: more than once reference has been made to publishable and unpublishable press releases, but it would be wrong to suggest or expect that every release was intended for publication. The press officer will sometimes issue background information to which journalists can refer. Releases sent to nationals should offer a number of story leads which can be followed up according to the policies of individual editors since rival newspapers will not wish to print exactly the same story. On the other hand, product publicity releases may well be printed as submitted, sometimes because trade and other specialist magazines are short-staffed and the editor is glad to print a well-written piece as it stands.

But whatever the intention or fate of the press release the literary standard should be a publishable one, either because it makes it easier for journalists to extract the facts, or because it saves an editor time if subbing and re-writing does not have to be performed.

Two common faults are also worth mentioning here. One is the long-drawn-out opening paragraph which indicates that an unskilled author is writing his way in. Such a release is not only in the rough draft state but would not have been drafted in that manner if the writer had been trained to write logically. The other is the woolly story which uses a great many words to present very few facts. This is a case of a writer knowing too little, or understanding too little, about his subject. The method which we are now coming to depends on the writer having first assembled the facts upon which the release is to be written. You cannot build a house without the specified materials and components.

The Frank Jefkins Seven-Point Formula for Writing Press Releases

The following seven points form a logical sequence for the presentation of facts in a press release. The formula is also useful as a check list to ensure that a story contains all the necessary factual elements. With the aid of this formula a rough draft release can be produced very quickly, but of course it is essential to collect the facts first. On the other hand, inability to base a release on this formula will immediately reveal the inadequacy of the material on which the writer is trying to produce a story. The formula thus works both ways, demanding and utilising facts. And that is all a press release is: a coherent assembly of facts expressed in the fewest necessary words. There is no requirement for dramatic prose, although apt choice of words does call for a first-class vocabulary to avoid repetition of uninteresting words and to use precisely the right words to secure the proper meaning.

Most people have bad habit words which they repeat, and this weakness has to be controlled. Clichés like "a wide range" must be avoided, but not "like the plague" which is another cliché. Words like "unique" can be overdone, and are hardly ever applicable. But by following this formula it should be easier not to permit these faults because the concentration is on facts and orderly presentation.

Here, then, are the seven points to follow:

1. Name of product or *subject* of the story.

2. Name of the *organisation.*

3. *Location* of the organization (which may be different from the address for further information).

4. Development such as *advantages* of the policy, scheme, action, product or service.

5. *Applications* such as how the scheme will affect people or the product has been or may be used. Applications under test conditions would also be applicable here.

6. *Details*, such as price, colour, size, availability.

7. *Source* of further information, samples, price lists, or address of showroom or information centre.

These seven points can be memorised by the key words:

Subject—Organisation—Location—Advantages—Applications—Details—Source.

The initial letters give us a mnemonic, SOLAADS.

While this is obviously a very handy framework for a product publicity story, it can be applied to any press release as will be demonstrated later. But before applying the seven-point formula to a practical demonstration example, let us look analytically at each point. They are not the themes for seven separate paragraphs. They represent the *sequence* in which the facts should be set out so that the essential news is summarised quickly at the beginning and is substantiated by additional information which is given in an orderly fashion afterwards.

The Opening Paragraph

This, in most cases, should contain the *subject*, *organisation*, *location* and *brief highlights* of the story. This is so whether it be a report of a political speech, the escape of a lion from a zoo, an announcement about a business merger, or a product publicity story about a new gas cooker or the latest electric motor car.

A great mistake with some press releases is that they open with a rambling sentence, even a rambling paragraph, and nowhere in these hundred or so words is there any mention of the subject of the release let alone the substantial introduction recommended in the preceding paragraph. This is no exaggeration. It happens all the time. Here is an example:

```
In all spheres of industrial activity it is widely
recognised that for increased productivity and improved
overall efficiency Materials Handling Methods must be
scientifically organised, using the latest techniques,
such as unit loads, containerisation etc.
```

What is there in this opening paragraph that merits publication as a *news item*? It might make an opening paragraph of an *article* on materials handling methods, but it is supposed to be a press release. In any case, there is a barrier of *18 words* before some semblance of a broad subject is reached. Would any editor bother to read on? Why should he? Unlike the essay, a press release does not require an "introduction", and that is the main fault with the example given above. It applies an essay style which is misplaced in a news story. And no sentence should end with "etc."

Ideally, the *subject* should be stated in the first three words as in the following examples.

Showerings Vine Products and Whiteways have countered the refusal by International Distillers and Vintners to their take-over bid by forecasting a dividend of 35 per cent for the current year (ending 31 March 1968).

Tallon Limited, the Bristol ballpoint pen manufacturers, today (Tuesday, July 4) announced two appointments to the Board, They are Mr. John Montague, the general sales manager, who now becomes marketing director and Mr. Ronald W. Pritchard, the works manager, who becomes works director.

The above are very crisp newsy opening paragraphs. The following is a good example of the opening paragraph which summarises the story:

The Ilford Manual of Photography, published by Ilford Limited and edited by Alan Horder, C.G.I.A., F.I.P., F.R.P.S., Senior Lecturer in Photographic Technology at the Regent Street Polytechnic, has been reprinted with a number of useful revisions. The price of the revised Manual - the 7th reprint of the 5th edition - remains £2. 2. 0d.

This Ilford story is also a good example of the ugliness of full points when a sentence contains abbreviations, but note that the price is set out correctly with "od". Two shillings should never be written "2/-", but always "2/od".

Here are two more excellent opening paragraphs:

BOAC today (April 1) starts jet services across the South Pacific on the route between Britain and Australia. The 33-hour flight establishes BOAC in the booming South Pacific tourist market and forges the airline's second round-the-world-route.

The new British Overseas Airways Corporation direct service from the United Kingdom to South Africa, to be known as the Springbok service, is to open on Saturday, 10th November 1945. It will be operated jointly with South African Airways, with one service a week in each direction at first.

And while we are looking at some older ones (just to prove that the real experts at press relations were doing it the right way many years ago), here are two more:

An agreement between Ford Motor Company Limited and the Trade Union Movement has been signed today (Monday, April 17). This is the result of discussions in the first place between Lord Perry, Chairman of the Company, and Sir Walter Citrine, General Secretary of the Trades Union Congress. Following these discussions, the Company's officials met leading representatives of several Trade Unions when a Joint Negotiating Committee was appointed consisting of Mr. A. R. Smith, Mr. H. S. Cooper, Sir Patrick Hennessy and Mr. J. Rigg, representing the Company, Sir Walter Citrine and Mr. V. Feather of the Trades Union

```
Congress, and Messrs. W. B. Board, A. Deakin, C.B.E.,
H. N. Harrison and J. R. Scott representing the Trade
Unions. A spirit of co-operation and goodwill
characterised the discussions throughout which is a happy
augury for future relations between the parties. The
procedure agreed upon by the Negotiating Committee has been
endorsed by all Trade Unions concerned and it is embodied
in the agreement now concluded.
```

This was issued by the TUC in 1944 as a joint press statement, and although it has the rather stilted phraseology of an official release, and is liberally sprinkled with capital letters, it is nevertheless packed with facts and a summary of the essence of the full release. Unlike the BOAC release, it does give the month first in the date reference. It is, incidentally, an historical press release since it announces Ford's first recognition of trade unions.

Even more historic, is the following opening paragraph from an Air Ministry release of June 21st 1937, not perfect but nevertheless appreciative of the need to present the essential facts from the very first word:

```
On the evening of July 5, "Caledonia" will take off
from the base established by the Irish Free State at
Rynanna on the Shannon for Botwood, Newfoundland. This
survey flight will mark an important step forward in the
first stage of the arrangements for the establishment of
regular air services between Europe and North America.
```

With such minor faults as one or two of these examples may have their newsworthiness is easily compared with the following:

```
Behind every successful electrical appliance
development stands an army of manufacturers responsible for
the manufacture of component parts. Theirs is not the
glory of recognition, theirs is not the accolade of acclaim
and yet without their knowledge, without their skill and
without their ready co-operation, almost every major
breakthrough in the electrical industry could not have been
made possible.
```

That extraordinary opening paragraph, devoid of any news content, containing no subject, product or name of organisation, and completely unidentifiable, was followed by two paragraphs in similar style, the third one actually mentioning the industry in which the manufacturer operated. The manufacturer was named for the first and last time at the beginning of the fourth paragraph, 176 words down in the story! From then on it took on the appearance of a press release, but *the first four paragraphs were redundant.* Why do people do it? No editor would persevere beyond the first sentence, let alone the first four paragraphs! Whoever wrote or authorised this release had no conception of what was publishable.

Back to BOAC (and Freddie Gillman again) for another glimpse of how not to waste a word. This time it is the story of the first *Comet* service, May 2nd 1952, another historic occasion:

```
The world's first regular jetliner service will be
opened by B.O.A.C. at 15.00 hours local time (14.00 hours
G.M.T.) today, when the de Havilland Comet G-ALYP leaves
London Airport on the inaugural flight from London to
Johannesburg.
```

Let us look a little more closely at the all-important opening paragraph. It is like the overture to an opera, commanding attention and offering a sample of what is to follow. Because a press release is a short, brief piece of writing, the opening paragraph must do its job succinctly. If the reader is not spurred to continue reading beyond the opening words the rest of the story need never be written. In other words, a story must begin with a bang. It does not have to be clever or even dramatic, but it must be interesting and compelling.

To a rose grower an opening sentence which began: "*The first real sky-blue hybrid tea rose can now be seen growing in the National Rose Society trial grounds at St. Albans, Hertfordshire*," would be big news. It might be almost dramatic news to rosarians, but it would not be anywhere near as dramatic as "*Forest fire devastates whole towns*." To some extent this explains the difference between a good deal of PR material which is sufficiently interesting to find a place in specialist features, but lacks the hard news appeal necessary for a general news column.

Notice, too, that our opening paragraph is not introductory. It does not lead up to the story, but tells the gist of the story at once. Sometimes this means that if only the first paragraph is published you have achieved valuable coverage. This is extremely important, and releases should be written with this in mind. Most of the stories which fail seem to be written as if the entire release must inevitably be published. This seldom happens and press stories must be capable of mutilation without complete loss.

Newspaper stories are written like this. A report does not state that a boy was walking home from school, decided to cross the road, did not look both ways, and was knocked down by a lorry. The opposite happens. The report that is published states that Peter Bryson, aged 9, was knocked down and killed by a lorry when he crossed a road on his way home from school. And that is really all the seven-point formula is all about, especially regarding the opening paragraph.

Just in case there may be some confusion over the use of "Location" at formula point three and "Source" at formula point seven, it should be made clear that the first reference may be to an address different from the latter. An organisation may be known or identified as being located in a certain town, but there may be a showroom or information centre somewhere else, as in the case of an organisation located in the provinces but having a London showroom. When companies have names like Smith, Brown or Jones it can be very helpful to associate a location with the name. Location does not necessarily occur in the opening paragraph of every story, nor need it be repeated in the final paragraph if sufficient reference has been made in the first paragraph.

Much of this instruction is being given to the opening paragraph. It really is vital, and it is in these very first few all-important lines that the majority of press releases go wrong. It is absolutely essential to make sure that the reader knows what you are talking about right from the start.

It is true, however, that there can be two types of opening paragraph, the one that names the product at once, and the kind that first of all describes the purpose or some other aspect of the product. To illustrate this the following quotations are taken of similar subjects, and come from releases issued at the time of the *Ports and Terminals* Exhibition at the Hotel Metropole, Brighton in April 1967.

This refers first to the service, then to the company.

Door-to-door container services planned by Associated Container Transportation Ltd. will be highlighted on the company's stand (No.127) at the Exhibition of Freight Movement & Handling, Equipment & Services at Brighton this month (April 24-28).

This names the company in the first breath.

Babcock & Wilcox (Materials Handling) Limited, a member of the Babcock & Wilcox Limited Group, designs and supplies complete large-scale materials-handling systems and equipment for a wide range of bulk materials such as ore, bauxite, coal, slurry, chemicals, grain, wood chips etc. This service extends beyond the handling of materials to such specialized fields as handling passengers at ship or air terminals by means of mobile, merchanised passenger gangways.

Each has its merits and faults. The first begins very well, then fails to offer any news at all, and clogs up the opening paragraph with details about the exhibition which should be in the title, not the story. The second makes bold use of the company name at the onset, but makes such a mouthful of the name that interest is immediately stifled. The paragraph then tries to pack a lot in a few words, but includes the cliché "wide range" and ends the sentence with a slovenly "etc." Who cares about the Group? This belongs to the *last* paragraph.

Here is one which begins to offer some news:

A comprehensive range of steel sections designed to meet the technical and cost requirements of freight-container manufacturers has been added to the large variety of section material already available for the transport industry from Metal Sections Ltd, a TI company of Oldbury, Birmingham.

It is a pity the story had to open so badly with the cliché "comprehensive range", but the paragraph does show how product, manufacturer and location can be included in the opening paragraph plus the heart of the story. The reference to the Group was neatly included.

And here is an opening paragraph which could have been very complicated but is written with commendable brevity and clarity considering the many items of information given in less than 60 words. Paragraphs of 50 or 60 words are ideal in releases.

From their range of more than sixty trucks, the Lancer Boss Group are exhibiting five on stand 26/27 and another four at the Black Rock demonstration area. Although the emphasis of the Group's products is on container handling, those exhibited are capable of covering every conceivable type of application where lift trucks are usable.

Press releases for exhibitions are not easy to write and there is the danger of sameness, but it is wrong to imagine they have to be different from everyday releases. They should be written to help journalists reviewing the exhibition, and since there are so many exhibitors it is a very competitive occasion when newsy opening paragraphs are imperative. Yet the majority of opening paragraphs in releases found in exhibition press rooms are cluttered up with details about the exhibition, not the exhibit. Most of them are exceedingly dull. The trouble here is that very few press officers, detailed to prepare exhibition press releases, understand that PR support for exhibitors is not something which begins and ends with a press release for the press room. This is a subject near to the author's heart which will be more fully discussed in a separate chapter.

The following is a variety of examples of interesting first paragraphs produced by consultants Eric Buston & Associates Ltd., Denzil Stuart Associates, and Peter Roderick Public Relations respectively.

A Gloucestershire farmer has won a first prize of £100 in the R. A. Lister and Company Limited International Centenary Competition to find the Company's oldest engine still in working order, and in regular service.

A fast fire-fighting and rescue hovercraft has been developed by Hovermarine Ltd. in conjunction with Merryweather & Sons Ltd. A full specification has been submitted to the London Fire Brigade, who have been considering the use of hover fire-boats on the River Thames, and other potential users are expressing interest in this new concept of fire-fighting.

```
... that's "GIGI", the new range by Potter & Moore.  The
perfume is light yet warm, individual yet widely appealing
- and very very young. (Bring the paper, closer, take a
deep breath, and find out what we mean).
```

The unfortunately quoted Gigi in capitals is perhaps forgivable in this once-in-a-while novelty of a scented release which gave a practical demonstration of the product, and marketed the story into the bargain. Mary Noble of Peter Roderick Public Relations received many letters and telephone calls from editors congratulating her, so once again we have an exception that is cheerfully successful.

When Mary Noble was engaged upon the launch of the Rouge Baiser lipstick colour *champagne* she sent a quarter bottle of champagne to beauty writers with a card asking them to retain it until further notice. About three days later each beauty editor received news of the launching of the new lipstick colour and was invited to join the directors of the company in drinking to the success of the new colour with the champagne already provided. Better than a press reception!

We have deliberately concentrated on the opening paragraph because it often follows that if the necessary discipline and skill is applied to achieve a good first paragraph it is not so difficult to continue in the same vein.

It is possible that the advantages, applications and details can be contained in a combination initial sentence or paragraph, but it all depends on what the story is about and where the news emphasis lies. In order to achieve an easily remembered formula and check list there may be some over-simplification in the suggested seven points, but alternative items can be used if they are more applicable to the kind of story issued. There should be in every press officer's mind a certain pattern to which all his stories should conform; an array of information which makes the release explicit and capable of gaining instant understanding and interest.

The Seven Point Formula in Use

Now, how do we do this in practice? We have analysed the opening paragraph, but how are points four to seven introduced? Let us briefly take a popular product and apply the formula to the skeletal facts:

1. Subject: jam
2. Organisation: Fulton Ltd.
3. Location: Evesham.
4. Advantages: packed in new plastic squeeze-jar. No sticky knives, no waste, no jam dishes, no wasps. Unbreakable decorative jar.

5. Applications: can be used anywhere, table, hospital bed, picnic, in restaurants, on ships and aircraft. Practical and presentable.

6. Details: flavours, sizes, prices. General retail distribution.

7. Source: name and address of manufacturers.

From this list, arranged like this in sensible sequence, we see the bones of the story. It also indicates items on which we may require more detailed information, although in this case a sample product will itself supply most of the information. The list gives a simple pattern which enables the information to flow without anything getting buried, repeated or muddled. The clarity of the story springs from the formula-based list. If the press officer proceeds to finalise his information accordingly, and then writes about each item in turn he finishes up with a press release which an editor of a grocery trade paper or a home page writer will welcome.

Such a story is free of gimmicks. It does not call for any clever ideas to get the story off the ground. The name of the product, or the subject of the story, should appear naturally in the *first three words*. The opening paragraph of this jam story can follow the formula exactly as previously explained, and succeeding paragraphs can set out the information bit by bit as the formula decrees. In this way a short release can be written on the following lines:

FULTON JAM IN UNBREAKABLE SQUEEZE-JARS

Jam from Fulton of Evesham is now being packed in unbreakable plastic squeeze-jars fit to put on any table. This means goodbye to sticky knives, jam dishes, messy washing up, wasted jam and, of course, glass jam jars.

The new squeeze-jars are made from hygienic pliable plastic, and are disposable when empty. There are no lids to lose, no glass to break. With these new clean containers there will be far less risk of wasps raiding the larder and being a nuisance in the kitchen.

Fulton squeeze-jars are so daintily designed with floral effects that they look 'right' anywhere, attractive on the table, handy for the picnic basket, clean to handle for the children. For those eating out or requiring jam while eating on journeys, there are individual miniature squeeze-jars.

All the usual Fulton full-fruit flavours are now packed in the new throw-away squeeze-jars, but prices remain the same as before at grocers and supermarkets.

Jams in the new squeeze-jars are made and marketed by George Fulton Ltd., Orchard Works, Evesham, Worcs.

Philip Johns, PRO.

July 18th 1967.

This is typically a press release which falls midway between advertisement copy and reporting, a product publicity story. It has all the ingredients that a copywriter might wish for, yet the release is factual without any inducement to buy. As a press report it is endowed with newsworthiness because it describes a revolutionary new pack and relates this to the many and varied needs of readers.

The same version of a story will not suit every kind of journal. The Fulton jam story is capable of being written differently for home page writers, the grocery trade press, catering journals, the factory's local press, and other sections of the press such as those covering food processing, the plastics industry, packaging and there is also an interesting safety angle. To use a term of the trade, with a little thought and imagination considerable *mileage* can be gained from a comparatively simple product publicity story of this kind.

The above suggestions form a small marketing exercise in press relations, and they show, too, how a press release can be made even more publishable if the trouble is taken to satisfy the needs of various editorial groups. The original press release is infinitely more publishable than many which are issued, but that is only a start! In adapting the original to suit other media the press officer can really display his skill. As a result he will convey the message to many more publics, and increase his return of press cuttings.

Although this formula is used here to provide the skeleton of a product publicity story its planned sequence of information can be applied to any kind of news report. Notice how similar it is to the average newspaper report, whatever the subject. We have already mentioned this but the point is worth repeating because one of the best ways to check that we are writing correctly is to read and analyse actual reports in the press. The first two of the following examples are taken from the front page of the *Daily Mail*: the third is from *The Observer*.

"*Tommy Docherty, Chelsea's firebrand chief, has been suspended by the Football Association for 28 days from next Monday.*"

"*The charge of alleged theft against Cass Elliot, 15-stone singer with the American Mamas and Papas pop group, was dropped by the prosecution at West London magistrates court today.*"

"*Sir Leslie O'Brien, Governor of the Bank of England, claimed last night that a speech he had made abroad about unemployment in Britain was being used for political ends.*"

All three begin with a positive presentation of facts and go on in the same manner, making miserly use of words so that every sentence, every paragraph counts.

Whether it be an obituary notice or the review of a film, a report of a political speech or of a murder investigation, it is still essential to say what we are writing about in the first few words, and that is well borne out by the three examples quoted above.

7

Some Press Releases Analysed

The author has sifted through several hundred press releases from a multitude of sources but has found it difficult to find more than a few which exactly fit the requirements of his seven-point formula which is, after all, an ideal guide rather than a set of emphatic rules. It is now proposed to reproduce a number of releases, in part or whole according to their length or usefulness for quotation purposes. In this and the previous chapter the author has made a number of recommendations which are not always apparent in these examples, and while they are not serious blemishes (and it would be remarkable if everyone did everything in exactly the same way!) the following comments are offered for consideration when these examples are being read.

1. *Headlines are often underlined*, probably more by habit than because it is intended to suggest that they should be set in italics. Underlining is unnecessary, unlikely though it is that the press officer's heading will be used. The underlining of headlines is therefore a typewriting drill which is irrelevant to a press release and is best avoided. Let us style releases properly.

2. *Location* of organisations is seldom given, yet it should not be taken for granted that editors will know, especially when the address on the heading is that of a consultancy!

3. *Address of organisation* is almost invariably missing from most of the releases studied by the author, yet it is very important information which may or may not be on the printed heading. Surely inclusion of the address is likely to provoke enquiries? It can also prevent confusion with another company of a similar name. For example, the author is aware of at least three large companies by the name of "Crane". This is very much a matter of communication. Clarity depends on spelling

things out, on including all the relevant facts. Releases with no locations or addresses for further information are incomplete, and the writer must remember that while the editor may require further information from the press officer, the reader will have to apply to the organisation for other details. The easiest thing to do is to complete stories with a final paragraph which reads: "*ABC tools are made by XYZ Ltd of Hilltop Industrial Estate, West Broker, Hampshire.*" If the editor does not want to print it he can cut it out, but in many cases he will at least transfer this piece of information to his reader service system.

4. *Full points* are used in abbreviations when press practice is to dispense with them. They take up needless space, they look "spotty", and—quite frankly—this is another secretarial practice which does not belong to the presentation of a press release. Many secretaries need to learn that while they may have been trained to set out letters in a certain way few of those secretarial college rules apply to press releases. And only a well-trained press officer can teach his secretary how to set out a press release!

Finally, several of these releases include "For immediate release" and "Ends" which are superfluous bits of jargon.

Beyond these advance remarks the following press releases are reproduced, with due acknowledgement, as examples of some of the better written, presented and more interesting releases which the author has selected from his collection. Thousands of press releases are issued daily, and no doubt readers will be aware of even better examples, but the following have certain attributes which make a useful contribution to the purpose of this book. The author is grateful for the opportunity to print them here. They also show that although there is a right and a wrong way of producing a press release there is no reason why individual literary style, and even humour, cannot be employed.

A Selection of Press Releases

CAPE KENNEDY IN S.W.5.

A one hundred foot Dunlop Dracone barge, towering right to the ceiling of Earls Court as if poised for the blast-off is an eye-catching feature of the International Engineering and Marine Exhibition (25th April - 4th May, 1967). This dramatic effect has been achieved by inflating the flexible Dracone barge with air and mounting it vertically.

In normal operation, Dracone barges are used for the bulk transport by sea of liquids such as freshwater and oil products. The D-type Dracone exhibited on the Dunlop stand is 100 feet in length, 5 feet in diameter and has a capacity of 11,300 gallons (some 51 tons of freshwater). Dracones are a British invention, manufactured by Dunlop Dracones Consortium (formed by Dunlop and the National Research and Development Corporation) in sizes up to 300 feet in length with a capacity of nearly a quarter of a million gallons. These barges are particularly manoeuvrable, tough and resilient in operation, and can be folded into a small space when not in use. Currently they are in use in many parts of the world carrying, for example, oil products in the Bay of Fundy, Canada, and freshwater in the Aegean.

Issued by Dunlop Press Office.

PRESS RELEASE: IMMEDIATE 7th July, 1966.

FERTILITY RITES AT STONEHENGE

The grass areas around the stones of Stonehenge became so worn by the feet of visitors that special fertiliser was recently sprayed on the area by the weed control section of Rentokil Laboratories Ltd. at the request of the Ministry of Public Building & Works.

Using a Land Rover and hand lances to apply the turf food, servicemen B. McLean and D. Morris feel that their scientific fertility rites have been more successful than those of the Ancient Druids who used Stonehenge as a temple.

Many public monuments are now being kept weed-free by chemical herbicides by Rentokil in addition to their work on highways, footpaths, industrial sites and public parks.

Issued by Advice & Action Ltd for Rentokil Laboratories Ltd.

KYNOCH INTERNATIONAL PRINT

The Kynoch Press, one of the U.K.'s largest printing offices, has for nearly 90 years been deeply involved with foreign-language printing. About 70% of all its work is now produced in a language other than English. Moreover, because of its long association with ICI print requirements, it has acquired exceptional expertise in despatching print to all parts of the world.

This was the background of last year's decision to establish the Kynoch International Print Service, designed to relieve exporting firms of virtually all the intricacies of producing foreign-language print. All the exporting firm has to do is to supply the text - in English. Kynoch International Print then makes itself responsible for providing a first-class translation, and for designing, printing, documentation and despatch on time to any required delivery point.

The service has been widely welcomed, particularly by firms new to exporting or breaking into new export markets.

Translations, when time permits, are carried out by translators of known ability resident in the country where the literature will be used, and with knowledge of the industry concerned with the literature.

Design is carried out by The Kynoch Press unit - fully qualified graphic designers whose ability has been recognised throughout Europe.

Type is set and read by men who spend 70% of their time working in languages other than English.

Printing in letterpress and litho is produced in a works which has won most of the major awards in British Printing.

Documentation is in the hands of experts who have been dealing with most countries of the world for many years. The same team arranges shipment and delivery - even on to the exhibition stand in daily consignments.

Through its foreign-language printing, the Kynoch Press is not only making a direct contribution to exports. It is also emphasising a fundamental "fact of life" in the drive for increased exports - the absolute necessity of approaching potential markets as directly as possible.

The Kynoch Press International Print Service is backed by the world-wide facilities of Imperial Metal Industries Limited and Imperial Chemical Industries Limited.

Issued by the Kynoch Press.

FOR IMMEDIATE RELEASE 1st June, 1967.

SPECIALISED PROTECTION FOR NORTH SEA GASOMETER

Hangers Paints Limited, a member of the Hull-based Storry Smithson Group, have been awarded the contract to supply protective coatings for a 4,000,000 cu. ft. gasometer - the largest in the East Riding - being erected in Hull by the North Eastern Gas Board.

The gasometer, which will be linked to North Sea gas supplies, is located next door to Storry Smithson's factory at Bankside, Hull.

Changing techniques in the gas industry have led to the introduction of specifications for oil-resistant coatings, and it is understood that Hangers Paints Limited won the contract because their products are particularly suitable to meet these requirements.

The Company are supplying large quantities of "EPISOLVE" metal primer and Epoxide Enamel. The two-coat system gives greater thickness than three or four coats of conventional paints, with consequently improved durability at reduced labour cost. The work is being undertaken in conjunction with Hangers Paints Limited.

Issued by Denzil Stuart Associates on behalf of Hangers Paints Limited.

PRESS RELEASE: IMMEDIATE 6th October, 1966

MONGOOSES PUT FIJI IN THE DARK

Until recently, the largest lighting and telecommunications unit in Fiji was frequently put out of action by mongooses.

Every time a mongoose touched two vital terminals, all the lights and power failed. As a method of killing the mongooses this was expensive and evidently ineffective so pest control experts from Rentokil Fiji Ltd. were called in and now have a contract to keep all the power company's estates clear of mongooses.

Rentokil Fiji is managed by Martin Vaney who was formerly dealing with woodworm in Hampshire for the parent company's Bournemouth region.

Issued by Advice & Action Ltd on behalf of Rentokil Laboratories Ltd.

Only exhibitor specialising in agricultural machinery exports

A Bristol company, Tradabroad Ltd., is the only exhibitor specialising in the export of agricultural machinery at the 2nd Export Services Exhibition.

Tradabroad act as export managers for several West Country manufacturers of agricultural machinery. They handle sales in all overseas markets, but with particular emphasis on Western Europe.

Managing director of the company set up last year, is Mr. Hank Piëst. He was formerly European sales manager of New Holland Machine Company and has been connected with the agricultural machinery market in Britain, the United States and Europe for almost 20 years.

Among Tradabroad clients are Alvan Blanch Development Co. Ltd., of Chelworth, near Malmesbury, who manufacture grain driers; H. J. Godwin Ltd., of Quenington, Gloucestershire, a member of the John James (Industrial) group, makers of high quality pumps; and Archie Kidd Ltd., of Seend, near Melksham, manufacturers of forage harvesters.

At the same time Tradabroad have been appointed to act as export consultants for a number of European manufacturers in the agricultural machinery field. These include Epple-Buxbaum, makers of combines, of Wels, Austria, and Stockey and Schmitz of Gevelsberg, Germany, who produce mowers.

Although specialising in agricultural machinery exports, Tradabroad act as export managers for a number of companies in other fields.

...ends...

October 1966

Issued by Eric Buston & Associates Ltd on behalf of Tradabroad Ltd.

BRITISH OVERSEAS AIRWAYS CORPORATION

The British Overseas Airways Corporation announces that it will inaugurate its Trans-Atlantic pure jet airliner scheduled service to-day Saturday 4th October 1958.

Authority to operate this service has now been received from the British Ministry of Transport and Civil Aviation and also from the Port of New York Authority.

A de Havilland Comet 4, under the command of Captain R. E. Millichap and with the Chairman of B.O.A.C., Sir Gerard d'Erlanger, on board, will leave London at 0930 hours British Summer Time for New York today.

A second Comet 4, under the command of Captain T. B. Stoney and with the Managing Director of B.O.A.C., Mr. Basil Smallpiece, on board, will depart from New York at 0700 hours Eastern Daylight time today for London.

The two aircraft are expected to pass each other over the Atlantic at approximately 45 West longitude.

This release was telephoned to news agencies by the Press Branch of BOAC immediately the Port of New York Authority gave its permission to operate the service, and this was received late at night on October 3rd 1958.

FOR IMMEDIATE RELEASE 18th May, 1967

PRESENTATION OF BOSTON TEAPOT TROPHY

Argentine Navy Day was celebrated in London last night at a reception in the Embassy when Admiral Sir Charles Madden, Bart., G.C.B., on behalf of the Sail Training Association, presented the Boston Teapot Trophy to the Argentine Naval Attache, Captain J. A. Acuna, for the A.R.A. "Libertad".

The Argentine Navy's training ship "Libertad", 3,765 tons, covered 1,335 miles in 124 hours last October during a very fast west-to-east passage across the North Atlantic between Nova Scotia and Ireland.

The Boston Teapot Trophy is presented annually by the S.T.A. to the sail training ship which covers the greatest distance under sail during any period of 124 hours during the year.

The trophy is a replica of a silver teapot (of the type used at the time of the Boston Tea Party) made in 1782 by Paul Revere. It was presented by Brooke Bond & Co., Ltd to the STA in 1966 and is awarded each year by the Association to encourage vessels to make fast passages under sail.

The "Libertad" made her maiden voyage in 1963 and represented the Argentine in the 1964 Tall Ships' Race from Lisbon to Bermuda. The Argentine Navy is an affiliated member of the Sail Training Association.

—ENDS—

Issued by Denzil Stuart Associates on behalf of the Sail Training Association.

London International Engineering Exhibition
Stand No. 59
Ground Floor
Earls Court

SASCO VISUAL PLANNING FOR ENGINEERS

The SASCO system of charting and planning utilizes a series of plastic-laminated and gridded charts and maps, in conjunction with a range of self-adhesive and magnetic components which allow for efficient and inexpensive visual planning and programming for all branches of engineering.

The plastic laminated surface can be written on and wiped clean. The components (plastic holders and coloured "shapes and tapes") can be easily applied to this surface by finger pressure only and removed without leaving a trace. This means that the basic plan is never damaged, and that the inevitable alterations necessitated in preparing plans and keeping the displayed information up-to-date and accurate can be effected quickly without detriment to clarity and neatness.

SASCO planner charts are supplied unmounted or mounted on rigid board. The mounted charts are eyeletted for easy hanging and hinged to fold for portability. Extensive operations can be planned by placing two or more charts together. Special Chart-Track and Chart Frames simplify installation, and the operation of transparent cursors. Standard charts include the Year-Planner and Six Months Planner which set out the whole year or half-year in diary form on one easy-to-read chart; Planners for: Critical Path Planning and Network Analysis, Floor Layout, Time-Tables, Staff Location, Maintenance, Budget and Stock Control; and a series of geographical Planner Maps.

For many other operations, a series of components is available; each kit contains the kind and quantity of components necessary for each specific operation. For each problem SASCO recommend the "Planner" with the most appropriate grid.

This release, which went on to describe three "recent additions" to the Sasco range, was issued by News of Industry Ltd *on behalf of* Self-Adhesive Systems Co. Ltd.

<u>Sortrac III for Rome Airport</u>

A contract for an automated freight sorting system at Rome Airport has been won against strong international competition by Welding Construction Co. Ltd., of Avonmouth. The contract is for design, manufacture and installation of a Sortrac III sorting conveyor for Alitalia's new Freight Terminal at Fuimincino Airport.

Sortrac III is a tilting slat sorting conveyor. It can handle packages with a maximum weight of 250 lbs. measuring up to 3 ft. x 3 ft. x 8 ft. to any number of destinations at rates of 3,000 per hour and above. In the Fuimincino installation the conveyor system will distribute packages up to 5ft. long and weighing up to 250 lbs. to 26 destinations at the maximum throughput rates.

The Fuimincino installation incorporates a straight sorting conveyor arranged to distribute packages to both sides. The conveyor segregates incoming aircraft loads to delivery or forwarding flights, and locally-collected freight into outgoing flight loads.

Sortrac III conveyors have also been installed at the B.O.A.C. Terminal at Kennedy Airport, New York, and K.L.M. at Schiphol Airport, Amsterdam. The system has been successfully used for road and rail freight terminal operations in the U.S.A.

Welding Construction Co. Ltd. is a subsidiary of Bristol Aerojet Ltd., a company jointly owned by the Bristol Aeroplane Company and Aerojet General Corporation. Aerojet General manufactures the Sortrac range of conveying equipment in the U.S.A. with Welding Construction as the licensees to manufacture and sell Sortrac systems in the U.K.

...ends ..

14 February 1967.

Issued by Eric Buston & Associates Ltd on behalf of Welding Construction Co. Ltd.

ROCKWARE'S LATEST IN LIGHTWEIGHTING

Rockware Glass Ltd., Britain's second largest glass container manufacturers, and pioneers of the popular 14-oz. lightweight pint milk bottle, have produced an experimental 12-oz. pint milk bottle. It is now on extended trials with United Dairies Ltd.

SAVING TO DAIRY INDUSTRY

Pioneers in lightweighting techniques, for the past two decades, Rockware's development of the 14-oz. 'lighta pinta' accepted by more than 2,000 dairy companies throughout Britain, was estimated to save the dairy industry some £500,000 annually. Bottle purchase costs were reduced seven per cent and the load of Britain's 44,000 milk roundsmen who deliver 33 million pints of milk daily to 13 million homes was reduced by 1¼ cwt. on an average 45-crate milkfloat load.

Mr. Adrian Bailey, Rockware's Marketing Director, stated:

"Trials of a Rockware Group 12-oz. pint milk bottle are, I would stress, in the experimental stage. The project forms part of our continuing research into the light-weighting of glass containers in general".

"It is part of the trend to discover the practical frontiers of lightweighting. For this reason, we would not consider putting the 12-oz. milk bottle into our range until the most stringent tests have been completed in all aspects of processing and field tests. These are now in progress".

Issued by Eric Williams and Partners on behalf of Rockware Glass Group.

For immediate release Wednesday 17th May, 1967.

ELECTRONICS AT THE PACKAGING EXHIBITION

Latest in Decca range of batch counting systems

Decca Radar Limited are exhibiting their latest Mastercount systems for packaging by count at PAKEX '67*. Fully automatic and semi-automatic versions of these high-speed electronic systems, introduced only two years ago, are now widely used in a number of industries on both sides of the Atlantic to save manpower and avoid waste due to over-batching. In all cases operation and supervision of the equipment is extremely simple, and batches of the required number of objects can be made up at sustained high speeds by unskilled operators.

Objects handled by standard Decca Mastercount systems in typical packaging, assembly and production situations include parts and accessories, confectionery, plastic mouldings, precious stones and metals, electronic component parts, glass tubes, gaskets, pellets, nuts and bolts, and hardware generally.

Decca are also exhibiting, for the first time in Europe, a model of a new sophisticated automatic batch counting machine for the confectionery industry. This machine, the Decca Mastercount 790, feeds a uniform output of accurately counted batches of sweets to high-speed conveyors and packaging machines up to 100 times per minute. At present there is no high-speed batching machine in general use which can operate at high batch rates in complete synchronisation with all types of continuously moving conveyors, and the Company claim their unit is first in a new generation of electronic systems for packaging by count. Synchronised batching is made possible by the use of an integral data handling facility to control the load in four internal stores. These stores act as buffers which ensure that the variable input of objects, for example from hoppers, is related to the demand of the conveyor for counted batches at regular intervals.

* Stand No.105 at the International Packaging Exhibition, Earl's Court, London, May 22nd-26th, 1967.

Issued by the Press Officer, Decca Radar Limited.

COATES CIDER FOR CHRISTMAS IN AUSTRALIA

The first consignemt of Coates Somerset cider to be sent to Australia will leave Nailsea during the next few days.

It will be shipped on the "Tasmania Star" and will arrive in Melbourne on December 15 in time for Christmas.

The order, for 250 gallons, follows an urgent request from an Australian import company and is made up of Coates Triple Vintage, Festival Vat, Special Dry, Somerset and Export ciders, in bottles, cans, and the distinctive Coates Quartet container.

The cider will be sold at Ye Berwick Inn, formerly an old coaching inn which is over 100 years old. The inn has a special cider bar, the only one in Australia, and is a popular tourist rendezvous. During the last few years thousands of English emigrants have settled near Berwick and, according to the Australian importers, "would jump at the opportunity of buying a bottle or two of the cider they were used to at home".

The Australian company, Norman Adeney and Associates of Harkaway, Victoria, handle Australian produced cider but tell Coates in their letter that though it is "very acceptable" to the settlers it is quite different from the English product.

...ends...

1 November 1966

Issued by Eric Buston & Associates Ltd on behalf of Coates Cider.

Comments on the Press Releases

Without wishing to be carping, let us now look instructively and constructively at these examples, noting in particular any imperfections in this mixture of news stories actually produced by press officers, and bearing in mind that these examples do reach a publishable standard ranging from fair to excellent.

The Dunlop story appeals because it is short and novel, but the long second paragraph needs breaking up, new paragraphs beginning with "Dracones are a British . . ." and again with "Currently they are . . ."

The Rentokil story is an amusing item which does not need to be headed "PRESS RELEASE: IMMEDIATE". The headline need not be underlined, and the opening paragraph should not be indented. But it is a neat little story with a touch of humour.

Kynoch have a lot to say. Being printers, they instinctively know that opening paragraphs are not indented. The first two paragraphs are rather long compared with those which follow, yet it is good to set out the separate services as separate paragraphs.

In the Hangers Paints release we have a story briefly told on one sheet of paper. The same three criticisms apply as with the Rentokil story. There are two unfortunate mistakes—4,000,000 instead of four million or 4 million and EPISOLVE in caps. In the third paragraph "particularly suitable to meet these requirements" is a meaningless generalisation which could surely be made more explicit.

In the second Rentokil story none of the paragraphs is indented although the second and third paragraphs should be.

Eric Buston headlines are always so neat, never in capitals, often running to two lines, with a simple rule beneath the second line only. Note that in the Tradabroad story we have "managing director" and not "Managing Director". The sparing use of caps is admirable, and correct. As usual with this consultancy, the release is impeccably headed, presented, written and reproduced. In this case the name and address of the client together with his exhibition stand number was given at the foot of the release. It seems almost churlish to fault this release by mentioning the author's objection to the ". . . ends . . ." If it wasn't the end it would be necessary to say "Continued"—but not "More"!

As explained, the BOAC story was not mailed but telephoned, so we can reproduce here only the typescript. But what a model of brevity and precision!

The interesting Sail Training Association story invites a comment on those spotty full points in those abbreviations, with one odd inconsistency: G.C.B., A.R.A., S.T.A. and then suddenly the much better STA.

The SASCO release has the merit of clearly giving the exhibition material in the top left-hand corner away from the story. Note that this release is properly indented, but unfortunately the writer had a partiality for capital letters. SASCO, being the company's initials, is acceptable although some editors might be tempted to put it down, incorrectly, into upper and lower case, but there is no necessity for the use of capitals in the third paragraph, for instance: "*Planning and Network Analysis*".

The next Eric Buston release—Sortrac III—practically follows the seven-point formula, and is in every respect an ideal press release.

In the Rockware release the headline is not underlined, but no paragraphs are indented and there is a needless subheading. This release tends to try too hard, and yet the second paragraph handles a lot of statistics very tautly. One has to be careful about quoting comments from company spokesmen. They are seldom printed, and an editor is unlikely to be interested in the views of the *marketing* director which could be something on a red flag to a bull.

The Decca release carries the Oliver Twist injunction since three-and-a-half lines are carried rather unnecessarily to a second sheet. With so little to continue it would be better to either cut the story or use shorter paragraphs and spread it. The headline is not underlined, but the paragraphs are not indented and the paragraphs have the appearance of uninviting slabs of words. Indentations do carry the eye into the story. This is a release with something to say and yet the message is cramped by generalisations and a restricted vocabulary.

Finally, another Eric Buston story, a nice pre-Christmas one with the usual Buston hallmark of snappy informativeness. Although this same quality is seen throughout the quoted Buston releases they are written by different members of the staff of this Bristol consultancy.

One final point: seven of these thirteen releases closed with the name of the author.

More Press Releases and Comments

Having made certain recommendations and comments an assortment of press releases is now presented from the consultancy with which the author was associated, for five years, where the style of presentation given in Chapter Seven, and the seven-point formula, was daily practised under his supervision, a certain flexibility being permitted according to the nature of the story.

SMITHS CLOCKS FOR THE DEAF

The problem of awakening the deaf, hard of hearing or the very heavy sleeper is solved by the Smiths Pageboy/Flashalarm. Leaving nothing to chance, it not only sounds an alarm but flashes a combined bedside lamp on and off. Moreover, it makes an extremely attractive bedside clock and lamp set.

The clock has a black face with raised gilt figures and batons and is luminous. The clock case and the base for clock and lamp are in white moulded plastic, giving it a very clean appearance. The lamp, which flashes when the alarm is operating, has a shade trimmed with gilt embroidery.

Height 10¼ inches. Width 11 inches. Depth 5 inches. Sectric mains electric. £3. 19s. 6d. complete.

The Smiths Pageboy/Flashalarm is made by Smiths Industries, Clock & Watch Division, and is available from jewellers, electrical dealers, department stores and other Smiths stockists.

ADVANCE INTRODUCE 'IC CUBE' SUB-MINIATURE OP AMP

A fully-compensated, sub-miniature differential FET operational amplifier of hybrid integrated circuit construction has been introduced by Advance Electronics in conjunction with Zeltex Inc., of California, to permit restricted space installation without the need for external stabilising networks.

In contrast to conventional monolithic chip amplifiers, the new Model 162 'IC Cube' is designed with a constant 6dB per octave roll-off characteristic to allow excellent frequency stability without external stabilization. It requires only the addition of input and feedback components to become operational and is thus generally easier to install and requires less space (0.1 cu.in.) than monolithic chip amplifiers.

An additional conveniency feature of the Model 162 'IC Cube' amplifier lead spacing on a 0.1 cu.in. grid permits flush mounting of the amplifier to the circuit board, thus eliminating the need for troublesome lead splaying.

DC open loop gain is 200,000 (typical); voltage drift 20uV/°C maximum; input impedance 10,000 megohms; common mode rejection 5,000:1 (typical). Output capability is ± 10V at 4mA with full short circuit protection.

The Model 162 'IC Cube' operational amplifier is manufactured by Advance Electronics Limited, Roebuck Road, Hainault, Ilford, Essex.

CF SECONDARY PROPPING SYSTEM FOR SLAB WORK

Slab work construction can be increased by 50 per cent using the new standard formwork system designed and marketed by Concrete Formwork Ltd. It allows the shuttering to be stripped off half way through the curing period.

When erecting CF standard formwork for slab work the first bay only is laced with waling tubes. The CF system consists of props with a secondary head, 4 ft., 6 ft., or 8 ft. lightweight steel joists and filler panels, and a bay may be spanned with, say, three 6 ft. x 2 ft. CF standard formwork panels dropped into position and self squaring. The secondary prop heads have capping plates which provide them with a flush top.

The CF secondary head permits removal of the panels halfway through the curing period, and since another set of props with secondary heads is supplied, further bays can be assembled so that work can proceed in half the time required if the formwork had to remain in position throughout the 7 to 28 day curing period.

The "top hat" section of the steel framework of the panels has a small hole for a specially designed slab anchor hook which passes through to hold the panels to the concrete slab. It increases the cost by only about ½d a square foot yet it is an invaluable safety factor because, being imbedded in the concrete, the hook holds the panel in position when the supporting beams are removed. Thus, the system is time-saving, doubly efficient and perfectly safe.

CF secondary heads complete with caps can be supplied for contractors' own props, or with CF adjustable steel props, in five sizes, adjustable in height from 3 ft 5 ins. to 16 ft.

Approximate costs of the CF slabwork system with secondary props are 8d a square foot for a 9-inch slab (hire) or 21s. a square foot for a 9-inch slab (sale). CF panels supplied for slab work can also be used as a panel system for walls, and this is a typical example of the versatility of the new CF standard formwork system.

Further information is available from Concrete Formwork Limited, 197 Knightsbridge, London, SW7. Telephone: Knightsbridge 7811.

ANOTHER CRANE FACTORY EXTENSION
FOLLOWS DEMAND FOR 'GAS PACK' FROM BUILDERS

To meet the demand which Crane Ltd. are receiving for their gas-fired residential heating equipment, the company has signed a £250,000 contract with Edgar Lawson Ltd. of Darlington for another big extension to their factory at Aycliffe, Co. Durham.

The new extension is 87,000 square feet and follows the 42,000 square feet extension announced last October.

When it is built, equipped and fully operative, Crane's latest development will provide work for another 100 employees, bringing the total up to at least 400 at Aycliffe. The company as a whole employs nearly 7,000 people at various locations.

The extension just announced will include offices, warehousing and loading bays, plus additional factory floor space. This is the third stage in a planned expansion programme towards an Aycliffe factory totalling 350,000 square feet.

At Aycliffe, Crane manufacture the Cavalier gas-fired boiler for residential central heating, and the unobtrusive Sunnybase skirting radiator which gives both radiant and convected heat and is replacing the conventional type of panel radiator.

This further development at Aycliffe follows the introduction of the Crane 'Gas Pack' offer to builders. This scheme enables housing estate developers to fit tailor-made gas central heating systems into new homes. Each pack consists of a Cavalier boiler, Sunnybase skirting radiators and other equipment as required for halls, kitchens and bathrooms.

The Crane 'Gas Pack' is the only one offering skirting heating and is growing in popularity with builders of new houses because of its low installation costs. Each pack is individually designed by Crane heating engineers, cutting builders' costs and assuring house purchasers of a reliable standard of performance.

NEW PREMIUM GIFT FOR RETAIL PRODUCTS

Described as "the cigarette card of the second half of the 20th century", give-away 35mm size colour slides provide producers of small unit retail lines with a practical means of sustaining brand loyalty. They are inexpensively printed by Kenrick & Jefferson, the specialist printers of West Bromwich, who have an exclusive patented process, and are distributed by Riverdale Products (Mayfair) Ltd., the incentive marketing consultants.

Among the first users of sets of transparencies are bubble gum (a James Bond series), a breakfast cereal (a Moon Shot series) and an aluminium cooking foil (a family pets series). Coupled with the growing interest in colour photography, series of transparencies appeal to collectors of all ages, just like the pre-war cigarette card.

Transparencies lend themselves to either short series of, say, six different pictures for promotional campaigns, or more regular series of perhaps 52 in repeat purchase small unit items such as confectionery. They can also be used as special gifts when complete sets can be offered, as consolation prizes in contests, as introductory gift offers, and in various other ways as promotional aids.

Kenrick & Jefferson have evolved a technique which revolutionises the reproduction of otherwise expensive slides. Riverdale Products (Mayfair) Ltd are discussing further series in many different product fields, offering exclusives to each type of product.

CHOBERT RIVETING SYSTEM IS THE ONLY ONE OF ITS KIND IN THE WORLD; IT OFFERS BIG DIVIDENDS TO MOST TRADES AND INDUSTRIES

The Chobert rapid riveting system by Avdel Ltd. of Welwyn Garden City, Herts - manufacturers of industrial fasteners used in fabricating and assembly work - is the only blind riveting system in the world which gives an automatic feed of rivets that enables them to be placed from one side of a workpiece by a single operator. With a placing speed of approximately 1,500 per hour, this system is probably the fastest of its kind in the world. In fact, the speed of placing rivets is controlled only by the speed at which the operator can insert them into the pre-drilled holes, Available in materials such as steel, brass and aluminium alloy, Chobert rivets are capable of joining metal to metal, and metal to plastic, wood, nylon or fibreglass. In the electronics industry, for instance, they are ideal as terminal lugs, pivot stop or location points. Well suited to fastening applications in most trades and industries, the advantages of the Chobert system include a continuous supply of rivets from one magazine, accurate and accelerated operator performance by unskilled labour, controlled expansion of rivet to provide uniform and smooth placings, noise inhibitive characteristics and, adaptability of placing by hand or pneumatic-powered tools, which are well styled and easy to use. In short, great efficiency, quality, economy, and safety in industrial operations.

RIVET ACTION

Manufactured with a tapered bore - the apex of the taper being towards the rivet tail - Chobert rivets are loaded on to a steel mandrel which has an opposite taper on its head and is drawn through the rivet from the rivet tail, expanding the tail as it goes so that an external shoulder is formed at the back of the workpiece to hold firm around the rear-side of the hole into which it has been placed. As the mandrel is pulled through the rivet, the shank is expanded symmetrically; this ensures that the rivet has good bearing in the hole and that a parallel bore is left in the rivet. Should extra strength or sealing be required, a sealing pin can be driven into the bore of the rivet after placing.

Supplied in foil tubes of 12 inches long, Chobert rivets are loaded into the tools by inserting the tail end of the mandrel into the tail end of the first rivet in the foil tube. By pushing the mandrel right through the foil, all rivets are transferred onto the mandrel, so that the foil can be stripped off. A spring is then slipped onto the mandrel which is inserted into the repetition riveter. Rivets are available in countersunk and snap head-forms in standard diameters of 3/32 inch and $\frac{3}{8}$ inch.

PLACING EQUIPMENT

Equipment for placing Chobert rivets includes manually operated and pneumatic-powered rapid riveting tools, a small plier-type handtool available with standard, long and flexible nose extensions for application to inaccessible positions, and a heavy duty hydro-pneumatic riveter for placing large diameter Chobert rivets. The rapid riveting pneumatic-power tool (Type 715) which places Chobert rivets at the rate of 1,500 per hour can be supplied with

```
air-operated tail jaws, or with remote control for bench
mounted operations.  Nose assembles, curved extra long or
tapered, can also be supplied with this tool.
```

Issued by Scientific Public Relations Ltd on behalf of
The client's name

The last two examples call for some comment and explanation.

The colour slide story for Kenrich & Jefferson was used in a press pack with sample slides which was given to journalists attending a press reception, and was accompanied by another release from one of the manufacturers who were actually giving away the slides in their products. The object of the exercise was to reach potential users of the slides, and those attending were mostly from the trade and technical press.

The Avdel story is interesting in several ways. It has a distinct pattern, an introduction followed by descriptions of the rivet and then the means of applying the rivet. This excuses the use of sub-heads which are used for deliberate divisional reasons. It could perhaps be argued that the introduction might be split into two paragraphs, the first ending at "pre-drilled holes" to complete the section which establishes the speed of the method.

This story very cleverly uses a number of references to speed in the opening lines to create an atmosphere or mood of speed. It also has a particularly difficult job to do and that is to create an image of the expression "industrial fasteners" as permanent fasteners when the very word fastener suggests something which could be unfastened!

Both stories give the company's name and address in the opening paragraph, and this is not repeated at the end. All these SPR releases concluded with the author's name, and the six stories were written by four different people.

In this chapter many examples have been quoted, showing some of the varieties of story and of story treatment that may be required in a press release. Since collections of press releases are not easily come by it is hoped that these examples will be interesting and instructive to those studying the craft of press release writing.

The golden rule is be *concise and precise.* Note, for instance, in the Avdel story how technicalities can be described in comparatively simple language. The whole story filled less than two A4 size sheets, generously set out with good margins.

Finally, here is an export story in which the overseas sales success takes precedence over the sequence of information suggested by the formula. This shows how the formula can be adapted to suit circumstances. There is also a great deal of information which can be told about the trainer, but this is condensed for the purpose of a press story. This is perhaps a good example of how much can be said in a few words.

AMERICANS BUY BRITISH KEYBOARD TRAINERS

Six Davall Model 25 individual keyboard trainers have been installed as an integral part of a new American typewriting course commencing on December 1st at the Government and Business Training School in Washington, DC.

The Model 25, fitted with a display, keyboard and programmes suitable for the Spanish Language, has also been installed at Academia Cultura, Esquina La Gorda, Caracas, Venezuela.

Made by Davall Teaching Machines Limited of Rothersthorpe Crescent, Northampton, England, the Model 25 is the world's first one-piece portable electronic keyboard trainer for teaching touch-typing. It can be used for rapid individual tuition, or as a remedial aid for teaching backward or handicapped students.

This British trainer consists of an eye-level display which simulates the keyboard, and a typewriter with either blank or marked keys, mounted on a console which electronically operates punched tape programmes that are supplied in either cassettes or in loops or strips. The whole can be easily placed on a school desk. A set of exercises punched on plastic tape is supplied with each machine, together with an exercise text book and operating instructions.

Students type the character which is seen illuminated on the display. If they make a mistake this must be cleared and corrected immediately. The trainer records correct strokes and errors. The more accurate the typing the quicker the speed. In field trials 14-year-old British school girls acquired speeds of 10 to 12 words per minute after only eight hours tuition on the Davall Model 25 individual keyboard trainer.

8

Pictures and Captions

Photographs cost a lot of money and can absorb a disproportionate part of the press relations budget unless properly controlled. Many mistakes are made over pictures. Releases are sometimes accompanied by too big a selection of too large prints, and that can be a waste of money. Photographs are not always necessary for every journal to which the story is sent. Sometimes, especially if the mailing is large, it is more practical to tell editors that pictures are available. These strictures are made at the beginning of this chapter because while every user of press relations services loves to see a picture published, not every picture sent out has even a chance of being reproduced. Profligate distribution of pictures is a vice of bad PR.

Another common fault is the quality of pictures, both in composition and in suitability for reproduction. And there are still some newcomers to the business who are capable of mailing $3\frac{1}{4} \times 2\frac{1}{4}$ inches snapshot size prints, captioned on the backs with a ballpoint pen, and sent through the post unprotected by card.

In his address already quoted from in previous chapters, Peter Ransley, editor of *Plastics & Rubber Weekly*, made some quotable comments on pictures. He said:

"*Pictures are very important. They're the first thing a reader looks at. Yet the standard of industrial* PR *pictures is always low; on some bleak Monday mornings it looks appalling. Pictures should be taken with the lowest common denominator of reproduction in mind—newspapers. Yet many are technically not good enough for newspapers. And many show little imagination. Uninteresting pictures of a complete piece of machinery instead of a close-up of some of the guts of it that would bring out an important point. Pubs, laboratories, hospitals unrealistically bare of people; a stand at an exhibition which closed six weeks ago; a view of a new office block, minute, from several hundred yards away. I think one of the biggest single improvements that could be made in press relations work is in the quality of pictures.*"

Of course, Peter Ransley is right, but it is not entirely the fault of press officers. Or it might be better to say that press officers do not always buy their pictures wisely, and seldom understand the limitations of the photographers they use. A great deal of nonsense is talked about professional photographers as if they must not be told what to do. A photographer can take only the picture he is instructed to take by a press officer who knows what pictures he wants and what kind of picture he needs for the distribution he has in mind. A photographer is not a mind reader, but he is sometimes held in a peculiar professional awe which expects him to be one. The press officer will need to spend much time sorting out—often finding out by trial and error—which photographers are best for particular work—studio portraits, table top, industrial action, speakers at meetings, interiors, and so on. There are so many different kinds of pictures that few photographers are equally good at all these specialities. Buying photography can be a very exasperating business, but you tend to get what you pay for and a good photographer is worth his price.

The selecting and instructing of photographers is itself a highly skilled business which has to be learned in the hard school of experience. The press officer who masters this side of his business is well on the way to becoming a very successful practitioner.

An Eleven-Point Guide for Pictures and Captions

The following eleven points provide a practical guide to pictures and captions for press relations purposes:

1. Subject material
2. People in pictures
3. Copyright, reproduction fees and delivery
4. Size of prints
5. Sharp, contrasty, glossy prints
6. Pictures available
7. The caption
8. People's names
9. Never use a paper clip
10. Protect pictures in the post
11. Colour pictures

1. *Subject Material*

Pictures should be taken for pictorial effect as well as for information value. Composition and lighting can enhance comparatively dull subjects like technical components. Glamorous models are usually more of a hindrance than a help in the majority of PR pictures, unless perfectly relevant and natural. True, there have been some PR gimmicks such as bikini-clad girls at a filling station to announce a new petrol. But it remains a fact that more people will look at a picture of a child or an animal than at a piece of cheese-cake.

2. *People in Pictures*

Human interest in pictures can often be a big asset. Holiday guide books issued by resorts usually carry pages of advertisements which look more like those for estate agents than hoteliers. The tables are always empty of people, white napkins frigidly set out as if all the guests have died in their beds. In external pictures no-one is seen entering or leaving and no cars are parked outside. Contrast these pictures with those in the brochures issued by holiday camps or agents for holidays abroad which are bursting with happy holiday-makers. People make pictures.

The people in pictures should usually be doing something suitable, and be intent on what they are doing, not grinning up into the camera. If pictures are taken of factory operations it will look more authentic if the operators are seen in profile, and sometimes the backs of their heads—with the photographer breathing down their necks, so to speak—can be not only appropriate but dramatic. It can be a mistake to photograph only the most glamorous young ladies at work. They could be mistaken for specially posed models!

If it is desirable to make a scene—such as an airport—look natural, busy people should be asked to walk into the picture, and to do so naturally, ignoring the camera. The photographer should make sure that ordinary people photographed like this have no objection to their picture being published.

Permission to photograph people, or to use pictures containing people, is something which may have to be established to avoid legal problems. Normally it is quite safe to print pictures with people in them provided no opinion or testimony is attributed to them.

One also has to be very careful about offending against the professional or amateur status of professional men and women or amateur athletes and sportsmen and women if pictures appear to be giving them publicity. This is a point to bear in mind when pictures may be used for a variety of purposes involving press relations and advertising. What might be admissible in press relations might not be in advertising, yet there might be a temptation to use the same pictures. This problem has occurred when people of amateur status have been featured in a magazine article, but to picture them in an advertisement for that issue of the magazine would have been extremely embarrassing if not dangerous to their amateur status.

3. *Copyright, Reproduction Fees and Delivery*

All pictures issued by the press officer must be offered free of copyright restrictions. The press officer must beware of accepting prints from employers or clients which are the copyright of publishers, photographers or other owners so that they can be published only provided the editor pays a reproduction fee to the owner of the copyright.

When commissioning photography it is essential to ensure that the copyright is assigned to either the organisation or the client as the case may be. Photographers earn income from reproduction fees on pictures for which they retain the copyright. As a result, it is not uncommon for those unfamiliar with copyright to obtain prints of pictures taken by newspaper or press agency photographers, and then to pass them on to the press officer with instructions to issue them to the press. Such pictures cannot be reproduced without a fee to the owner of the copyright, and editors will not do this with a picture supplied from a PR source. They will expect the picture to be free of copyright, and this is possible only when the organisation concerned owns the copyright.

Similarly, one has to be careful about using pictures in any kind of printed material. Unless copyright belongs to the organisation a reproduction fee will be due to the owner. Higher reproduction fees are charged when a picture appears in advertisements or advertising material, than when it is used for editorial purposes. Although a PR consultancy may produce an educational leaflet it could be classed as advertising literature, especially if distributed through a showroom or on an exhibition stand. In this context, "picture" may be read to mean any illustration whether it be photograph, drawing, diagram or cartoon. It is a point to remember when wishing to reproduce a newspaper cartoon in a house journal: if it is a staff journal the publishers may be kind and agree to a token fee provided full acknowledgement is given. But newspapers do earn a very considerable income from syndicated material.

One also has to be careful of organisations which make a speciality of photographing business men in their offices: when the time comes to want to use the picture because, say, the man has been promoted, the print charge may be too exorbitant to justify its wide distribution, while purchase of the copyright may be as high as £50. The photograph itself may be excellent, and the businessman (not to mention his wife!) may be proud of the large original prints. But this kind of photography, which plays upon the plausibility and vanity of businessmen, is of no practical use to the press officer who has a budget to keep to and needs 25 half plate prints in a hurry.

This raises another problem with photographers: delivery. More often than not the press officer needs a same-day or at worst a 24-hour print service, otherwise the story is dead and the pictures worthless. Before commissioning a photographer it is crucial to find out *when he will deliver*. Some photographers are specially set up to provide rapid service and go so far as to provide a regular messenger service. But on the whole this is uncommon, as most photographers are small units, and if they do their own processing there may be a delay of up to seven days before the contact prints or proofs arrive. This is particularly true when using photographers outside London. It depends on the purpose of the photography whether this delay matters or not; it is also another case of the press officer having to understand how to buy photography.

From these remarks it will be seen that the press officer must maintain strict control over photography. Pictures can be very valuable and costly property: if the truth be known more money is probably squandered on irresponsible handling of photography than on hospitality. For example, when a large number of prints are required (and provided the original is first-class) it is possible to have quantities of repro-prints run off at about a third of the cost of ordinary prints. Again, when having photographs taken the photographer may charge by the "shot", and it is very tempting to be wasteful and shoot this, that and the other instead of working to a clear programme of planned "shots".

It is also advisable to make sure that photographers retain the negatives safely and can supply prints to order. Allied to this, the press officer must keep a photographic library so that he knows exactly what pictures exist, what they are about and who took them. The simplest record system is a ring file containing sheets on which are stuck prints and captions with the negative numbers and the photographer's name and address typed below. This is handier to use than a bulky guard book.

The consultant will also find that for accountancy purposes he should always issue written orders bearing the job number so that the photographer can include both order number and job number on his invoice.

This saves time in checking invoices and authorising payment. It is all too easy to order photography on the telephone—or even by letter—but have no means of comprehending the account when it is received.

4. *Size of Prints*

From sad experience of British postal practices the author strongly advises that pictures no larger than half plate size ($6\frac{1}{2} \times 4\frac{1}{4}$ inches) be used for general press relations work. For special work—fashion, for example—big prints are justified. If it is an exclusive article, a set of large prints is desirable. But on the whole, half plate prints of good pictures—very likely enlargements of sections of cropped or masked originals—are perfectly suitable for most press needs. There is very real risk that larger pictures will be damaged in the post, and therefore rendered useless.

Larger than negative size pictures are required because they are easier to see by the editor, easier to retouch if necessary, but most important of all blockmakers, when re-photographing the picture, like to reduce from the original to the actual size of the block. Blemishes lessen upon reduction.

It is sometimes mistakenly thought that if large pictures are sent to an editor he is more likely to print large pictures in his journal. The size of the photograph has no bearing on the size of the picture eventually reproduced. There is just one small exception to this and that is that a 4×4 inches square enlargement from the square negative produced by a reflex camera, and actually cut down from half plate paper, is a very acceptable size for provincial newspapers who may well reproduce the picture same size since this often coincides with the width of two columns.

5. *Sharp, Contrasty, Glossy Prints*

To reproduce well, especially on cheap newsprint, a picture must have good gradation of tone, otherwise the printed picture will be very poor. Unless a picture is first-class to begin with it will reproduce badly, even with skilled retouching. For reproduction purposes photographs should be black and white (not sepia) and glossy, not mat.

"Sharp" is an expression not always appreciated, and it is surprising how many people are content to accept a picture that is out of focus. A sharp picture enlarges well, and reproduces perfectly. Sharpness is not always possible in a news picture taken in hurried circumstances, but it is essential in a picture taken with deliberation.

An editor is bound to reject a fuzzy, dull print which he knows will print badly. One of his problems is how to secure a regular high standard of picture reproduction.

6. *Pictures Available*

There are several ways of letting editors have a preview of the series of pictures available without going to the needless expense of mailing all the pictures to every editor. Miniatures can be sent, or sheets of lithographed reproductions, but one of the best ways is to reproduce the pictures at about snapshot size on 12 × 10 inches photographic paper. Such pictures can serve a double purpose because for some magazines they will be reproducible as they stand, while editors of other journals, newspapers mainly, can request enlargements.

7. *The Caption*

First let us deal with the controversial question of whether captions should be fixed to the backs of pictures or flapped so that they can be folded down to be read so that the picture remains visible. Both methods are in use, and there is something to be said for each. The author prefers the first method, and has found that the majority of editors favour it, but the second method is advocated by the IPR and in other text-books. Because there is no clear-cut policy on this subject it would be foolish to be dogmatic, but sensible to set out here the advantages and disadvantages of each method and possible reasons for their adoption.

Flapped Captions. Flapped captions are obviously very convenient to a person studying a picture since he can see both caption and picture together and refer from one to the other. Flapped captions probably owe their origin to the vast picture libraries in newspaper and magazine publishing houses, and this suggests that flapped captions are ideal for reference prints, but not for prints that will be used by an art editor and eventually by a blockmaker. When the caption is flapped there is always the risk that it will get ripped off and then the identity of the picture is lost. In fact, flapped captions can get ripped off at almost any time, even at the point of extracting pictures from an envelope or file, especially when the captions are on flimsy paper. The author's own experience as an exhibition press officer is that flapped captions have been a nuisance, liable to damage, detachment and loss.

But considering that so many pictures are sent out without any captions at all, a flapped caption is certainly better than nothing! It is incredible that anyone can despatch a picture without a caption but it happens with astonishing frequency.

Fixed Captions. Fixed captions have the distinct advantage that they are reasonably permanent, but they can be fixed with Cow gum for removal if necessary. The fixing must be done carefully. Too much adhesive will spread with disastrous results. Some glues will crimp a photograph if it is on lightweight paper. The fixing of captions is therefore important, and the person responsible should be properly instructed. If the caption stays with the picture identification is certain, and the wrong caption will not be applied. And since the caption is a source of information for the benefit of the journalist composing the actual caption which will appear in print there is no question of a detachable caption being useful to send to the printer. In the author's opinion, therefore, a caption fixed to the back of the print is the safest and most practical method.

Direct Captions. Yet a third method of captioning is to duplicate the wording direct on to the back of the photograph, and for this purpose a Banda spirit duplicator is generally used. As one editor told the author, this method has the merit of maintaining the identity of the picture even after it has been marked up with the required reductions for reproduction. These instructions to the blockmaker are drawn on the back of the print. Sometimes they will be drawn over a caption which is pasted to the back of the print, but it can happen that a separate caption, whether flapped or fixed, may be taken off so that the instructions can be made on the back of the print itself.

Direct captions are used by those who frequently distribute pictures, the BBC for instance, and it is a good method when pictures are likely to be used soon after issue. But for pictures with a longer life and ones which may be held in stock, the attached caption can be replaced if the information has to be revised. And while spirit duplicators are excellent machines, it is possible for a bad operator to duplicate indistinctly so that this type of caption, which is usually produced in colour, can lead to editorial errors through the misreading of details in, say, pale blue. The rule, then, is that direct captions are well worth using when the expected life of the caption is short, and duplicating is perfect. It is, of course, a time-saving method ideal for urgent news pictures.

The only kind of caption which may provide actual copy for typesetting is the extended caption story, that is the sort which forms part of what is known as a picture-and-caption story. Here it is wise to submit the extended caption in press release form in addition to the fixed caption.

Wording of the Caption. The caption itself should consist of a title, a briefly worded description, and the address of the source from which further information may be obtained. Usually, the text of a caption can be contained in about 50 words, but there may be exceptions to this. Accuracy of detail is absolutely essential. Photo captions are apt to survive a long time and may be referred to long after press releases have served their purpose. In addition to putting an address for further information, including telephone number, at the end of the caption—and as a separate paragraph away from the information—it pays to identify the source by means of a rubber stamp on the back of the print itself. This is a precaution in case a caption is removed.

In captioning a picture the press officer should ask himself who is going to receive it and what is likely to happen to it. Some pictures may be used at once and may be even returned, others will go into picture libraries or into journalist's personal files, and some may be posted to freelance writers who are compiling articles, features or supplements. Pictures suffer a strange life, and captions must be capable of standing up both physically and informatively to the diverse demands that many people may make upon them at various times over a considerable period.

We have voted against the flapped caption, but from the point of view of durability there is surely nothing more foolish than the photograph which dangles by a piece of Sellotape from the foot of a press release, a practice to be observed quite often in the press rooms of exhibitions. The picture is very easily parted from the press release, and since it bears no caption—and seldom so much as a rubber-stamped identity mark—the picture is useless.

Equally useless is the photograph bearing no caption but having an identifying rubber stamp which has the effrontery to ask the editor to please mention the company's name!

After so much criticism this must surely be the place to applaud the exceptionally rare but commendable practice of running off captions on headed caption paper. This is done very well indeed by P & O who print the company name in the house-style shadow type logo and clearly set out the full address of the PR photographic library followed by the telephone number. Other press officers please copy! There can be no doubt about the source or identity of a P & O picture. This efficiency must delight editors and encourage use of P & O pictures.

An aspect that is easily overlooked is that an editor may not like the picture he has in front of him, but would like to print something else on the same subject. If it is easy for him to pick up a telephone and ask for another picture he will do so, but if there is no address or telephone number on the caption (and certainly if there is no caption!) he will use somebody else's picture. Pictures have to be marketed too, and the printed caption heading used by P & O is an excellent piece of press *relations* thoughtfulness, or good marketing if you prefer to call it that.

8. *People's Names*

It is vital to get names, initials, spellings, ranks, titles, jobs, qualifications, decorations and honorary positions correct. To be absolutely certain it is wise to go back to the most reliable source, such as the man's private secretary. Never rely on a telephone operator or anyone more distant than a secretary, personnel officer or company PRO. It is frighteningly easy to get personal details wrong, especially when they are given over the telephone. Names like Davis and Davies, Philips and Phillips, Allan and Allen, St. James, St. James' and St. James's, Gerry and Jerry, and many others call for the utmost care. Most people like to see their names in print but they are not amused by misspellings.

Equally, it is vital to be accurate about personal descriptions. This is seldom easy because people's titles, jobs and positions may change, and it can be fatal to take it for granted that one's information is right. Far better to check than be sorry!

Remember, too, that editors are relying on the press officer for thoroughly reliable information, so the onus is on the press officer to check and recheck and never take anything for granted, particularly if the details have been on file for any length of time. In writing captions the press officer shoulders a very big responsibility. He may think that there is nothing to caption writing and dismiss it as a chore, but it is one of the most serious tasks he can perform.

9. *Never Use a Paper Clip . . .*

or any other means to attach a picture to a letter, press release or MSS. Nor must pictures be stapled to press releases. Any sort of fastening will inevitably damage the picture and these marks will mar the picture when it is being re-photographed for plate-making purposes. When requesting pictures it is a very wise precaution to warn that secretaries must not destroy pictures by clipping them to letters. Secretaries, knowing nothing about the reproduction destinies of photographs, are unwittingly guilty of spoiling most of the photographs they post.

10. *Protect Pictures in the Post*

While card-backed envelopes are advisable for very large prints, they are too expensive to use for general press release mailings when cut card can be inserted in stout buff manila envelopes for adequate protection. Again, this may be unbelievable but editors do receive many pictures in crumpled envelopes with no protection whatsoever.

11. *Colour Pictures*

Finally, to complete this chapter, a word about colour pictures. Except on rare occasions when perhaps an editor wants a cover picture, colour photographs are of no use for press relations purposes. Colour pictures can be useful for other PR activities such as house journals, literature, exhibition displays and especially for slide presentations at seminars, but for normal press work black and white pictures are required. So, unless there is a special arrangement with an editor to supply colour pictures, the press officer will restrict himself to black and white photography.

However, it is possible that with the growing use of web-offset printing, and the printing of colour pictures in the general make-up of the page, that the editors of journals printed by this process will welcome colour photographs as well as black and white since they can be reproduced quickly and cheaply in comparison with other processes. The web-offset four-colour magazine, while a little gaudy and having a newspaper rather than a glossy magazine effect, does make colour photography a very different and exciting proposition for the press officer.

9

Communication Media

Few aspects of press relations are more complex yet so fascinating as the continuous study which is required of the various media of communication. How do we convey our story, how many different methods can we use, and how many different versions, treatments and perhaps translations will be required? What different timings will be demanded by the special requirements of each medium?

In addition to the press in all its many forms—and the press is still by far the largest and most influential medium—we have television (both BBC and commercial), radio, documentary films, newsreels, film magazines (like *Look at Life*), film-strips and slides. The press officer will also be concerned with pictures and captions, visual aids for permanent display and as speakers' equipment, and the writing of speeches and preparation of speakers' notes which are necessary for the medium of the spoken word. He may also be associated with publications such as the annual report, information and educational leaflets, folders and booklets, and also with sponsored books.

In this chapter we shall consider the following media which are available to the press officer:

1. The Press
2. Films:
   - Newsreels
   - Film magazines
3. Radio
4. Television
5. The spoken word

Of these, the press can be sub-divided into a number of categories and remains by far the most versatile and far-reaching of all the communication media, despite the challenge and the insistent appeal of television. The big advantages that the press has over all media are its permanence and its portability.

1. The Press

The British press is a much more complicated medium than the newcomer to press relations may at first appreciate. To the press officer based in London it is fairly easy to think chiefly of the national press, that is, all those newspapers and magazines distributed throughout the UK, and forget that in addition there is also a national press within Scotland, Wales and Northern Ireland.

If he is associated with a specialised industry he may find it difficult at first to realise that there are hundreds of trade, technical and professional journals in scores of separate categories, while the practitioner in a PR consultancy will, in the interests of a variety of clients, have to be familiar with many categories comprising some thousands of titles. Similarly, it is easy to think of local newspapers as "local rags" and fail to understand the power and influence of the provincial press in all its many forms, perhaps be unaware that there are about 90 daily newspapers published outside London, and even be under the false (and all too commonly held) impression that the London evening newspapers have national circulations like their sister morning papers. Conversely, the press officer working in the provinces may find it even more difficult to appreciate the complexity of the national and provincial press.

British newspapers can be broken down into the following categories:

National Mornings
National Sundays
London Evenings
Provincial Mornings
Provincial Sundays
Provincial Evenings
Provincial Weeklies or Town Weeklies (including bi-weeklies)
Regional Weeklies and Weekly Series
Suburban Weeklies
Scottish Mornings
Scottish Sundays
Scottish Evenings
Welsh Morning
Welsh Evenings
Northern Ireland Mornings
Northern Ireland Sunday
Northern Ireland Evening

For convenience, Scottish, Welsh and Northern Ireland weeklies are included under the provincial and regional headings.

The National Press

From this list emerges the pattern of the British newspaper industry, and it is unique to the United Kingdom. The compactness of the British Isles makes possible a national press which is not found elsewhere, although as in Germany there is a tendency now for newspapers to acquire larger and more regional circulations.

But throughout the rest of the world, the majority of newspapers have their main sales in and around the city of origin whether this be Paris, New York, Rome, Sydney or Montreal. In large countries like the USA this tends to lead to big chains with common news services and much syndicated material but individually titled and edited local daily newspapers. Thus, in Britain, we enjoy a remarkable means of speedy communication. A story written and published in London (or transmitted to Manchester for the northern editions) can be on the nation's breakfast table. This is an advantage peculiar to British journalism, PR and advertising. It is, of course, one of the reasons why it can be very difficult to publish a PR story in a national newspaper unless it is of *national* interest. This applies not only to daily morning and Sunday newspapers, but also to most of the magazines which will be discussed later.

The number of national dailies and Sundays has been shrinking over the years to the extent that to list them here might be to date this book in a very short time. Moreover, we seem to have reached a stage in British newspaper history when it is economically impossible to successfully launch a new national newspaper while re-launches under new titles (e.g. the *Daily Herald* as the *Sun*) have not proved to be very successful. The tendency has been for popular newspapers to get fewer and bigger, and for the more serious newspapers to increase in both number and circulation, an interesting phenomenon.

Unfortunately, the reason for this phenomenon is not that the nation is becoming more serious-minded but rather the reverse! It is largely a question of advertisement revenue and the competition received from commercial television for the advertisement revenue available for products selling to the mass consumer market.

Again, because of rising print costs and a dearth of advertisement revenue a number of provincial newspapers of all kinds have ceased publication in recent years, although the introduction of the more economical web-offset printing has given a fillip to the provincial press, and we have even seen the emergence of a few new evening newspapers.

The Provincial Press

In the list of types of newspapers the provincial press has been divided into very distinct categories. Although many people may normally think of them all as provincial newspapers, they do have very different characteristics which can have a bearing on whether the press officer should include them on his press list. Town weeklies circulate chiefly within the town which gives these newspapers their names, but regional weeklies like the *West Sussex Gazette*, the *Kent and Sussex Courier* and *Pulman's Weekly News* do not confine their circulations to one county even, while the *Warrington Guardian Series* and the *Kent Messenger* comprise large groups of newspapers with localised editions. The suburban newspapers circulate in the suburbs of large cities such as London and Manchester, and tend to have less of a distinct community appeal than the town weeklies.

The press officer should take every opportunity during his travels about the country (also when on holiday) to study the newspapers of the UK. The standards of many of these papers are high, and some believe that the London evening papers could learn much to their advantage from the provincial evenings!

One distinction is to be noted in the provincial dailies. Most of the provincial mornings have comparatively small circulations, having to compete with the London nationals, and they appeal mostly to the middle and upper class reader. The reverse is true of the provincial evenings which may have circulations between 100,000 and 400,000, and do not, except near London, have to compete with the London papers. They usually have a popular readership and, moreover, by introducing much magazine material of interest to housewives, have during the past two decades built up very strong family readerships. Consequently, press officers for many organisations will find the provincial evenings most valuable media.

Thus, the press officer for a popular household product is likely to find the usefulness of the provincial press to be in the following descending order of merit: evenings, regionals, large town weeklies, mornings, small town weeklies, suburban weeklies. This means that to avoid uneconomic mailings a press list of provincial papers needs to be very carefully selected. It also implies study and knowledge of these hundreds of newspapers.

The press officer who knows his media will always be a more effective operator. Unfortunately, it is customary by too many press officers (consultants are often the worst offenders) to carry out mass blanket mailings of the provincial press and hope for the best. This incurs the wrath of large numbers of provincial editors who simply have not the space to print press release material (unless it is about a local industry or topic), and is a regrettable waste of time and money.

The advertiser is nowadays protected from wasteful expenditure by readership survey tables which enable the agency to choose media most economical and appropriate to a campaign, and although the press officer has got to rely much more on personal knowledge and research he, too, has to try to offer his organisation or client a sensible expenditure on carefully chosen media.

Magazines and Journals

The magazine field is even more capable of division into categories, but to avoid too long a list the analysis can be restricted to the following:

Women's Weeklies	*Children's Magazines*
Women's Monthlies	*Trade, Technical and Professional Journals*
Specialist Weeklies	*House Magazines*
Specialist Monthlies	

Local and Regional Magazines

With the big four, *Woman*, *Woman's Own*, *Woman's Realm*, and *Woman's Weekly*, we have an extremely powerful and influential press addressed to the women's mass consumer market with the advantage over both the national newspapers and, for the time being, commercial television of being able to offer the advertiser full colour, although this is rarely of any significance to the press officer. Other women's weeklies are aimed at either different age or intellectual groups. Most are printed gravure.

Women's monthly magazines, being less frequently published, are less able to compete for the mass market advertising and a number have disappeared while at the top end of the market we have seen *Woman's Journal* and *Homes and Gardens* soar rather like the business newspapers. The home interest cum women's magazines like *Ideal Home*, *House and Garden*, *House Beautiful*, *New Homes*, and *Homefinder* have won important circulations among those making, improving or re-equipping homes, and to these magazines can be added *Do-It-Yourself*, *Homemaker* and *Practical Householder*, although now we are entering one of the numerous specialist magazine categories. But this does indicate that the press officer dealing with, say, furniture, cookers, central heating, lighting, decoration or some such product will need to build his press list to include many categories in which reader interests tend to merge.

Think of a subject and there's bound to be at least one specialist magazine devoted to it! In this respect, the British periodical press is truly fantastic, and this is one of the advantages that the British press officer can share only with his American colleagues. It is something which both baffles and excites the envy of press officers from most other countries where their media is far more limited.

Some people talk rather loosely about "glossy" magazines, often quite erroneously describing the popular women's weeklies as such although they are actually printed on cheap paper and not the art paper implied by the old-fashioned term "glossy" which really refers to the society and fashion magazines so popular in pre-war days. *Country Life*, *The Field*, and the *Illustrated London News* are among the last remaining examples of the gracious "glossy" magazines of a past era, although we had for a time the combined and modernised *Tatler and Bystander*, until their purchase for individual publication by the Illustrated County Magazines Group, publisher of 19 county glossies.

There is nothing static about the publishing world, and the press officer has to appreciate something of its history and the reasons for the great changes which are constantly taking place. Immediately after the war colour-gravure Odhams magazines like *John Bull* and *Illustrated* were great successes, selling more than a million copies weekly. *Everybody's* was popular, too, and *Picture Post* was an adventure in pictorial journalism dating from the 30's that seemed indestructible. Yet television, and especially the onslaught of commercial television, killed journals based on adventure serials or picture news.

Two other kinds of journal have failed in this country, the news magazine and the humorous magazine. Only American news magazines and *Punch* continue to sell in Britain.

By understanding why publications come and go, are acquired, relaunched and so on the press officer will be able to anticipate possibilities for the publication of his information and news. He will watch out for the advent of new journals and get in touch with editors long before publishing day, offering assistance with articles or pictures. He may thus be able to help an editor who is seeking original material. That is the way to make editorial friends rather than mere contacts.

Specialist monthlies are those which deal with identified interests such as hobbies, crafts, arts and ideas and beliefs. Some of these magazines are fairly expensive to buy nowadays, particularly if there is limited advertising available to them. On the other hand, some are bought as much for the advertisements as the editorial, philatelic magazines being a good example.

When building press lists and plate libraries it is necessary to differentiate between the readerships of magazines. In the photographic field, for instance, there are journals read by amateur photographers and film-makers, professional photographers, the retail camera trade, and the makers and users of industrial films, plus the associated worlds of cinema-going, film-making and the cinema industry. It would be a nonsense to mail all these journals with the same story even though in some directories they might be listed under the same heading. Their very different readerships must be understood.

This sort of problem often perplexes the student when confronted for the first time by the trade, technical and professional press—three quite distinct categories—and he finds it hard to realise, to take another subject, that the *Chemist and Druggist* is read by retailers, the *Chemical Worker* by trade unionists in the chemical industry, the *Chemical Trade Journal* by those in the chemical and chemical-using industries, while *Chemical Products* interests manufacturing chemists. Once again, he has to be very careful in selecting the right media for a "chemical" story.

Titles can have a sameness about them which can be most misleading. Fortunately, there is in the *Newspaper Press Directory* a complete guide to the contents and readerships of most British journals, and also to those of the major publishing countries overseas. (The publications of other countries are listed but not necessarily the subjects covered and the readerships interested.)

Three types of circulation will be observed, bookstall (i.e. retail sale); subscription (i.e. by post paid annually); and controlled circulation (i.e. free circulation to a selected list of readers). Among trade and technical journals the controlled circulation journal is usually sent to a larger section of the trade or industry than would normally subscribe to a magazine and so much wider coverage is generally accomplished.

Children's magazines come and go with amazing frequency, suggesting that the young of today are more fickle than in the past, and only a few of the more educational magazines such as *Treasure* and *Look and Learn* are likely to interest the press officer. He should take an interest in these papers because they often publish apparently informative articles on a multitude of subjects, but the information given is sometimes unreliable. If the press officer represents an information service likely to be useful to the junior press he should make these services known repeatedly to the particular editors. It is too late to correct an "educational" article once it has been published.

Other people's house magazines may be useful to the press officer.

Some of the large works newspapers make a point of publishing general interest material such as do-it-yourself, gardening, fashion or motoring features. For example, when the author was editor of *Rentokil Review* (and outside features were scarcely ever used) he did publish road safety articles supplied by RoSPA because such a large proportion of Rentokil staff spent many of their working hours at the wheel of car or van. *Communication*, the membership journal of the British Association of Industrial Editors—house journal editors—publishers a monthly feature called *Definite Articles* which reports the availability of articles for house journal publication. As press officer to exhibitions the author has, through this facility, offered and had published a number of articles describing forthcoming exhibitions.

Local and regional magazines form a growing group of publications which in some cases seem to have almost replaced the national picture magazines. Most counties have "county magazines", and some of these like *Yorkshire Life, Cheshire Life and Lancashire Life* published by the Whitethorn Press are very beautiful magazines. Others are published by local newspapers, as with *Kent Life* published by the *Kent Messenger*, while a national series of glossies reminiscent of the pre-war *Sphere* and *Tatler* is published by the Illustrated County Magazine Group Ltd from the Ruddington Press at Nottingham. Its titles include the *Illustrated Bristol News*, the *Birmingham Sketch* and the *Guernsey Life*. These journals are more likely to be interested in feature articles than press releases, subject to discussion with the editor.

2. Films

The title press officer does not imply that the holder of this office should confine his activities to the supply of information and news to the press alone. It is necessary for him to familiarise himself with the many outlets for his stories through all kinds of film which may be used for the cinema, TV, or for private audiences. He may also be expected to advise on film scripts for his organisation or in conjunction with a film unit which has been commissioned to make a film for his organisation.

There are also press relations on behalf of the organisation's films which we will deal with at the close of this section. And in another chapter on export press relations we will see how he may need to co-operate with the Films and Television Division of the COI, Visnews or an independent film unit. So the more he knows about films as a PR medium the better equipped he will be to succeed with this form of communication which is becoming increasingly valuable. Attendance at film festivals and other activities organised by the British Industrial Film Association is recommended as an instructive way of comparing techniques in documentary film-making.

Newsreels

While these are less frequently seen by British audiences the cinema is a powerful medium overseas, especially in the developing countries of Africa and Asia. The COI supply newsreels to all parts of the world every week. Newsreel cameramen are always in attendance at exhibitions because these events are constant sources of new ideas, products and applications. The press officer should never forget to invite newsreel companies when he has suitable subject matter for them, and he will find their addresses in the *WPN Directory of Newspaper and Magazine Personnel and Data* which (together with the *Newspaper Press Directory*) he will by now have learnt must be on his annual subscription list.

Film Magazines

Apart from the COI film magazines there are those of Pathe and the Rank Organisation which are shown first in British cinemas and may afterwards have overseas distribution to cinemas and TV companies. Pathe produce magazines of short interest items, while Rank's *Look At Life* films each concentrate on an interesting and entertaining subject such as the strange things that go on under city pavements, how our new skyscraper buildings are maintenanced, or the Farnborough Air Show. *Look at Life* films appear every week at major cinemas throughout the country which means that they need 52 new subjects every year. They are not purely documentary films, an element of entertainment being an important characteristic which the press officer must consider when putting up ideas to the producer.

Press Relations for Sponsored Films

Because a documentary film has many news story opportunities it can provide a legitimate vehicle for extra press coverage for the organisation which commissioned it. Publication of these stories will also create a demand to borrow a print or to attend showings. Fine films like John Laing's *Coventry Cathedral*, Shell's *Rival World*, BP's *Giuseppina*, Rentokil's *The Intruders* and Smiths Industries' *Time of Change* have gained much for their sponsors and themselves through press notices.

Here are a few ways in which an alert press officer can make good use of a film for press relations purposes:

1. It can be announced that the film is to be made, or picture stories can be released of the film unit on location.

2. Industrial film critics can be invited to a premiere.

3. A synopsis should be written so that copies may be given to members of audiences, and copies can be sent to all journals read by people likely to wish to borrow the film. A press release should accompany the printed synopsis, presenting a publishable summary.

4. Press releases can be distributed reporting various showings of the film at meetings, conferences and other assemblies.

5. Dates and venues of film showings can be contributed to the diaries of events carried by many trade and technical journals.

6. If the film wins an award there are further opportunities for a variety of stories and pictures, and this award can be mentioned in all future stories. It now becomes "*The award-winning film . . .*"

7. If the film is shown at exhibitions or press receptions the stars of the film can be present as special guests, especially if they are members of the staff and not actors. This was done when the Smiths Industries' film *Time of Change* was shown at a press reception, and it provided useful pictures for the local press in South Wales where the film was made.

8. Foreign language versions may be made and their availability can be announced at home and abroad.

9. An executive of the organisation may go on an overseas lecture tour, perhaps with Board of Trade assistance, and if he takes the film with him each separate showing provides material for a story, including an advance one airmailed to the local press before the executive arrives. In such a tour there are all sorts of opportunities for home and foreign press coverage.

10. Acquisition of the film by the COI makes yet another story.

11. A release, containing a brief synopsis, can now be sent to appropriate overseas journals to encourage borrowings of the film from the British Commercial Officer.

12. Foreign showings including those on TV can provide opportunities for further stories in the British trade press.

In other words, one good documentary film can provide material for a continuous campaign of news stories.

3. Radio

Television has not made radio redundant as the popularity of Jack de Manio's *Today* programme proves and here, of course, is a programme which forms a regular target for press officers with stories of immediate interest such as an event which is taking place that day, the opening of an exhibition, for example.

To make the best use of radio as a PR medium it is wise to do two things: (1) accept that the BBC will not broadcast blatant advertising, and (2) take the trouble to study the *Radio Times*, noting the names of radio personalities and producers, and also of series and regular programmes likely to welcome ideas, but remember that many series are produced some time in advance. A study of a file of back numbers can be an excellent way of anticipating seasonal programmes. As with all press relations activity, the golden rule is to study the medium and exploit the opportunities.

One of the interesting and useful things about British radio is the established network of regional stations in Wales, the West of England, Scotland and Northern Ireland, and the growing number of new local radio stations such as Radio Merseyside and Radio Brighton. All these stations take up news material of local interest, some of which may well be derived from PR sources. Short talks on subjects of local interest are slotted in on the regional programmes, and when appropriate the press officer should submit his ideas to the local BBC studio. As an example of this, a holiday industry conference was being held in a seaside resort and the author was able to give a four-minute talk after the news to explain what this conference was all about.

Many programmes such as *The Archers*, *Woman's Hour*, *Gardener's Question Time*, *Holiday Hour* and *Today* are interested in ideas which are applicable to their special programmes. When Rentokil introduced their woodworm insurance scheme this was discussed on the programme *Money Matters*. Listeners to *The Archers* may recall the visit of the Archers family to Guernsey, this being organised on behalf of the Guernsey Tomato Marketing Board by Leedex Ltd.

4. Television

With TV there are even more outlets than with radio because in addition to BBC TV and Independent Television News there are numerous programme contractors in London and throughout the U.K., all of whom are responsible for series and magazines and thus liable to be interested in ideas and facilities that press officers can provide. As with radio, it is a matter of patient research, studying the programmes, noting the people concerned, and having the right material at the right time—usually well in advance before a programme is taped or canned.

It is surprising what diligence and good fortune can produce. The author approached the producer of a Granada series, had the producer and scriptwriter to see the material available, but got a refusal because the producer had certain personal views on the subject. But the scriptwriter remained interested. Nearly a year later he joined ATV and, in connection with a new series, rang up the author and asked if the facilities were still available. The result was a 23-minute programme devoted to one organisation!

The final result can be very satisfying but both radio and TV work will be very time-consuming, and those interviewed must be warned that there may be hours of tedious rehearsal before the show goes on "live" and "spontaneous" as the audience fondly imagines! It can happen that those involved are so hot and tired by the time the red light shows on the camera that the programme actually screened is inferior to that rehearsed maybe an hour earlier.

One word of caution must be uttered regarding TV. By its very nature TV, like the stage and the cinema screen, is essentially an entertainment medium. Except for very occasional and exceptional items such as political party broadcasts and messages from the Prime Minister, TV is neither a platform nor a pulpit. It can be used as a schoolroom, but not for the mass audience to which TV is mostly directed. TV has a fascination for certain extroverts, and the press officer must be extremely careful not to allow heads of his organisation to blunder into TV interviews which they intend should be serious but which the programme demands otherwise. TV is an excruciatingly candid medium which can crucify the insincere, the bumptious, the frivolous and the evasive. Some of those who have been revealed disastrously on the TV screen can no doubt be called to mind, and that is warning enough that this is not a medium which can be exploited by the publicity-seeker for it will exploit them to their dismay and disadvantage.

5. The Spoken Word

The rest of the media in our list has been dealt with elsewhere in this book, but there remains the spoken word, whether this be a luncheon address, a speech at a conference, a talk at a more intimate seminar, a radio broadcast, or possibly a TV talk or discussion. Elocution and platform behaviour has no place here, but it can be a duty of the press officer to assist in the collation of material, even the writing of speeches, for members of his organisation, and this is something which requires not only knowledge of oratory but knowledge of the speaker.

Prepared speeches may be very necessary to the press officer so that he can issue advance copies, prepare summaries, or even interpolate into the speeches quotable phrases. But even a prepared speech must be in character, following on from other speeches, perhaps repeating known sentiments, and if a press officer is called upon to prepare speeches the first thing he must do is find out what the man has said on other occasions!

Two things should be avoided: statistics which are indigestible unless presented visually, and the use of jokes which is now recognised as the hallmark of the amateur speaker.

A speech is neither an article nor a press release. It should be the most human of all forms of communication, direct person to person communication. It should be capable of comfortable, relaxed, natural exposition, and this means choosing words and phrases which can be mouthed naturally without seeming to be artificially literary. To write a good speech the press officer needs to have an ear for the music of words.

A prepared speech should be read as if the speaker had written it himself and with the aid of a tape recorder it is possible to compose such a speech for someone else.

10

Organising Press Events

The organising of press events calls for methodical and meticulous planning. The model for one event is much the same as for another so that success often depends upon experience. There is nothing particularly difficult about organising PR events, provided the press officer is prepared to do—or, rather, to *be aware* of the necessity for doing—the painstaking donkey work.

There is a lot of hard work in organising a press event, as there is in organising any event involving the movement and handling of people within the limitations of time, venue and cost. The press officer who has had experience in organising other kinds of events such as amateur dramatics, public meetings, galas, sports gatherings and the like will find his knowledge and experience invaluable in planning and running press relations functions. Equally, it can usefully broaden his experience if he does participate in voluntary activities in an organising capacity.

The trouble with unsuccessful PR events is usually that the organiser has failed to plan in sufficient depth, on a D-Day basis, and has probably relied too much on the good intentions of other people, or merely on lavish hospitality which is sometimes mistakenly thought to be all that interests the press.

The Three Types of Press Events

Let us first be sure of what is meant by the three main types of press event. The loose expression "press party" is often used in a vague sense to mean any sort of press gathering whether assembled or conveyed, but by *press conference*, *press reception* and *facility visit* we refer to press gatherings of accelerating complexity. In this order of things, the first is a fairly simple affair, the second occupies a bigger place, more time and is consequently more elaborate, while the third invariably involves travel.

1. *Press Conference*

A press conference is organised like a meeting, the guests being seated to receive an announcement and to ask questions. It may be held in an office, a boardroom or a hotel room. Hospitality is usually modest such as coffee, tea or sherry served with biscuits, according to the time of day. A bar is not always necessary. Copies of the announcement will be available in press release form.

A press conference is a fairly unpretentious occasion, capable of being called at short notice if the urgency of the news demands it.

Television viewers had the novel opportunity of actually seeing a press conference in action when Sir Francis Chichester landed at Plymouth after his single-handed voyage round the world in *Gipsy Moth IV*.

2. *The Press Reception*

As the term implies, this is the type of press event which more nearly resembles a cocktail party, but its success will largely depend in its being much more than a mere drinking occasion. PR has, in the past, gained a regrettable reputation for over-generous hospitality. Contrary to the impression held by some people, most journalists who attend press receptions come in search of a story, not a free drink.

A press reception depends for success on a programme and the promise of a story sufficient to attract a good response to the invitation. For this reason it pays to include a timed programme on or with the invitation, although strangely enough this is rarely done except by the more imaginative and efficient press officers. Some invitations do not even state the purpose of the press reception and it is a wonder anyone bothers to accept apart from the minority of hangers-on who can always be found to attend anything. A programmed invitation is more likely to attract the journalists who are seriously interested in your subject and best able to give it press coverage. However, we will deal with the invitation in fuller detail later in this chapter.

A typical timetable would include: the initial reception (without formal announcement); initial refreshments according to the time of day (hot soup has been served on a winter's morning); the business of the occasion; and a final period of hospitality of the bar and buffet kind. The business may require the guests to be seated, and this session can be in a separate room away from the catering. It may include speeches, demonstrations, a film and an opportunity for questions to be asked and answered. Those responsible for answering questions should have anticipated the most likely questions and have their facts by them and not be like the sales manager at a press reception who, when asked the cost of the equipment, said he had left his price list behind! A good question and answer period can do much to create goodwill if speakers are prepared to reply frankly and fully.

A short documentary film—not more than 20 minutes—can be a very useful part of the proceedings, and should be included if possible, but it must be relevant and recent if not actually new. It may be someone else's film, either producing the raw materials or using the finished article, if the host company does not have a suitable film of its own. For example, a film showing the manufacture of laminates might be shown at a press reception for a furniture maker. The documentary or industrial film, free of advertising, is undoubtedly one of the best PR mediums we have, and guests at press receptions provide most receptive audiences. A film gives information entertainingly and most people enjoy watching films.

The author emphasises the value of films at press receptions because he has successfully shown them at press receptions for a variety of organisations. If the film is the first item on the programme after the reception it will create a very pleasant atmosphere for the remainder of the party. And while there should never be a poor speaker, and platform activites should be rehearsed and timed, a film can sometimes be a tactful means of limiting the amount of speaking time when a company executive is inclined to enjoy being on his feet before an audience! A good 20-minute film is infinitely better than a dull 10-minute speech.

Returning to the general programme, it can be a wise plan to divorce the business section from the refreshments, and it is a weak press reception when someone "says a few words" in the middle of a cocktail party, inevitably with his back to half the guests, or lost from view because the speaker is on the same floor level as the audience. The catering bill is doubled when there is no separate business session, and the worst offenders can be the representatives of the host organisation (who mistake the event for an opportunity to indulge in some free drinking). The organiser should restrict company representatives to essential hosts such as technical experts needed to talk authoritatively to guests.

Incidentally, the press officer should drink sparingly if at all at press receptions, and if the event is organised by a consultant for a client it is a very bad thing for the client to see consultancy staff consuming drinks for which he will have to pay. It is an odd thing but when the catering bill for a press reception is high it is usually because there has been a lot of drinking by people other than the press. Press drinking can be restricted to the short periods before and after the business session, which means that few guests will consume more than two or three drinks. These are points of great significance when budgets are being considered. A press reception does not have to cost a ridiculous amount of money, and it is totally wrong for press receptions to be regarded as extravagances.

3. *Facility Visits*

Facility visits provide the press with the opportunity, and often the privilege, of attending an official opening, visiting a factory or other premises, visiting an installation, going on board a new ship, flying in a new aircraft, or being taken abroad to an overseas exhibition. For the trip, anything from a private car to a chartered aircraft may be used. These events can be costly because the party has to be conveyed from point to point, fed and entertained, and on a long trip overnight accommodation is necessary.

The Electrical Development Association division of the Electricity Council organise excellent facility visits to their annual conference and exhibition, held in alternative years at Brighton and Harrogate, and the total press attendance from London, Scotland and the provinces exceeded 250 at Brighton in 1968. This is always extremely well done, and is a real service to the electrical supply and electrical appliance industries since the press are given a preview of the new models (in February) which the public will not see until the *Ideal Home Exhibition* some weeks later. This event requires elaborate travel arrangements (sometimes with supplementary plans as when a rail strike was threatened in 1966). The organisation includes a cocktail party attended by the press and representatives of all the exhibiting companies, and a press tour of the exhibition which—for a private show—is always up to the highest exhibition standards. This must be one of the most practical and best run PR events of the year.

More modestly, when the Elvaco central heating system was first introduced into Britain a private car was hired to take two or three women journalists to a house near London which had been equipped with the new system. Several visits like this were made over a period of weeks. The house was occupied and it was neither possible nor desirable to take a large party to visit a private house. The journalists were able to have a cup of tea with the owner and discuss the advantages of the system, and also experience its special characteristics.

There are two basic kinds of facility visit and the organiser should be clear in his own mind and in his invitation about the kind that he is holding. First, there is the visit which is purely to provide background information; second, there is the kind with a definite news story and this will require facilities for some guests to get the story back by telephone, telex or fast transport in the case of TV news. The press will expect the visit to be of one kind or the other, but if they are merely feted and fussed over in the course of a pointless journey they will not have an enhanced opinion of the organisation. It is foolish to take a plane-load of journalists from one end of the country to the other to see a jam or paint factory no different from one they could see on their own doorstep. Unfortunately, this happens all too often, and PR gets a bad name for extravagant thoughtlessness.

Organising a Press Conference or Reception

The following considerations must be borne in mind when organising these two kinds of press event.

1. *The Purpose*

There must be a good reason for the conference or reception. Wouldn't a press release suffice? Is there a big enough story to warrant taking up the time of the press, let alone the expense? Are we absolutely clear what we want to tell and show the press?

2. *The Date*

What is the best date? Many factors will control this choice: the purpose of the event, the availability of speakers, the availability of the press, and the availability of the venue. Right choice of date is vital. For example, if a new central heating system is to be introduced the press reception should be early in the year in order to achieve coverage in the autumn-published heating features and supplements in the women's and home interest monthlies. January would be preferable, February would be getting rather late. (If the product were a Christmas gift, the event should be in July.)

To make sure that the right speaker is free it may be necessary to work a long way ahead. Some globe-trotting tycoons are hard to book at short notice! And there is not much sense in holding the event on a day when the journalists you want are attending something else, such as the opening of an exhibition. It is by no means easy to avoid a clash of dates sometimes, but it does pay to check as far as possible. The *Financial Times* publishes a weekly table of forthcoming activities and *Exhibitions Bulletin* is a monthly guide to exhibitions being held at home and abroad during the current and the following year. The *Daily Telegraph* Information Bureau is always very helpful. We will deal with the venue separately.

Linked with the right date is also the right day of the week, and the right time of day. The time of day for a press gathering is much more important than is sometimes supposed. Businessmen are inclined to think first of their own convenience and availability, and to regard these events as cocktail parties which must commence at 6 p.m. and be held out of office hours so as not to interfere with the day's work. But the guests have homes to go to. They do not all work on national newspapers whose offices are open day and night. They, too, like to keep office hours. It is no pleasure to them, and not really a duty, to have to forsake dinner at home with their families to attend a commercial cocktail party.

A London reception at, say, the Waldorf between 4 p.m. and 6 p.m. is as late in a conveniently located venue as one would wish to make a press reception. Such an arrangement makes it possible for most journalists to catch their usual trains home.

If the organiser does insist on an evening affair he must expect to attract office juniors and freelance contributors to whom the invitations have been passed by more senior people who prefer to attend the other press functions which are held at more convenient times of the day.

So, generally speaking, the best time for a press conference or reception is between 11 a.m. and 1 p.m. on a Monday or Tuesday (Wednesday is bad for journalists working on weeklies) during the first or last ten days of the month (mid-month is bad for journalists working on monthlies). For numerous reasons, press gatherings occur at other times on other days, but the ideal is suggested above, especially when aiming at a party of journalists from daily, weekly and monthly publications. Newspapermen should be given their stories before lunchtime, and an evening paper reporter will want his story as early in the day as possible.

3. *The Venue*

A venue should be chosen because it suits the occasion, provides the correct facilities, is conveniently situated, has the right appeal, and makes reasonable charges for exemplary catering. That is a short list of requirements, no more.

Choosing the venues for press events calls for knowledge of the advantages and disadvantages of a large variety of premises, and for this purpose it pays to continuously put on file information about all likely hotels, halls and other accommodation. This calls for a regular process of seeking out and sifting after enquiry or investigation. Many proprietors would like to obtain press function business, probably because they hold a totally false impression of the likely bar sales, but a capable organiser will regard the bar facilities as the least of his worries. Careful selection is necessary and usually one finds that only a limited number of establishments are worth retaining on the recommended list. Why is this? Surely in large cities like London, Bristol, Birmingham, Newcastle or Glasgow one is almost spoilt for choice? This is not so as two examples will reveal.

In London there is a modern skyscraper building which possesses a magnificently appointed lecture theatre which is admirable for conferences. But there is no public transport and empty taxis hardly ever pass the door. It has earned the reputation of being a place from which it is difficult to return. Quite another problem prevents one from using certain otherwise attractive venues in some provincial cities: lack of car-parking facilities. In selecting a venue outside London the organiser has to cater for guests travelling in from other towns, usually by car.

Let us summarise the eight main considerations to be borne in mind when booking venues for press gatherings:

1. Availability of a room or rooms of the required size, and whether this accommodation is also available earlier in the day or on the previous day for preparation or rehearsal purposes.

2. Does the accommodation meet the special demands of the occasion: e.g. does it black out for films; is it sound proof; is the floor strong enough for weighty exhibits (ballroom floors seldom are); are there convenient cloakroom facilities, especially for coats, hats and umbrellas during winter months?

3. Is the catering good? Are there any specialities?

4. Is the venue or its location of special interest?

5. What are the costs per head for finger buffets, fork buffets, lunches and dinners? Is there a hire charge for rooms? What is the method and rate for gratuities? (Comparative costs are more important than one might think.)

6. Has the venue special facilities such as lighting effects, staging, microphones, projectors, screens or tape-recorders? Some are extremely well-equipped especially for press events.

7. Is there a car-park or are the premises adjacent to one? Apart from guests' cars, space may be required for a demonstration vehicle.

8. Are transport facilities good, e.g. taxis, public transport, and is the venue easily accessible at busy times of the day? In London it pays to hold press conferences and receptions within a reasonable distance of Fleet Street, Long Acre and Gray's Inn Road, but if the event is associated with an exhibition at Earl's Court or Olympia the Kensington hotels are more convenient. Accessibility can have a critical effect on attendance figures if a number of press events happen to be claiming the same people on the same day.

Other considerations may occur according to the needs of the occasion. A hotel may be required to provide lunch for a press party visiting a factory or an installation. What is the capacity of the dining room? Or it may be an attraction to invite the press to a brand new hotel which has novelty appeal. It may be that outside caterers can be brought in to provide for a party in an historic venue, for example a City livery hall or the Royal Pavilion at Brighton. Maybe catering can be arranged in a marquee in the factory grounds. The author has even used a barn on a farm.

Few venues are suitable for every event, and if press parties are being held in various parts of the country satisfactory answers will be required to many questions. The important thing is knowing what questions to ask! It is not sufficient merely to write or telephone: venues should be inspected before making firm bookings.

Of course, not everyone is as fortunate as the Port of London Authority which has both the advantage and the pleasure of taking its press parties for a river and dock cruise in the steam yacht *St. Katherine*!

So we have three major problems to resolve before anything else is decided: is there a big enough story to warrant holding the event at all; when and where do we hold the function?

4. *The Invitation List*

This should not be a big problem for the experienced press officer, and certainly not if he is dealing most of the time with a limited, specialised press. It can be more difficult for the consultancy dealing with a much bigger assortment of journals and journalists. By this is meant that the consultancy may have to pay more attention to the accuracy of its invitation list because, with a number of clients operating in different fields, the consultancy tends to deal with more people less often. And by accuracy of the list we mean not just the addresses of the journals but the names of the individuals who are to be invited. One does not invite "the editor" but a person whom one has checked is the right person to ask.

To produce a reliable invitation list it is necessary to do a lot of telephoning because journalists do change their jobs with remarkable frequency. In fact, it is true to say that if the same organisation held a reception twice a year there would be considerable changes in each succeeding invitation list.

Invitations, whether cards or letters, do have to be made out to individuals. After all, an invitation is a *personal* communication. It cannot be sent vaguely to an unidentified person. This may come as a shock to those who run off grubby looking invitation letters on a duplicator and send them in unsealed envelopes to unnamed editors. Not surprisingly, such invitations produce little or no response and the organiser has to "pack" the reception with his own staff to make it look as if there is a good attendance. Good attendances are won by taking infinite pains.

When compiling an invitation list it must be large enough to produce a satisfactory turn out. If the aim is to have an attendance of 40 it may be necessary to invite 60, perhaps more. Clearly, the attendance will depend upon the various factors of newsworthiness, attractiveness of venue, and convenience of place, date and time, but in addition there are always other considerations such as staff shortages in the office, personal illness, and holidays which are beyond the control of the organisers and so deplete numbers even after acceptances have been received. It is necessary, therefore, to invite more than you need and expect fewer than promise to come. On these occasions the press officer must never be over-optimistic and it is foolish to boast to employer or client that this and that paper will be represented. National newspapers tend to accept everything and then make their choice on the day!

5. *The Invitations*

The news may be so "hot" that a telephoned invitation will be justified, and this is possible when the invitation list is a small one. Or the list may be extremely specialised, and all the journalists will be personally known to the press officer so that he can ring round in the friendliest way and invite them all at short notice. But these are exceptions to the usual run of press events, possible with press conferences but unnecessary with press receptions which have to be planned over a matter of weeks so that there is ample time in which to give journalists seven to ten days notice, sometimes longer.

The timing of the despatch of invitations is of importance to the overall organisation of the event. There must be a day prior to the event when a reasonable knowledge of likely numbers is required so that catering, transport, seating and other arrangements can be confirmed with banqueting managers and contractors. This day may be three to seven days in advance of the actual date. And if, for some reason, numbers are limited, it may be necessary to stagger the despatch of invitations in order to control the total number of acceptances, further invitations being sent out to make up for refusals.

Mention has already been made of those dreadful duplicated invitations on plain paper that are sometimes sent out. Out of courtesy to guests the invitation must either be a decently produced letter (which can be reproduced if done carefully) or better still a printed invitation card. A card is always preferable, and letters should be resorted to only when there is not time to print a card or when numbers do not justify the design and print cost. A card has many advantages over a letter. It is a special piece of correspondence, arriving in an important-looking white envelope. Out of politeness it cannot be ignored. It does its job well. Invitation cards are often put on mantelpieces and window sills where other people see them. And if the design and printing is neat and distinctive it will help to make the event seem worth attending. If the host is prepared to go to some trouble to invite his guests properly he will surely go to the same trouble to make sure that the event is worth attending.

There was a time when it was thought that invitation cards had to be given the copperplate look, but the vogue of script type faces has now been superseded by the use of neat modern typefaces which are at least legible.

When designing cards thought should be given to the way in which replies will be returned. The organiser needs to know the refusals as well as the acceptances, and the best way to obtain definite answers one way or the other is to provide an easy means of reply. There are several ways of doing this: reply slips, reply cards, or addressed envelopes, but by far the best method is to incorporate an addressed reply card with the invitation card. This can be done by having a long card with a perforated reply portion, measuring $8\frac{1}{4}$ inches long by $4\frac{1}{8}$ inches wide to fit a DL size envelope. Thus the recipient can keep the invitation and post back the postcard part which has to be filled in with his intention of coming or not, together with both his name and the name of his publication. This last detail is worth remembering because those accepting are not always those invited.

This shape card offers four sides for printing. On the face we have the invitation to the left of the perforation, and on the right the "I can/I cannot" reply part. On the reverse side the reply part must bear the organiser's full postal address and in the top right hand corner a frame to indicate that a postage stamp is required, otherwise people will post it back in an envelope. When so many offices use franking machines a stamped addressed card is irrelevant, although advisable when writing to freelance writers and correspondents at home addresses.

A fourth area remains, the back of the invitation, and this is where a timetable programme of the event should be set out. These timetables—so seldom incorporated in invitations—are very much appreciated by journalists. For one thing, they show that there is a programme, and that it is not just a junket with a press pack to take home afterwards. And having a timetable means that the event has to run to time, and this is a useful discipline for all concerned including VIP speakers! It is no plan at all to run a press reception as a cocktail party with a speech being made when the time seems appropriate. Half the guests will have gone by then!

The following is an example of simple, informative and effective wording:

The Directors of XYZ Ltd
have pleasure in inviting

....

to attend a PRESS RECEPTION
in the Buckingham Room,
Hotel Western, Park Lane, London, W1
at 11.30 am on Tuesday November 5
to view the new XYZ models for 1967

Cocktails — RSVP John Smith, XYZ Ltd.,
Refreshments — 88, Hall Street, London, W1.

This card does require the organiser to write in the names of each guest, and names must be neatly written in by hand and *not* typewritten. If there is a very large invitation list this handwriting may be too big a task and the alternative is to have a card which reads:

The Directors of XYZ Ltd
have pleasure in inviting you
to attend a PRESS RECEPTION

The wording of the invitation should clearly set out all the facts which will encourage the recipient to decide to attend if he possibly can. The purpose of the event must be clearly stated. Some press invitations simply invite attendance at a reception at a certain place on a certain date, but do not bother to explain why a press reception is being held! Why should anyone accept such an empty invitation? A press reception has to be marketed like anything else, hence the attention to detail which is emphasised throughout this chapter. This marketing attitude is vital because invitations must compete with many other claims upon a journalist's time, including rival invitations.

The invitation card should also indicate the kind of refreshments that will be provided, and the address for reply should be printed at the foot of the ticket even though a reply card is attached.

The appearance of the card will be enhanced if it carries the organisation's coat of arms, or the company logo, and it should comply with the accepted house style regarding type face and colour.

Should there be any sort of enclosure with an invitation card? The answer is yes if it will do anything to encourage the journalist to come. It could be a personal note, or if it is a complicated or controversial subject it may be a good idea to include some preliminary information which will stimulate curiosity and questions. But it can be fatal to send out the press release in advance.

Once the cards have been posted the press officer must be organised to receive replies. As they come in they should be sorted into acceptances and refusals, and a daily alphabetical list compiled. A check should be made with the invitation list, and if replies have not been received from those whose attendance is particularly desired it will be necessary to telephone them.

A telephone follow-up may seem to be an unnecessary chore in the midst of all the other jobs which have to be dealt with at this stage of the organisation, but the extra effort is almost certain to be worthwhile. When telephoned some of the people will say they have never seen the invitation, and this may be perfectly true. Letters do go astray in the post, and publishing organisations are so vast that it is possible for letters to go astray within an organisation. There may be other reasons why the prospective guest has not replied, and a few friendly words on the telephone may very likely encourage an acceptance. One has to "sell" a press reception.

For the day a complete list of acceptances should be made up, and this can be checked against signatures in the visitors' book so that absentees may be sent the press releases and pictures they would have received had they attended. Just because guests do not turn up is no reason why the purpose of the reception should be completely lost on them. In fact, it often happens that on the morning of the event one or two guests will telephone their apologies and ask to be sent any information which would have been handed to them at the reception.

6. *Identifying Guests*

It has become accepted at receptions, meetings and conferences that everyone should wear some form of identification. This practice has the distinct advantage that it makes contact and conversation so much easier. Putting names to faces is always a problem at social gatherings, and the British are not good at introducing themselves. Name badges are a great help to the press officer who cannot always know everyone by sight, especially when as so often happens substitutes or new faces are present. By means of badges which name both guest and publication he can move among the guests, quickly scanning badges and welcoming people by name.

The three main types of badge are those with pins, the adhesive label and the pocket card which fits the breast pocket. Of these the adhesive label is best when both sexes are present. If the names are typed with a bold-faced electric typewriter they are easy to read. Badges of a different colour, or bearing the organisation's house symbol, should be worn by members of the host party.

The badges should be prepared from the acceptance list, and set out in alphabetical order on the reception table at the entrance to the room where the reception is being held. This table should be adequately staffed so that arriving guests are quickly received and not obliged to queue up. If there are two receptionists, one can ask for signatures in the visitors' book and the other can find and hand out badges. It is seldom advisable to hand out press packs at this stage: they can either be placed on the chairs or better still presented on leaving. Spare packs can be kept on the reception table for those who do ask for information in advance as sometimes happens when a guest cannot stay for the full programme.

7. *Press Kits or Packs*

One of the abominations of all kinds of press event is the over-elaborate so-called press kit. Presumably the press kit is intended to be a convenient way of carrying the press information, but as it turns out guests often have thrust upon them bulky and weighty wallets which can only be described as a nuisance. Some of our biggest companies go to considerable expense in the attempt to impress journalists with beautifully produced wallets when a simple press release would be much more to the point. It is a stupid practice. It is also unnecessarily costly and therefore wasteful of funds that could be better spent on other PR activity. The average journalist wants a few facts on a piece of paper, *that's all*! Something he can put in his packet. He does not want to look like a schoolboy visitor to the Motor Show.

Let us look for a moment at the question of cost since in running a press event we should be working to a budget and press packs can be a formidable item if we are not careful. Press packs can cost unmentionable numbers of shillings each, sometimes as much as £1 apiece, whereas a hundred press releases are of negligible cost, say £2 including printed heading and duplicating. There is a lot of difference between £100 and £2, especially when the £100 represents not only a waste of £98 (which is criminal but common) but a waste of effort because the single piece of paper is preferable.

At a press reception a simple plastic wallet is a convenient means of presenting a small collection of essential but loose items of different size such as press releases and photographs. But because a press gathering is being organised it is not imperative that there be a press pack. It can be a temptation to produce too many press releases, provide too many pictures, and to add pieces of print as well. But more often than not a press release alone is sufficient, and it is better to display photographs, numbered on a board, and take orders for them rather than give every guest a set whether wanted or not. Available pictures, or the availability of pictures, can always be given at the end of the press release.

However, if press packs are absolutely necessary the best are undoubtedly the pliable plastic ones which can even be rolled and put in a jacket pocket if need be—very necessary if the guest is trying to eat and drink during the buffet session. The simplest is the transparent kind, but there are more sophisticated ones with button-down flaps which are useful and more secure when material is being collected during a prolonged visit or tour. The use of clumsy cardboard wallets is incomprehensible, and no journalist appreciates the kind with glued or even stapled flaps which always seem to burst open.

These remarks therefore refute what is so often common practice, but surely the guiding rule must be: use a wallet if it provides a service to your guests, but don't use a wallet merely to try to impress them with the importance of your organisation. Journalists will *not* be impressed by sheer swank. They will be impressed by thoughtfulness. It may be thoughtful to provide a wallet, but it may be even more thoughtful not to overload them at the wrong time with yet another thing to have to carry.

8. *Catering*

When giving numbers to the caterers it is safe to work on a number slightly below that of the acceptance list, since not all the guests remain for the buffet. While it is extremely bad to have insufficient food, it is equally bad management and economics to have a lot of food over. The bar can be controlled by one of two methods: the bar tender can be given a maximum figure, at which point he asks the organiser whether the bar should remain open; or the bar can be closed at a certain time and coffee can be served.

The serving of coffee is an excellent device for bringing the proceedings to a close, and, since by coffee time numbers are sure to be depleted, it is almost certain to be sufficient to order only half as many coffees as total number of people present. These remarks are not intended to be pinch-penny but to indicate that by proper management press events can be budgeted and controlled in a sensible and responsible manner.

Returning to the question of food, this is more important than the bar. If an organisation really wants to impress the press good food is by far the best method! A weakness of some hotel receptions is the triviality of the food, sometimes no more than cocktail canapes, and that is downright shameful. The food should include some substantial items and not miniature sandwiches lost under a maze of mustard and cress! The organiser should insist on not only seeing a variety of menus and prices but should clearly understand from the banqueting manager what is meant by each item. It only takes one press reception to learn how and what to order if the organiser has the gumption to ask exactly what he is getting for his money. It is no good hopefully accepting a banqueting manager's vague assurance that he can "*do something for about 17s. 6d. a head, sir*". It is sometimes surprising how much better one can do for 15s. when one demands that each item be detailed.

9. *Gifts and Mementoes*

Should the press be given presents at press receptions? It depends on the suitability of the gift or memento to the subject of the reception. A gift is not vital, but if it is a sample or is related in some way to the organisation running the reception, then it can be appropriate and desirable. There are some organisations from whom such a gift might well be expected, but otherwise gifts are more appropriate to facility visits where they are an accepted courtesy. A gift should not seem to be a bribe, merely a nice gesture, and if it is a matter of proving one's case by providing a sample it will, of course, be a very good tactic.

10. *Managing the Event*

It has been stressed at the beginning of this chapter that a press event must be planned right down to the last detail, and that there must be a properly planned prgramme. This sounds all right, and probably looks very nice on paper, but how is all this to be managed? Well, the press officer has to be both producer and stage manager, and it is not very different from directing a staged production. People have to do certain things correctly at stipulated times, and a press reception is not just "played by ear". Only the press officer can co-ordinate and manage the various elements, and everyone from managing director to distinguished guest must comply with his control. A good press officer will operate almost invisibly, and the event will seem to run itself, but all the same the press officer must be here, there and everywhere making sure that everything proceeds as it should.

By setting out the programme on the invitation ticket the press officer commits everyone concerned to a timetable. VIP speakers may try to be a law unto themselves, but there are three ways of maintaining control. First, speeches must be prepared so that copies may be available to the press; second, there must be a rehearsal, with or without the VIP speaker; and thirdly the press officer can take the chair and so make sure that the programme runs to time.

One of the controlling factors will be the accessibility of the venue. If more than one hotel exists of the same name the location of the chosen one must be clearly stated. If the hotel has more than one entrance the right one should be clearly stated also. If there is an indicator board in the foyer of the hotel the organiser must check that his event is correctly described. If there is any risk of guests losing their way along corridors, there should be directional notices. If the event occurs in the winter or on a wet day cloakroom facilities should be clearly indicated. We have already referred to the reception table at the door, adequately staffed to receive guests. The organiser should be present to welcome guests and do anything necessary to expedite their entry.

If the organisation or the client has been made responsible for the supply of products or materials, the organiser must make sure that they have in fact arrived and are ready for use. The same applies to the arrival of a film, projector and projectionist.

The reception period will usually run for 20 or 30 minutes, the shorter the better. During this period drinks will be served according to the time of day, and guests will be introduced to members of the host party. The reception period must not drag and will continue only so long as a reasonable number of guests have yet to arrive. If it goes on too long the press will become restless and want to know when the programme is to begin. The organiser must therefore take the feeling of the assembly and watch how satisfactorily the attendance is building up. He must judge the right moment to go on to the next item on the programme, doing his best not to overrun the stated time.

Throughout the course of the event he must make sure that the timetable is obeyed, the showing of the film, the giving of speeches, the demonstrating and finally the invitation to enjoy the refreshments and ask questions of members of the host party. During this latter period the organiser will endeavour to meet as many of his guests as possible and see that they are satisfied with answers to their questions and are supplied with information. He should also endeavour to say good-bye to each guest on leaving and thank them for coming.

Finally he will have to agree the account for the hotel's services and his appreciation of the way in which the hotel contributed to the success of the event will establish good relations of value to the next occasion.

Organising A Facility Visit

While most of the items already discussed under press conferences and receptions will also apply to the organising of a facility visit there are several additional items to consider.

In this category of facility visit can be included all those visits by parties of journalists to factories, installations, sites and so on requiring conveyance of guests, or at least the management of guests at some distant or outside location as distinct from receiving them in the head office boardroom or in a hotel in the vicinity of the publishing offices. It also includes trips on new trains, ships or in aircraft, provided by the owners as a facility to the press to gain first-hand knowledge and experience. It can involve no more than a single journalist who is being given facilities to write an article, or a party of almost any size.

Such visits can be very complicated organisational feats calling for patient preparation over a long period. Journalists are unwilling or unable to give up a day, perhaps two days, on a facility visit unless there is justification. Complaints are made from time to time about wonderfully organised charter-plane trips with generous hospitality and souvenir gifts, but no story!

As we said when considering the press reception, there must be a clear and valid purpose for a press event, but particularly so for one which will occupy so much of a journalist's time. It must add to his knowledge and experience, supply background material, show promise of future news development, or give him an immediate story. *It must be of value to a journalist in his daily work.* He must go home feeling glad that he accepted the invitation, and not feeling that it was all very nice but rather a waste of time. Some well-known organisations do spend several hundred pounds to achieve no more than that. These ill-conceived jaunts do the PR business no good at all.

Let us analyse the practical requirements of facility visits.

1. *Party Numbers*

The primary consideration when planning a press visit is the number of people in the proposed party. This number may be determined by the capacity of the premises to accept visitors, the catering or overnight accommodation facilities, the seating capacity of aircraft, motor coaches or railway coaches, the number of potential guests (which may be restricted with highly specialised subjects), and the budget.

From the above variations upon the single theme of numbers we begin to see both the complexity and the logic of the necessary planning. One does not say "*Let's invite some editors to see our factory*" and then go ahead and invite them. Each "variation" is worth studying in turn.

Capacity of the Premises. Visitors to a factory can be a nuisance to those working there, but this must never be apparent! A certain number of people can be handled comfortably, whether it be in a laboratory or factory or on an outdoor site. No more than 15 people might be acceptable in a research establishment, whereas six parties of 15 might be all right in a large factory.

On most factory visits small groups need to be organised because production operations would be lost on a crowd, and so the usual practice is to organise parties of from six to 12 people, each with a guide. This may therefore decide how many groups can be taken round in the available time between arrival and lunchtime, or in the afternoon before the party must leave. One method of overcoming the time problem is to let these groups follow different routes, rather than have them following one behind the other. In this way all groups can complete their tour at very nearly the same time, and visitors are not left hanging about waiting for the others to catch up with them.

This clearly calls for some good planning and rehearsal. Guides must know what they are talking about, be capable of answering questions, yet all take about the same time in dealing with each section of the tour. There should be a manual for the guides to study, and rehearsals should include practice tours which are carefully timed and observed by the organiser. It is no use detailing members of the staff for guide duties and then hoping for the best on the day.

Catering and Accommodation Facilities. Party numbers may be controlled by the seating capacity of the dining room at the factory, or at a local hotel or restaurant. If there is suitable outdoor space a marquee may be the answer. Again, if a large party is desirable, seating limitations can be overcome by having a cold buffet with a minimum of tables, although a party which has been tramping round a factory will prefer an opportunity to sit down and relax at lunchtime. But these are the sorts of alternatives which need to be thought about carefully, remembering that factory canteen facilities will not be available while there are few parts of the country where large gatherings such as weddings, 21st birthday parties, annual dinners and the like are not being organised and catered for by a local hotel, baker and confectioner or brewery.

But it is not always easy as the Electrical Development association find when they take their big press party to the EDA conference and exhibition at Harrogate. The conference town is unable to accommodate the press party, either overnight or for the press reception, and this has all to be arranged in York. Coaches carry representatives of the exhibitors from Harrogate to York for the press reception, and next day coaches bring the press from York to Harrogate. This seemingly complicated action between two towns 22 miles apart is handled splendidly.

Naturally, it is pleasanter to keep a party together if an overnight stay is necessary, and a member of the organising party should stay at the hotel too to act as host. Local conditions may demand scattering the party among different hotels, but this should be avoided if possible. Many members of the press party will know one another and will enjoy the opportunity of staying in the same hotel. If a party does have to be split up it is a good idea to find out if any of the guests do wish to keep together, and accommodation can be organised to meet individual wishes.

Attention to small personal details can be most important to the success of an event, and if block bookings have been made the actual allocation of rooms at different hotels can be made during the coach, train or plane journey. To do this well a team of organisers is required with hosts, couriers or guides attached to each grouping of guests. The guests must never be left unattended, never expected to move from A to B unescorted once they have joined the party at the assembly point. Sometimes it is even wise to have someone detailed with a car to pick up latecomers or stragglers so that there is no danger of anyone failing to join the party. This danger is perhaps greatest at the end of the day!

A point worth remembering in this respect is that if guests have to travel a long way to join the transport (as when airports are some distance from city centres) it is safer to collect people in a central place and provide transport to the airport. Otherwise it is almost inevitable that someone will have a breakdown, lose his way, run into fog, mistake the time or miss the plane through some mishap or misunderstanding, whereas it is comparatively simple for guests to assemble at a suitable well-known spot which is accessible by most forms of transport. Motor coach companies can usually advise on the best meeting places because they have picking up points agreed between them and the police.

Capacity of Transport. Numbers may be determined by the peculiarities of the seating capacity, or the party booking arrangements, or the mode of transport. If a coach has 42 seats it is obviously impossible to accept 43 guests. The same rule applies to aircraft. It is not always possible to put on a larger coach or aircraft. Trains are more flexible up to a point, but the organiser must discuss with the railway booking staff the make-up of the train and the kind of stock being used since this differs considerably according to the region. It is essential to know how the seating will be dispersed, and it may be desirable to restrict the party to a single coach. Alternatively, the *minimum* size of the party could be the total seating of an entire coach.

When chartering aircraft there may be a choice of aircraft, and this choice will again depend on members. Similarly, if seats are being booked on a scheduled passenger service there may be an advantage in a number which secures a price reduction. These points should be discussed at the earliest possible moment with the airline.

The commercial staff of transportation organisations can be exceedingly helpful, but it is wise to check everything and not rely too heavily on other people to take over one's responsibilities. On one occasion the author discovered at very short notice that railway tickets had been wrongly dated, which would have invalidated them when presented to the ticket collector at the barrier! Fortunately the wrong date was discovered in good time otherwise that press visit might have been calamitous. Tickets should not be posted to guests: it is safer to ask guests to exchange a voucher for a ticket supplied by the organiser at the place of departure.

From the last remark an important lesson can be learned: an organiser must be a born pessimist. He must literally make himself miserable trying to think of everything that could possibly go wrong so that he can then find a satisfactory solution to it. For example, in a certain town the police insisted that coaches must unload their passengers at a specific place. But it meant a short walk involving the negotiation of busy cross roads at traffic signals in order to reach the venue. It could have rained and the party could have arrived at the venue feeling very uncomfortable. There was a risk that some members of the party could have gone any one of three wrong ways, even in that short distance. And it was not a very good thing to have to herd 60 people across a busy crossroads. So the organiser argued, and the police relented and permitted the coaches to unload on the other side of the traffic lights outside the venue itself, despite the fact that this happened to be a bus stop! The coaches had to go away and return at an agreed time which meant that the activities within the venue had to run strictly to time. But this sort of thing can be done if the organiser has a sufficiently nimble mind to foresee trouble.

On another occasion transport was impossible because the guests were coming from all points of the compass, and yet the venue was situated in a very out-of-the-way back street of a northern city, but this was overcome by printing a very explicit map on the invitation ticket.

Limited Invitation List. When the topic is so specialised that there is a limited invitation list the problem is to find a date when the majority can attend. This problem is best overcome by offering alternative dates by telephone, and negotiating in this way until a sufficiently large party has been assembled. In this case the visit will hinge on the date acceptable by the guests.

The Budget. It may be practically possible to accommodate and to transport a hundred people, but if the cost is £10 a head a total cost of £1,000 may be prohibitive. Whatever facilities or limitations may exist it is essential to have the event strictly costed, and to work within an agreed figure. Every cost can be known in advance and nothing should be agreed upon without a prior quotation. Indeed, the value of the enterprise is bound to be related to its cost, and if the press visit is but one item in an annual budget it is imperative that costs be known in advance and controlled throughout the exercise.

2. *Invitations*

For this type of operation the invitation must give specific details about the object of the visit and the facilities for transport and accommodation which will be provided, accompanied by a timetable from start to finish including the picking up and returning of guests. Depending upon how complicated the arrangements may be, an invitation ticket as already described for press receptions may be adequate or it may be safer to include a covering letter setting out the special arrangements.

Because so many bookings have to be finalised when numbers are known it will be necessary to despatch invitations much earlier than in the case of a press reception. Transport contractors and caterers will want a week's notice of the final arrangements, so if time is required for sending out a second round of invitations should acceptances be unsatisfactory, the original invitation will need to go out a month before the date of the event. This means that copy must go to the printer at least a fortnight before delivery is required, and time must also be allowed either side of the printing dates for first of all the finalising of details and the design of the card and then, when delivered, the making out and posting of the cards.

Thus, at least two months in advance of the event, we must know exactly what is going to happen. Working backwards yet again, it is not going to be too soon to begin making plans three months in advance, and no doubt some thought will have been given to the idea of a press visit much earlier than that.

It is important to see that the right people join the party. Such an expensive event merits the attendance of senior editorial personnel: it is not just a day out for juniors, free-loaders and hangers-on. This can be emphasised by pointing out that numbers are restricted and that it will be a privilege to attend. It does happen sometimes that when a very attractive press visit is learned about a number of journalists will ring up and ask to be invited! And some who were not invited will ring up and complain about this afterwards! This only goes to show yet another of the pitfalls of press relations: you can be too successful!

3. *Party Briefing*

No matter what details may have been sent at the time of invitation each person who has accepted must be sent detailed instructions three to seven days prior to the event. The instructions should not be sent too soon, otherwise they may be mislaid, nor too late otherwise they may be delayed in the post or in the publishing house internal postal system.

Before leaving home every guest should know exactly the programme of the visit.

It is unwise to issue only assembly instructions in advance, and then to issue the rest of the instructions during the journey or upon arrival, although it is sensible to re-issue instructions in case anyone has left his behind. There are many reasons for advance issue of instructions, and they will vary from event to event, but knowledge of the scheme of things will enable people to bring with them suitable clothing, accessories and equipment which might include such things as raincoats, sunglasses, cameras or field glasses. The organiser should avoid anyone uttering the cry of disappointment, "*If only I had known I would have brought my so and so.*" Thoughtful organisers make successful events!

Some organisers hand out elaborate press kits as soon as they meet guests, and when these kits are clumsy cardboard wallets it really is a problem to know what to do with them. A sheet of paper that will go into pocket or handbag is much better appreciated. To quote one example of a very fine organisation which arranges a large number of tours, the moment one joins the party a great cardboard wallet is presented which can contain as diverse an assortment of literature as a map, a large 24-page guide printed on heavy paper, a house journal of some 60 pages, an annual report, a staff newspaper and a press release. The weight of one of these press packs, presented to a party of members of the British Association of Industrial Editors, was one pound ten ounces! Guests were expected to carry that load around all day, in the course of which they also had to negotiate a stand-up buffet luncheon served with a glass of wine. When organisers involve their guests in acrobatic exercises they are not being particularly thoughtful, and a foolish press kit of this description can mar an otherwise memorable occasion. There was no reason why this press kit could not have been presented to guests upon *leaving* because only the map was of value during the tour. No-one had time to read any of the documents.

4. *News Story Facilities*

If journalists are likely to need working facilities so that they get stories, pictures, tapes or film back to their offices in time for use that day these facilities must not only be laid on but made known in advance. Telex, telephones, typewriters, lighting facilities, darkrooms, and cars to station or airport may be necessary if it is one of those real news events such as a royal visit or an official opening by a VIP of national importance. It is useless inviting people to cover a story which they cannot communicate to their editors in good time.

5. *Timing*

Following on from this is the need to time events such as VIP visits and official openings so that they occur before lunch and there is time to communicate the story to evening papers and radio and TV news services which are broadcast from 6 p.m. onwards. This timing of press visits will be controlled by the location of the venue, and also by whether the party is staying overnight or travelling to and from the venue during the day. Day return press visits present problems requiring very tight and foolproof schedules, and much will depend upon the speed of the transport. We must accept that the earliest a party may be able to leave a city centre—to which members have already travelled from their homes—is 9 a.m., and it should be back by 5.30 p.m. since some members of the party may well have to undertake a considerable additional journey to reach their homes. Add to this the fact that most factories close down for lunch at 12.30 p.m., and close for the day at 4.30 p.m., and there are very strict time limitations within which a visit has to be planned.

Every item in the programme must therefore be timed, and this does mean going over the ground and timing every movement of the party, making special allowances for the time it takes for a given number of people to leave or enter a vehicle or building, cross roads, ascend stairs or attend demonstrations. An experienced press officer can estimate these times without having to resort to a mock rehearsal, but it does pay to go over the sequence of movements where they will actually happen. Even then it is wise to insert in the timetable some extra minutes so that the programme is flexible enough to allow for losses of time through lateness of transport, unexpected weather conditions or some other minor disaster on the day.

This programming should be so expertly done that the party proceeds comfortably throughout the sequence of events without anyone being conscious of being "organised" and only that everything runs smoothly. The press officer should be a relaxed, unofficious controller who seems to be as much one of the party as the guests. He will move about among them, chatting, smiling, never letting anyone notice his occasional glances at his watch, or the flicker of his eyebrow as he signs to someone to get things moving a little more speedily. The fact that an intended demonstration is skipped because five minutes have been lost, or that the coach driver pulls up to allow guests to admire the view because he has five minutes in hand, will be details lost upon the visitors in the general smooth running of the trip if the press officer has a programme with hidden flexibility and is himself adaptable enough and sufficiently unflappable to make minute adjustments as he goes along. Although a programme may be carefully planned and scrupulously rehearsed it seldom actually goes like clockwork because trains can run late, aircraft are notorious for being late, traffic does get held up, people do get lost, and something always takes longer than expected. But this does not matter if the organiser has taken the unexpected into account.

As an example, the author was concerned with a women's press party to a south coast town. The timetable permitted the train to be ten minutes late and allowed twenty minutes for the coach to convey the party from the station to the demonstration theatre if the train arrived on time. In the event the train was on time, it was a glorious day, and the coach took a detour via the sea-front which made a delightful start to the visit. But had the train been 20 minutes late the coach could have conveyed the party to the venue in a few minutes and the demonstration could have been curtailed by the few lost minutes. Whatever happened, everything would have run perfectly so far as the guests were concerned. Their programmes set out the various arrival and departure times but they did not necessarily know how long each operation took to complete.

One member of the party wrote a story afterwards congratulating the organisers on a press visit that ran like clockwork. Unbeknown to that journalist it was a day of constant adaptation. One guest missed the train altogether, but joined up with the party later on, thanks to possession of the timetable. There were a number of substitutes in the party and the table-plan and place cards for lunch had to be changed during the factory visit. One lady missed the coach back to the station, but was driven to the station in the organiser's car. It was a very happy day and is still commented upon when guests meet the host on other occasions.

11

Information Services—Their PR Value

There are varying opinions on the value and purpose of information services. Properly done, the collating and imparting of information is a skilled task, and it implies a two-way service. Sometimes the terms information officer and press officer are synonomous, and sometimes the two terms are synonymous with public relations officer, as in the Government service. We shall not argue about labels but discuss that activity which has mainly to do with supplying information in the sense that a seaside resort publicity department runs an information bureau for the benefit of visitors or a transport service for the benefit of travellers. And as a service it is very much a PR activity, communication in its most direct, simplest and personal form.

In those organisations which rely upon spreading information about themselves, such as political parties, religious bodies, voluntary societies, tourist bureaux and overseas Government offices, the task may be of a very general nature, issuing information as demanded whether by personal visit, telephone call or letter. These will be the information officer's main tasks, and a *press* information service may be only a small part of his total activity.

Nevertheless, the information officer represents access to information, a source of value to the press, and he is in an ideal position to practise press relations and exploit his facility to give the press what it needs. It is therefore up to him to *market* his information service.

Marketing Information Services

All his efforts will be aimed at establishing his information bureau as a permanent source of reliable press information. So the first thing he must do is to offer and announce his services. There is a special section for addresses and descriptions in the *WPN Directory of Newspaper and magazine Personnel and Data*, and an annual insertion costs very little. Copy is required in October for February publication.

The most practical step of all is to make direct contact with those in the press world who can at some time use your information. This can be a long job, and its extent will depend upon the subject matter, but there are few subjects of such restricted appeal that only a few publications will be interested. Even on a single publication there may be a number of people who should be made aware of your service.

If press relations are being created for a new information service it is sensible to reduce the amount of work by making each operation serve more than one purpose. This is the time to do two things at once, to both announce your existence and to set up a mailing system.

The mailing list (or plate library) should cover every possible publication likely to be interested and the feature writers, plus columnists and special correspondents on national and provincial newspapers; agencies which supply magazine features (such as Roger Smithells Ltd and the Joan Storey Organisation); freelance writers and authors of relevant books; lecturers; trade associations; radio broadcasters; TV programme producers and suitable TV personalities; and other opinion leaders relevant to your subject such as MP's, University dons, clergy, doctors, teachers, and others who express informed opinion—or whose opinion could be better informed! The list is a formidable one, calling for prodigious effort in producing it and maintaining its currency. All these people should be told by means of a well-produced facsimile letter, addressed and hand-signed, what the bureau represents and what information can be supplied.

If the sponsoring interest is not apparent from the name this must be declared. "Front organisations" are rightly condemned by the IPR Code of Professional Conduct. It is totally wrong to pretend to impartiality if your "centre" is not an official one or one organised for joint benefit, as in the case of a trade association information bureau. This means that you must not invent a fancy name for an information service and try to obscure the true identity of the sponsors. Such a device is usually a tool of the unscrupulous who want to direct opinion in a certain direction without it being known who is behind the direction. A consultancy was suspended from membership of the IPR for doing this.

The list will be added to from time to time, and changes of names and addresses will be made by vigilantly watching sources of this information such as the weekly trade journals *World's Press News* and

Advertiser's Weekly and that great aid to advertising agency space buyers, *British Rate and Data.* But be warned: keeping a large mailing list or plate library up to date is an endless task. Publications fold, change titles, are acquired by other publishers, and move office so frequently that a hundred-per-cent accurate set of addresses would be a miracle. The *PR-Planner* is a useful and inexpensive means of keeping editorial data up to date.

The information to be distributed, using a specially designed press release heading, will very likely go out to divisions of the mailing list according to the topic. There may be news stories, announcements of exhibitions or film shows, new literature, reports of meetings, window display pictures, statistics on enquiries received, each of which may require a selective list, while the organisation's newsletter or house journal may be mailed to certain members of the press.

The press cannot be expected to understand the information service unless they have seen it for themselves, and it will be a good policy to invite groups of journalists to attend press receptions coupled with film shows and exhibitions, special displays and talks on the work of the organisation. If space is limited for gatherings a series of press visits can be organised, perhaps at fortnightly or monthly intervals, so that as many members of the relevant press as possible may have a personal introduction to the bureau's services. Personal confrontation with the press is always well worthwhile. The press officer who offers a useful information service can be a very real friend to these fellow workers.

One of the best ways of arousing their interest is to offer some authentic source of information which is unobtainable elsewhere. For example, if the information officer represents a technical organisation he can offer to provide technical data, pictures and charts, and better still he can offer the resources of his organisation's scientific staff for the checking of MSS or proofs so that no technical inaccuracies slip through. This kind of offer must be made irrespective of whether the organisation is mentioned or not. The reader might exclaim: "What, do all this for nothing?" That is taking a very short-sighted view because in the long run the organisation will be mentioned as often as not, and the mentions would not have been obtained at all but for the generosity of the service made available at all times. In addition it is sometimes important to an organisation that its subject is treated intelligently and accurately, and is not misrepresented simply through lack of factual knowledge.

Propaganda

Where do we stand regarding propaganda, and what information constitutes propaganda? How do we meet the charge, sometimes made, that we are issuing propaganda?

Propaganda is information biased in favour of an opinion, belief or cause for which it seeks support. The best known form of propaganda is the propagation of the Gospels which is acceptable to a Christian, and possibly to a convertible heathen, but appears to be biased to a Buddhist or a Mohammedan just as the messages of Goebbels were distasteful to the Allies during the Second World War.

The trouble with propaganda is that it depends on whose side you are on, whether you support Vera Lynn, Lili Marlene or Tokyo Rose! In fact, to be perfectly honest, the British wartime Ministry of Information (afterwards re-named the Central Office of Information) was sometimes better described as the Ministry of Misinformation as when it issued photographs to the press which were supposed to show German aircraft crashing in flames, when in fact they were pictures of staged models! Presumably there was a dearth of real pictures and the fakes were good for morale, but that's propaganda for you.

There is the risk that propaganda-issuing organisations may misunderstand the purpose of PR, and it may be similarly true that information officers engaged in propaganda practices are not strictly speaking elegible for membership of the IPR. However, propaganda of the belligerent, offensive and dishonest type is usually reserved for border incidents and wars.

National and Local Government Services

Facts about Government policy and home administration, mainly to do with social services, are largely aimed at explaining how things will be managed and how the public will suffer, benefit or may be expected to co-operate. This is interesting because the Government is really engaged in a marketing operation. Here we do have information services in a marketing situation which may surprise those who regard Government services as being free from commercialism. True, there are no monetary profits! But there are the pollsters, and the by-elections and the next General Election to consider. There is very little difference, then, between marketing a commercial product and marketing a Government policy, and although this may shock some Civil Servants who hold themselves aloof from marketing we have only to look at the Board of

Trade, and the COI, to see immediately how these Government services are committed to marketing. The Home Office, the Ministry of Health, the Ministry of Housing and Local Government, the Ministry of Transport and the Department of Education and Science are only some of the Government departments which have very big marketing tasks to perform, aided by information services.

Local authority information services also are beginning to grow since an increasing number of local authorities have become sufficiently enlightened not to fear a public outcry over spending money on telling the ratepayers what goes on.

Their press relations take several forms such as locally issued information about (a) Council and committee proposals and decisions; (b) facilities provided by the Council; (c) amenities for the benefit of visitors; and externally issued information about (a) holiday attractions; (b) residential attractions; (c) industrial attractions and (d) special facilities such as shops, sports, docks, a civic airport, entertainments, halls for conferences, concerts and exhibitions, gardens, or historic monuments.

On the Sunday prior to the 1967 GLC elections, Rudolph Klein in an article in the *Observer* on the need for LA reform by means of larger regional authorities like the GLC quoted this extract from the Mass-Observation survey which was conducted on behalf of the GLC in 1966. "*It is very difficult to see how Londoners can identify themselves with the Greater London Authority when they are so very unaware of the amenities, functions and services provided by the GLC.*" Klein commented on this quotation thus: "*The GLC's reaction to this—bitterly attacked by the Conservative opposition—was to increase spending on its information services. At best this can be only a partial answer. Facts are dead things unless people feel that they matter to them personally. And it is this which is lacking.*"

The GLC responded to the Mass-Observation report by advertising appointments for PR positions which one might have expected the GLC to have made a long time before. Yet the Conservative opposition was idiotic enough to threaten that if it came to power they would disband the newly appointed information service. As everyone knows, the Tories did win London and they were extremely grateful for an information service with which to announce their policies on education and housing!

This party political foolishness apart, Rudolf Klein is right when he says that information services are only a partial answer. The underlying problem is a marketing one to which information services should be allied. Unless the GLC markets its amenities, functions and services—

in other words makes them desirable and arouses desire for them—the information service will in fact be churning out dead facts.

To quote from the *Directory of Activities undertaken by Local Authority Public Relations, Press and Information Departments or Sections*, published by the PR Department of the National and Local Government Officers Association in September 1967, the Greater London Council, catering for a population of eight million people in an area of 620 square miles covered by 32 London Borough Councils and the City of London, has a Public Information Branch (operating on a regional basis) comprised of the following personnel:

Director of Public Information
Press Division: Chief Press Officer
Press Officers
"Outposted" Press Officers
Press Office Manager

The Press Division is responsible for all activities involving relations with the press (lay and technical), radio, television and other means of communications (independent of the Council), except films, exhibitions, and advertising which are handled by the Publicity and Campaigns Divisions which also come under the Director of Public Information.

It is the duty of a local authority to inform the people of rights, services, benefits and amenities, yet for some strange reason authorities think this is a waste of money! It could save money if, to take but one simple example, civic pride could be encouraged as a weapon against vandalism. Slowly, an increase in the number of PR appointments is occurring, but as is also revealed in the NALGO *Directory* quoted above, only 81 local authorities of various categories had, in 1967, information services as distinct from the publicity departments to be found in holiday resorts and towns concerned with publicising trading interests.

Local authorities seldom have a lot of money to spend on publicity. Under the Local Government Act, 1948, resorts are permitted to spend only the product of a 3d. rate. There are more than a hundred British seaside resorts and watering places, most of them with small populations producing small rate funds. With visitors a resort can double its population for a few months of the year. Very rightly, publicity has been described as the lifeblood of British seaside resorts which are having to compete with holidays abroad in more and more distant and exotic places as the world is opened up so that a day visit to a European capital is easily accomplished by almost anyone.

The resort publicity manager, PRO, information officer—or whatever he may be called!—can to a very large degree supplement his advertising resources by paying keen attention to the news possibilities of his resort. He will find that the opportunities are endless and that local reporters, being correspondents of the inland daily papers, will welcome his news items and leads. A resort is news all the year round to the would-be visitors who live and work in towns fifty or more miles away. A North Wales resort, for example, is news in nearly every daily newspaper published in Lancashire, Yorkshire, Cheshire, Warwickshire, Leicestershire, Nottinghamshire, Lincolnshire, the Home Counties, Scotland and a good many other parts of the UK. North Wales ceased to be the playground of Lancashire when post-war petrol rationing came to an end.

The extent to which a resort can augment its publicity through the news columns of newspapers, particularly provincial evenings, depends on the vigour and imagination of the press officer. If he becomes the eyes and ears of the town he will never be short of news. He will co-operate with all who can tell him what is going on such as conference organisers, entertainment promoters, the parks superintendent, sportsmen from golfers to show jumpers, or league sports teams, local artists, writers and musicians, the town band, archæological finds, the police, youth organisations, the schools—in fact the community as a whole will be his source of news, not just what he is directly concerned with in his small brown office in the town hall.

Towns which are centres of cultural, historic, industrial or some other special interest could easily enhance their local interests by providing information services. Yet there are large cities in Britain with no information services whatsoever. They rely on extraneous services such as the public library, the chamber of commerce, or maybe a free supply of guide books (sometimes of dubious value to the local tradespeople who pay for the "free" supply by taking advertisement space). In some towns it can be said that the librarian provides a truly heroic information service which should not be his responsibility at all.

There can be no doubt that much of the information work considered in this chapter is associated with marketing one thing or another. Again, this may surprise some local government officers who would not ordinarily regard themselves as marketing people.

The same thing applies to the public authorities although here no-one would deny the contribution to marketing that is undoubtedly made by the information officers of the nationalised fuel and power, transportation and other industries.

The reason for this affinity between PR and marketing is simply that good communication is necessary to the process of supply and demand, that human relations are involved in satisfying human needs. However wonderful the central government or the local government service, it will fail if no-one is aware of it and how to benefit from it.

12

Product Publicity

A study of what is commonly known as "product publicity" will help to show the difference between news and puffery.

In the 1820's and 1830's, when early newspaper advertising for commodities and services was better known as "puffing", it was hard to distinguish between editorials and advertisements because the art of displaying advertisements, the use of special display type and hand lettering, and the inclusion of illustrations were sophistications yet to come. They belonged to the day when the space broker found it was easier and more profitable to sell space if he also had creative talent, and especially a gift for sloganising.

In the early 19th century advertisement copywriters or puff writers were frequently famous authors and poets, and it was fashionable for advertisers to "keep a poet" as the expression went. This was all part of the growing industry and commercialism of the times, and the development of the popular market. Puffery was an invaluable aid to marketing, although much despised by men like Carlyle who referred to the "all-deafening blast of puffery" because they could not understand that a trader or manufacturer must make known in order to sell, and that newspaper advertising was an economic means of broadcasting a sales message.

To the newspaperman, puffery has continued to mean literary advertising, and the attempt to present advertising as news has incurred the wrath of editors convinced that their editorial columns are being misused. They have denounced such offerings as "puffery", meaning nowadays free advertising, not always recognising that while there has been a modification in the meaning of the word puff a great many things advertised are also of news value.

When the author was publicity manager of a certain seaside resort, and regularly sent news stories to the local newspapers about the activities of the resort's publicity committee and department, he was once chided by a local editor for being "the supreme puff merchant". Old prejudices die hard. Similarly, when the author was some years later PRO of a timber preservation company, a certain Cornish newspaper devoted several columns to the story of a local church which the company had preserved from the ravages of insect attack and fungal decay, giving the name of the company. But when the same newspaper was sent a product publicity story of interest to householders the author received an advertisement rate card!

A puff, or a "free puff" as it is more often described, means an unmistakable advertisement appearing in the editorial columns. It is the term used by an alert editor when he thinks that somebody, usually with something to sell, is trying to gain from a reference in his columns. It is also used less specifically by advertisement managers—those responsible for selling space—who regard editorial mentions as announcements improperly occupying space which they could or should have sold. For these reasons we frequently see the absurdity of a legitimate news story from which all commercial names have been deliberately and all too obviously deleted, sometimes to appease the advertisement manager. The press is, regrettably, much more influenced and dominated by the advertisement side than the editorial for the simple reason that publications exist very largely on their advertisement revenue. It is even said that news is printed on the backs of advertisements! Nevertheless, the economics of publishing are not so one-sided as those last sentences may imply: *unless the editorial secures and maintains adequate sales and readership the advertisement manager will be unable to sell his space.* He depends upon a sound editorial policy. A good editor, as we shall see, may well rely on good press officers providing him with material which helps him to achieve a successful journal.

We therefore have to balance the fears of the editor that he is being "got at" by those seeking free publicity with the anxiety of the advertisement manager that organisations may be getting away with unpaid advertising. In reconciling these fears we have to overcome the general antipathy of both sides of the publishing world towards the growing practice of press relations which is sometimes seen to be a menace to both their independent editorial functions and their profitable space-selling enterprise. These are not entirely unfounded fears because users of PR, by which is meant employers or commissioners of PR services, themselves all too often and quite erroneously believe that press relations is simply the means of achieving free and favourable publicity.

A four-sided situation confronts us. It comprises the organisation, the press officer, the editor and the advertisement manager, and the situation can be resolved only if we accept the fundamental principle that it is the press officer's duty to establish good relations with the press on behalf of the organisation. In the supply of genuine news to editors he is doing nothing to offend advertisement managers, and he has every right to expect his organisation to be named as a proper and necessary part of the published information. This means, then, that the press officer is not concerned with the advertisement manager, he is not dealing with advertising, and his sole concern is in satisfying the editor. The employer or client has to understand this principle and the relationship which follows from it.

This is imperative now that PR is becoming less of an information service and more of a system of communication necessary to marketing strategy.

We now arrive at the real consideration: *what is news*? News is not a novel story which has no publicity content. Despite the pretended scruples of some editors, news cannot be a negation of publicity because every story in every publication—unless it is the editor's pure theory and opinion—is bound to be good or bad publicity for someone or something. This is because publicity is no more than making known, creating public knowledge, publicising. Such publicity is informative, making no attempt to persuade, influence and induce action, that is, to make known in order to sell, which is the extension of publicity known today as advertising and formerly as puffery.

The words "publicity" and "advertising" are frequently but erroneously taken to be synonymous. There are, for example, Publicity Clubs affiliated to the Advertising Association. Publicity managers and advertising managers are often different titles for the same job, although an advertisement manager is employed by a media owner to sell space or time or to rent sites to advertisers. But strictly speaking the two terms can be distinguished, the one making known and the other making known in order to sell. Thus news can often be good or bad publicity, because news informs and makes known, but it is not so biassed, controlled and sales promoting as to be advertising.

The nearest one gets, perhaps, to "free" advertising is when a critic gives an unconditional testimonial and goes so far as to say "You must go out and buy this book" or "This is a film you must not miss". But even then it is unbiased and uncontrolled, a bit of luck really because the critic could have destroyed the book or the film by condemning it as something not worth buying, reading or going to see. Here it can be seen quite clearly that there is a great element of risk in press relations activity: the press officer cannot comment on his organisation or product but the editor can, and it may be favourable or unfavourable or purely factual without comment. An advertisement, subject to advertising law and ethics and media "house rules", will be so biased, controlled and sales promoting that it will say exactly what the advertiser wants to say. This is not possible with product publicity which is not, therefore, free advertising. The press officer cannot say, least of all publish, anything he likes, ethics or no ethics.

This is very important. The press officer may have to convince his employer or client that this is so, that it is pointless for him to say all those nice things, and use all those superlatives, capital letters and underlinings which the proud proprietor of the product may desire, even insist upon. In such circumstances the press officer must not be led astray by one who does not understand the nature and purpose of a press release. The editor will reject a press release that is written as a piece of advertisement copy. Large numbers of press releases fail because their authors either do not know the difference between press release writing and advertisement copywriting, or they are unprofessional enough to obey instructions instead of giving advice. Anyone can pay a piper to play out of tune, but not everyone will want to listen to the noise.

The purpose of a press release is to provide the facts. If it expresses an opinion as well, this will be propaganda. If it contains self-praise, it will be an advertisement. While it is sensible to name the product and its maker as early in the story as possible, names should afterwards be used sparingly. The golden rule is that the name should appear only when its mention adds clarity and meaning to the report. Name plugging is an abuse of press relations, and rightly arouses the ire of editors.

The object of this discussion, and the definitions it has produced, is to arrive at the genuine newsworthiness of product publicity since the name is apt to be misleading to those whose loose usage of jargon tends to equate publicity with advertising.

Product publicity is news about products, and in the right journals or in the right pages or features, products can be very important news to the particular readers attracted by these specialised columns. Product publicity seldom makes "hard" news and is unlikely to be published in the general news columns of daily newspapers unless it is a new invention, it is a national achievement, there is a huge export contract, or there is some social, economic or political angle. Stories about products and services are usually reserved for special features. The press officer should not send a product publicity story to the editor of a newspaper but to the correct specialist journalist who may be, say, the motoring, gardening, aviation or science correspondent, or perhaps the home page or women's page editor.

Selecting the appropriate recipient of a press release is all part of skilled press relations work. Each story requires its own individually picked mailing list, and it will be a list of individual journalists, specialist editors or correspondents rather than a list of newspaper and magazine titles. Like anything else, a press release has to be marketed, and the acid test of a good press officer is the extent to which he knows his media. And by this is not meant the extent of his personal contacts with the press. Contacts mean little: the correct placing of stories is vital. A contact cannot print a dud story whereas an editor you have never met will welcome a thoroughly good story. For this reason, another acid test of a good press officer is the extent to which he keeps out of Fleet Street bars and the modesty of his entertainment expenses. Advertisements seeking press officers "*with first-class Fleet Street contacts*" reveal a sad misunderstanding of what press relations are all about. The only thing that matters to an editor is whether your story is of such value to his readers that it will help to maintain and extend readership of his journal. And that is a matter of very elementary publishing economics.

Sometimes this restriction of product stories to the specialist features is a little unfair. We all know that when a product or service is in trouble the press will comment freely and names will be named. We are told very bluntly what make of car was in the fatal road accident; what kind of aircraft from whose airline hit the mountainside; whose department store or factory was burned to the ground; which company has been brought to a standstill by a strike, and so on whereas if one of these companies merits favourable comment the name is all too often omitted on the grounds that it would be advertising! This is grossly unfair and an abuse of press relations from the editorial side. Press officers are entitled to expect good relations to extend from editors to themselves. However, it would be wrong to suggest that a state of antagonism exists, for, as will be seen later in this chapter, a great many editors and journalists do work closely with press officers and value them as sources of valuable information.

Nevertheless, improved relations from the editorial side are desirable in the offices of some of our big circulation newspapers. Let us look at this example from the London *Evening News*.

On Tuesday April 25th 1967 the *Evening News* published a fascinating story on its leader page, headed "*Be sure your SINS will find you out*". Readers were told how it was possible for a submarine to navigate half way round the world without sighting land or stars. It was a background story to the homecoming of the British £25 million nuclear-powered submarine *Valiant* which had voyaged 12,000 miles underwater to and from Singapore.

The report praised the Ships Inertial Navigation System as the secret of the submarine's feat, equipment which was attributed with curious vagueness to "*a British firm*".

Surely there was no secret about the identity of this "*British firm*" which had made such an outstanding contribution to the success of this underwater voyage? Surely the name of this obviously very ingenious British firm was as important to the story as the name of the submarine or that of its commander?

In contrast to this omission of names—which may sometimes be due to the speed with which national newspapers have to be produced—the special correspondent is usually more accurate than the general news reporter, while one can have nothing but admiration for the devoted trade or technical press editor or staff man who can produce a brilliant article on a complicated subject almost at the drop of the hat. But the press officer needs to know the varying qualities, limitations and categories of journalist with whom he has to co-operate and work.

Accuracy of information has to be a press officer's fetish. If he is a member of the IPR he is bound by clause three of the IPR Code of Professional Conduct which lays it down that "*A member shall not intentionally disseminate false or misleading information, and shall use proper care to avoid doing so. He has a positive duty to maintain truth, accuracy and good taste*".

The IPR Code is right to insist on such scruples. Not only does this clause mean that the press officer must himself issue reliable information but he must check the reliability of his sources. He does not merely issue information because he is told to do so, or because he assumes it to be true. PR consultants may find that their clients are supplying incorrect information, even publishing it in literature, in advertisements and on containers. These inaccuracies may be genuine errors, but it is up to the press officer to satisfy himself that what *he* puts his own name to is true, accurate and in good taste. It is not his job to issue false or biased stories to please his employer or client because unless he pleases the editor and ultimately the reader he is lost. This is equally true of modern marketing: it is recognised today that you can only sell what people will buy, and you will only sell a second time what satisfied people the first time.

It follows that the press officer must adopt standards which may be higher than that of certain journalists. He has to be a purist about facts. He is not an advocate, a propagandist or an advertisement copywriter. It is possible, therefore, that the growing practice of press relations will have the effect of making published information more generally reliable.

But while there is this curious tendency, peculiar to the medium of the press, to dwell upon the drama of disaster rather than upon the sweet smell of success, the impact of good press relations, and an enlightened editorial outlook in some quarters, is beginning to permit the publication of stories which not long ago would have been condemned as commercial. The *Daily Express* is not shy of printing business success stories. In fact, it is the only British newspaper which has given a whole front page column story to the success of an advertising campaign and the way in which this was achieved by an advertising agency which it named. The *Daily Express* welcomes good business stories, particularly those about exports. An example of this is the following quotation—surprising in a British newspaper—from the *Daily Express* of August 14th 1967.

> **New Cortina Breaks all the Records**
>
> *Express Motoring Reporter*
>
> The Cortina Mark II, unveiled by Ford at the Motor Show last year, has broken all production records for a British car.
>
> More than a quarter of a million have been made in 10 months.
>
> Exports too have reached an all-time peak. Overseas sales for the first six months of this year are up 42.8 per cent.
>
> Biggest seller is the GT—Grand Touring—model, a hotted up luxury version of the car. European sales alone in six months are equal to what they were for the whole of last year.

That appeared on page five, a regular news page, and not in a motoring section where product publicity might be accepted or forgiven. The product name was even headlined!

No-one would deny that this story was excellent publicity for the Ford Cortina in a multi-million circulation paper which enjoys one of the highest advertisement rates in British publishing. It would be cynical to say that the only reason why the story was printed was because it suited the newspaper's policy to please a big national advertiser. No, this is a story which deserved to be printed on its merits as a news story irrespective of whether it happened to lick the feeding hand. The fact that it appeared also knocked on the head the old, old story that a paper must not offend advertisers by favouring one advertiser editorially.

Contrast this with the "no firms named policy" of the *Evening News* which, that same day, August 14th 1967, carried a front page picture with the following heading and story.

He Wants the Birds to go Away

> Once upon a time, to carry a black umbrella meant that you were Something in the City. But in these enlightened days they turn up in all sorts of unlikely places.
>
> Why, they have even been found in Tube trains that don't get within a mile of Ludgate Hill. Today the camera spotted one atop a 100 ft turntable ladder. The man holding it was laying bird-repellent plastic on ledges and balconies.
>
> The strip is a jelly-like substance laid at points where birds perch. "They don't like the feeling of landing on this substance and they fly off," said an official of the firm carrying out the work.
>
> The man was not, in fact, engaged on work in the City but at Buckingham Palace which, presumably, makes an umbrella perfectly proper. And, after all, it *was* raining.

The *Evening News* was not alone in failing to name the name, and the story appeared in several national dailies and was on BBC TV News. This product, Scarecrow Strip, the company, Rentokil Laboratories Ltd, and the turntable fire appliance has been photographed and written up for more than five years, and yet except in some provincial newspapers or trade and technical magazines the names are religiously stricken out of the records. Why? It has become a frequently used story in the press, on radio and TV, and in film magazines, but the product and company names remain taboo until, presumably, a Rentokil operator falls off the turntable ladder and breaks his neck. Then, Rentokil will be named and blamed!

Yet British holiday resorts are named—at their cost—when beaches are contaminated by oil, and holiday tour companies are named when their coaches or aircraft are involved in accidents. The press *in general* will claim these places and companies are named in the public interest (and they could be right up to a point), but isn't it also in the public interest to know the identity of companies which are efficient and provide goods or services which are of value to the community?

It certainly seems that there are days when names are out and other days when names are in, which does at least add a spice of excitement to the strange existence of a press officer. But it is difficult trying to explain these peculiarities to an employer or client who thinks his product rates a front page story in the nationals!

Nevertheless, despite the unpredictable attitudes of the news editors of the popular newspapers, product publicity is so widespread that it can exist only because of genuine editorial need.

Many journals with specialist interests such as gardening, home decorating, yachting or motoring have a duty to their readers to report the latest products such as new insecticides, paints, boat fittings or car accessories. These items are genuine news. Equally, trade magazines would be pretty useless if they did not inform grocers, ironmongers, electrical dealers and other retailers about new products, additions to ranges, modifications, price changes or advertising campaigns. All these topics are important news to the readers of these journals. The same applies to cosmetics, foodstuffs or domestic appliances in the women's magazines. These reports make excellent news, and undoubtedly they are excellent publicity too. The expression "product publicity" becomes a very apt one because these editors make no bones about giving publicity to that which is of sufficient news value to attract reader interest.

In a sense, the same is true of the popular newspapers because they will print stories which give publicity to politicians, film stars, TV personalities, authors, musicians and sportsmen who are of sufficient news value to attract reader interest, even though they are more coy about company names. Famous people such as Twiggy, Lord Robens, Sandie Shaw, the Beatles and Lester Piggott are constantly publicised freely in this way. All news is publicity of a sort: but editors tend to differ on when the kissing has to stop.

But the thing so often misunderstood by advertising people is that the write-ups must be supplied and will be published in editorial phraseology. The story will describe the lipstick or the wheelbarrow in factual terms, not in the excited "buy-this-bargain-now" style proper in a hard-selling advertisement. Each kind of writing has its special place. For this reason press releases submitted by advertising agencies in support of advertising campaigns are often useless to an editor because the writer has not known the difference between writing advertisement copywriting and news reporting.

This is one of the tragedies of the advertising-PR world in which neither seems to properly understand the writing requirements of the other. Advertising men want to introduce blurb writing into press releases, and PRO's are apt to regard advertising as something intellectually inferior. This is a foolish situation which is peculiar to Britain and does not exist in either America or Australia. The place of press relations in the marketing mix has to be accepted and respected by both advertising and PR practitioners. This understanding will come about when it is recognised on both sides that advertisement copy and press releases are different just as advertising and documentary films are different. A press release is really a literary documentary.

Now to the editor's gratitude for product publicity! Yes, we know there are editors who scorn press releases, news agencies which dispose of them by the dustbinful, and even willing trade press editors who find only a percentage of the press releases submitted to them are of any relevance or value. We have to take it for granted that for years editors of all kinds have been inundated with the most appalling rubbish.

All the same, why are so many press releases printed word-for-word in the press, even over the bylines of staff journalists who never wrote a word of them? Because they are publishable! We have already referred to advertising people having mistaken ideas about press release content, but sales people more than any others should be made aware of the truth of this statement.

The press officer is likely to be confronted by the sales manager who regards everything, displayed advertisements or editorials, as advertising. If he gets his hands on a press release he writes in the company or brand name in every sentence, in capital letters and underlined, naturally. He would like editorials to be advertisements, and he honestly does not want there to be any difference. When the advertisement manager from a technical journal tries to sell him space on the strength of the enquiries promoted by an editorial, the sales manager guffaws. This very common attitude among sales people is a prime cause of bad press relations because one can imagine how incensed an editor must be when he receives such obvious puffs, as he frequently does, from sales managers playing at press relations which they do not understand and are not prepared to pay to have done by a skilled practitioner. We see the same thing in exhibition press rooms when exhibitors who spend nothing on PR expect journalists to accept sales literature instead of press releases which have been prepared with understanding of press requirements.

Press releases must be publishable, although the editor has a perfect right to present the information how he wishes. By publishable we mean that it must be good enough to publish, that it is well-written, accurate, logical, interesting, comprehensible and lacking in ambiguity.

There is an indisputable need for press releases. Thousands of editors with small staffs could not possibly report all the news which is supplied to them free of charge by press officers. The City pages of our daily papers—and business features and sections saw a big increase in 1966–8—are full of information about the financial affairs and personalities of public companies, mostly derived from press officers. Our popular gossip columns would scarcely survive but for the flow of stories and invitations to attend PR organised events. It is no secret, and certainly no shame, that industrial news is made available to the press and the press are very glad to have it. The *Financial Times* has won an enviable reputation for the breadth and depth of its business, industrial and financial news coverage, and so it should because it must have the biggest mailbag of press releases of any publication in the UK. It makes excellent use of this information, and there is probably a better rapport between the editorial staff of the *Fnancial Times* and press officers than between any other British newspaper and the nation's press release writers. The *Financial Times* staff seldom if ever print releases as they come, and the information supplied is skilfully presented according to the feature or page in which it is used. Here it can be said that public relations has quietly and effectively contributed to the deserved success of a serious and important newspaper.

The proof of this need for press releases lies in the fact that many editors are by no means shy of ringing up or writing to press officers and asking to be put on mailing lists. When journalists change jobs they often make this known to press officers. And if one of two journals fails to get a story, because it has been accidentally missed out of the mailing or the release has gone astray, the luckless editor will ring up and complain to a press officer if the rival paper has printed a story he did not have the chance of printing too. Press releases play a vital role in modern publishing offices, even if the result is that editors are spoilt for choice and can enjoy the luxury of being ultra-selective so that they discard stories with disdain. And although many of those press releases are abject specimens of journalism, where would the press be today without the worthwhile releases?

This is borne out by the following letter circulated by Peter Evans when he became editor of *Furnishing Review* in 1967:

Dear Sir,
I should like to take this opportunity of introducing myself as the new Editor of Furnishing Review *and to say that I hope to have the opportunity of meeting you personally as soon as possible. In the meantime I look forward to your continued co-operation in keeping Furnishing* Review *informed of any new products made or marketed by your Company.*
As you know, Furnishing Review, *with a controlled circulation in excess of* 13,000, *and its high quality reproduction—in both black and white and colour—provides a unique service for the Furnishing Trade.*
Furnishing Review *provides you with a unique service, in that it is your link with your customers. Keep us informed of your activities and we will keep your customers informed,*
Peter Evans
Editor

The specialised magazines, whether they have circulations in the millions or the very few thousands, would be poorly informed indeed but for the press releases they receive daily. They exist in a surfeit of information supplied free of charge. They even have the wire facilities of Universal News Services to feed them with skilfully prepared industrial news. The British press, as never before in the history of publishing, has every opportunity to know what is going on and to have it straight from the horse's mouth. Even Scotland Yard runs a press service, the Church of England too. So does Buckingham Palace. There has never been any secret about the one at 10, Downing Street, and Mr. Macmillan's press officer, Harold Evans, was knighted for his services.

13

Exclusive Signed Feature Articles

A press release is broadcast, but an article is written specifically for one publication. It should bear an author's name and be exclusive to a single publication, although other articles on the same subject can be written by the same author for other journals and may appear concurrently. For example, the subject of holidays in Spain could form the theme of any number of original articles, each one being exclusive to a particular journal.

Such articles are not written speculatively. Editors do not sit back and wait for articles to appear out of the blue. Issues are planned and contents are commissioned. They may be written by staff writers, free-lance contributors or by PRO's and press officers. An editor may go to a literary agent in search of a suitable author. This means that there is no point in a press officer sitting down and writing an article which he then offers to an editor. Nor is he likely to be very successful in placing one of those articles which someone within the organisation has decided to write without so much as the slightest invitation.

There is a very substantial market for good articles from PR sources, but chiefly for technical articles for trade, technical and professional journals which do not have large staffs. On the whole, national newspapers, women's magazines and other big circulation journals prefer to have articles written by their own staff writers, or by commissioned professional contributors, and will rarely publish features from PR sources unless perhaps they are written by well-known or authoritative authors.

The press officer can therefore achieve publication of feature articles in one of three ways, and the third can be sub-divided into a further three sections.

First, they may be written by staff writers.

Second, they may be written by outside contributors.

Third, they may be supplied by the press officer, either written by himself, or by a freelance author specially engaged, or by people within the organisation.

Let us consider each in turn.

Articles by Staff Writers

Regular feature writers working on newspapers and magazines usually have to produce at least one article a week, and it is no mean feat to write interestingly on fifty or more different topics in a year. If a press officer can succeed in giving a staff writer a first-rate idea for an article it will be very welcome, but it must be an idea worthy of the writer, feature and journal. It is no use trying to fob off a staff man or woman with a contrived publicity yarn.

The press officer should study the press and collect the names of writers who either write about the organisation's subject, or could be interested in some aspect of it. This piece of research will reveal those who have certain penchants or express specialised knowledge and particular sympathies. Thus, the press officer will become aware of the staff writers to approach when appropriate stories occur.

Similarly, he will note the special correspondents who have columns to fill, the motoring, industrial, gardening, property, shipping, aviation, science and other correspondents whose contributions may appear in many publications. It is not unusual for the editor of a specialised journal to be a special correspondent and contributor on his subject to other journals such as national newspapers. One finds, for example, that the man who writes the Saturday gardening feature in a newspaper is also the editor of a weekly gardening magazine. Again, staff writers on national papers often contribute further material to provincial papers and may also broadcast and appear on TV. All these people are constantly seeking ideas and subject matter.

The more the press officer knows about the needs of these staff writers the more useful he can be both to them and to his organisation. There are some very real press relations to be cultivated here in the realm of ideas for articles. Of course, it may entail rather more than just handing over an idea: the press officer must be willing to devote time to escorting the staff writer to the scene of the story which may be a factory, site or installation.

For the press officer commencing in a new post it will be a long and painstaking task to get to know all the staff writers who may be interested in material about his organisation, but by studying the media, and through press conferences and receptions, press visits, correspondence and the telephone this profitable field of communication can be established and many friends made.

The most satisfactory state of affairs is when staff writers know that you are a valuable source of material and come to you for material to write about. It is even better when they choose you rather than your rivals because you have established a reputation for reliability. More than that, they will come to the press officer who is prepared to go to some trouble to help them. The press officer who provides a service and does not seek favours will have his service used and be given the favours.

Articles by Outside Contributors

These are more numerous and less easy to contact because they may write less frequently for the same journals, and correspondence will have to be forwarded to their private addresses. But as the various publications are studied it will become apparent that there are writers who specialise in certain subjects, and that they should be kept supplied with information and possible themes for future articles. There are, for example, freelance writers who specialise in writing the articles in special supplements and give-away booklets such as those in the "boom" issues of women's magazines. There are others who write regular features in specialist journals, sometimes writing under nom de plumes in other journals. Freelance writers of all kinds abound, and if the press officer bothers to offer them information facilities he may well find that they tend to write about his organisation and its services or products simply because he alone takes the trouble to feed them with facts. As one such writer said to the author, "I can only write about the things I have in front of me," and that may well be the case in a busy world. The enthusiastic press officer will seek out these writers and make a point of offering to help them with facts, ideas, pictures, samples, facility visits or whatever may be of use to them.

There are some press officers who regard freelance writers as time wasters, nuisances to be put off and ignored. Provided they are not amateur writers producing speculative articles, they can be extremely valuable. It does pay, however, to check that their work has in fact been commissioned and will be published.

In addition, there are also text-book authors, and script writers for radio, films and television who work independently and are glad to know of reliable sources of information.

Supplied Articles

Here we come to the kind of article which is most satisfying to the press officer because he has more complete control over its content. When helping staff and freelance writers one has to concede the treatment to them, and it may not necessarily be as the press officer would wish. But if he writes it or edits it himself he can take more responsibility for what is published.

Some press officers make the mistake of thinking that an article appears only once whereas a press release may appear repeatedly with consequent greater coverage and better result for one's efforts and expenses. There is no comparison really. The two are both good but quite different types of writing and communication. Even their PR value is different. Press releases provide news which is ephemeral, and to be effective must be repeated in regular doses just like advertising, but articles have greater authority, are read more carefully and are therefore more likely to be remembered, while they enjoy the permanency of being indexed. Technical journals are retained and often bound, and authoritative articles become part of the literature on the subject. Furthermore, reprints can be made of articles so that the organisation may use them as mailing shots or literature for distribution at meetings, demonstrations, and exhibitions.

There is no reason why a press officer who knows his subject and writes well should not write articles in his own name, and establish himself as a writer in his own right. Many PR people have done this to mention only Alan Hess, Rene Elvin and Sam Black, who are well known for their writings. Press officers should be big enough to be able to put their own names to articles.

But he may be too busy to write every article himself, or it may be a subject requiring an expert on the subject, and then he will need to use his file of freelance writers. The careful creation of a file of specialist writers on appropriate topics who can be commissioned to write articles is an important part of the organisation of a press office. With these additional writers the press officer can augment his staff and efforts; moreover, although his budget may not permit an addition to his full-time staff the occasional use of freelance writers can be a convenient way of easing the staff problem when he is exceptionally busy.

Within the organisation there are likely to be specialist authors, either willing or unwilling to write articles. Sometimes the too willing ones have to be restrained because it can be embarrassing when an important member of the scientific, development or design team takes it into his head to write an elaborate technical article running to ten thousand words which he is confident the press officer can get published for him. Such enthusiasts must be dissuaded. Conversely the man whose name would look well on a company article is often disinclined to prepare a manuscript. Between these two extremes, which are very common, the press officer has to operate so that he can obtain articles by the right people, prepared in a way that is acceptable to editors.

The correct procedure is simple, and when this is explained to authors within the organisation it is usually accepted as the professional procedure. Editors do accept articles which have been written speculatively, but that is exceptional. The majority of articles are first of all discussed with the editor, and if he likes the idea he will commission a piece. The press officer will therefore approach an editor with an idea, giving a brief synopsis, suggesting illustrations, and asking (a) how many words the editor requires; (b) how many pictures will be used; (c) when copy is required; and (d) in which issue is the article going to appear. When an editor writes back and says, yes, he likes the idea of the article, and wants 1,500 words with three photographs by the middle of next month for the issue of the month after, then the press officer has a definite instruction to go ahead and prepare the article. If it is to be written by someone within the organisation that person must understand that he is virtually under contract to supply an article of a given length on a certain subject by a specified date and that space has been allocated for the article in a particular issue.

But will this executive do what is expected of him? Let's face it, it would be remarkable if he wrote more than one article in a year. He does not have the facility to write two a day which, although exceptional because he has other things to do, should be within the capacity of a good press officer. Good intentions there may be, but if the press officer is not careful he may find that the executive will put off writing the article, always intending to do it "next weekend". This is where the press officer reveals his special ability. He can offer to edit the author's rough notes; he can "ghost" the article—that is, write the article for the executive or have it written by a freelance—and this is often the way in which famous or busy people do "write" their articles; or the article can be prepared as the result of an interview when the executive dictates his views in reply to questions. This last method, using a tape recorder, is a popular solution; in fact, a good many autobiographies of the famous have been produced by this method, and it does have the merit of the article being based on the author's own words.

It may be that the organisation has a personality who has something worthwhile to say so that there is a demand for articles by him, and the tape recorder method can be used to obtain articles from a man who is no journalist and does not have the time to sit down and laboriously write for the press.

Once the press officer becomes known within his organisation for the publication of articles he may have to beware of executives who do not understand that these articles are exclusives, and cannot be offered to other editors once they have been published. In this respect, an article is very different from a press release.

However, it is possible to syndicate an article when its appearance will be in journals with non-competitive circulations such as provincial newspapers or possibly house magazines. For example, an article on a business topic might be offered to all the chamber of commerce journals published throughout the UK, and there would be no harm in an identical article appearing in several of these journals published in cities many miles apart.

It is also possible to paraphrase a basic article and produce a number of exclusive articles for different journals, using the same information but varying the applications and case histories according to the readership of each journal. Here are three examples of how this has been done.

1. A manufacturer of louvre windows enjoyed a very useful series of articles in journals read in local government, confectionery production, and laundry and dry cleaning circles. The technicalities of how the windows were made and how they operated were identical, but the applications to various kinds of building and the interviews with people working in these buildings were quite different.

2. A pest control firm with a service for the control of flies had the problem of convincing various people in trade and industry that even a single fly could be unhygienic and uneconomical. The basic material about the nasty habits of flies, and the company's techniques for their effective control, made a straightforward semi-technical article, but it could not be offered as it stood to numerous magazines. But by applying the problem and the solution to a number of trades and industries troubled by these pests it was possible to publish a dozen different exclusive articles in journals covering the food retailing, preparation and manufacturing trades and industries.

3. The third example comes from the central heating business. A

manufacturer had a packaged deal for builders. The press officer visited a number of housing estates where the system had been installed, spoke to builders, plumbers and the owners of occupied houses and obtained first-hand impressions of how the system had been experienced by all concerned. Since the visits were made to estates in different counties, and pictures taken showed a variety of house styles, it was possible to publish a set of different articles in home interest magazines.

This is, of course, an economical use of time and money expended on travelling to obtain material and photographs. It does cost more to write an article than a press release, but when a series of articles results the cost of fares and hotel expenses as well as the press officer's time becomes a very good investment. Sometimes the work cost can be diffused even more cleverly when the field research and pictures provide further material for house journal articles, picture-and-caption stories, annual reports, training manuals, and slides for training programmes and client presentations. From this general list it will be seen how a single press relations effort can contribute to the entire PR programme for an organisation, entering right into the functions of finance, production and marketing. Within the press officer's own sphere, the material for one article in a specialised journal may, later on, be used together with the material on other specialised subjects in a comprehensive article which reviews the achievements of the organisation in many different fields.

When commencing work on an article the press officer should consider what possibilities exist for facts and pictures to be used for other PR purposes. He may, for instance, take the opportunity of obtaining 35 mm colour slides because these will be useful for future PR activities such as exhibitions or seminars, even though he has no immediate use for colour pictures for press relations purposes.

Articles and Advertisements

It was the author's experience a few years ago to be brought in to write exclusive feature articles for a company whose advertising was having very poor results. From the advertising point of view there were two difficulties: first, the company's products and services were sold to industry and were not popularly known, and, second, there was hardly an industry to which they could not be sold yet it was impossible to advertise in all the available journals. There was an educational task here for which display advertising was not suitable.

However, the detailed article with pictures and diagrams was ideal, and such articles could be written for large numbers of magazines. In this way industry learned about the scientific nature of the problem and its consequences, and also about the research undertaken to discover answers to the problem, together with the products, skills, equipment and techniques which had been evolved to satisfy the needs of industry. This was a very successful operation and the company's business expanded as a result. It was an instance of something that a number of industrial companies discovered for themselves during the Wilson "Squeeze" of 1966–8: PR can be a more economical promotional tool than advertising.

It is also the case with industrial companies that when they are launching a new product on the market, production is limited, and large sales are neither expected nor can be handled, the small amount of advertising justified by such budget conditions is too small to have any valuable impact. Frankly, such advertising is a waste of money. But for a fraction of the cost of even a modest advertising campaign PR techniques can be employed to do all that is required to get the product off the ground.

An example of this occurred with a company supplying the hospital service. A certain hospital in Kent had a hygiene problem, but traditional methods of finance meant that a small sum of money was allocated annually to deal with this problem. No-one had really considered whether the expenditure achieved anything and year after year the same ineffective work was carried out, having been put out to tender with a budgeted limit on cost. The fact that the hospital had suffered this problem for 90 years had not struck anyone on the management committee as being stupid.

An enterprising company, convinced that it had a method of totally eradicating the nuisance for ever, and not merely for a year, put up a scheme costing far in excess of the annually budgeted sum, won the contract and carried out the work successfully. At the time this was a phenomenal achievement in the British hospital world. The press officer published an article in *The Hospital* which brought hospital administrators from all over the UK to see the miracle in Kent. Treatments in other hospitals for the same or similar problems were later published in other journals such as *Hospital Engineer*.

By press relations methods a service of great public value was made known to those responsible, and the company's reputation was notably enhanced as it became recognised by the health authorities as the specialist organisation for this particular kind of work. The cost of producing the articles was negligible compared with the cost of inserting display advertisements which could not have told the story with anything like the same degree of authenticity and conviction. Later, this success in the hospital field was included in the company's advertising to the municipal and health authorities.

Enough has been said, then, in this chapter to show that the signed exclusive feature article is not only a major part of press relations practice but a major medium of PR practice in general.

There is, however, one other aspect of advertising in relation to PR articles which needs to be discussed here. It has been shown that articles can, in special circumstances, do a better job than advertising, perhaps serving as the vanguard of advertising. Sometimes an alert advertisement manager will discover from the pagination, dummy, or simply because the staff of trade journals are small and they work closely together, that an article from a PR source is to be published, and he will think that here is an opportunity to sell advertisement space. His psychology is all wrong and he has only an eye for the main chance. (An even more alert advertisement manager would wait until the article had appeared before approaching the company!) Consequently he goes to the company or its advertising agents and proposes not only that advertisement space should be bought in the same issue as the article but that the advertisement should appear opposite the article.

It happens all the time: companies in all foolishness buy such space and have advertisements facing their articles. In the author's opinion—and some of this has been explained already—the advertisement is unnecessary and a waste of money. But worse than this, the advertisement looks as if it is there because of the article, and the article looks as if it is there because of the advertisement. It looks like a double blackmail. The advertisement, *in that issue and in that position*, must destroy much of the authenticity of the article which depended so much on its editorial independence. A totally unnecessary and irrelevant element of commercial bias is introduced by the advertisement at a time when the content of the article is novel and acceptance is bound up with faith in the statements of the technically qualified author, a very different matter from being persuaded and convinced by the claims of an advertiser who is entitled to put the best face on things.

Unfortunately, some marketing people cannot see the validity of this argument because they regard press relations as no more than an extension of advertising, and to them it is all advertising of a kind, whether occupying advertisement space or editorial columns. *But the average reader makes very clear distinctions between the two* and rightly or wrongly it is the reader's point of view which matters here. The old-fashioned view is still taken by the majority of readers that editors wouldn't dare publish anything in the editorial columns that wasn't true, whereas no-one entirely believes what they read in advertisements. The fact that this is nonsense is beside the point: it is the duty of the press officer to produce press material which is worthy of the reading public's simple faith while at the same time enjoying the facility of publishing what will be accepted and believed. This is the great strength of press relations, especially the feature article, and it imposes ethical responsibilities and exposes the very real dangers of abusing the trust of readers if one tries to publish false information.

14

Exhibitors and Exhibitions

There are two clear-cut sections to this chapter: press relations in support of an individual participant in an exhibition, and press relations for an exhibition as a whole, that is on behalf of the organisers but also beneficial to the individual exhibitors.

PR Support for Exhibitors

It is an expensive business to take stands in private or public, national or local, permanent or travelling exhibitions, to say nothing of overseas trade fairs, British Weeks, and BoT Joint Venture schemes which will be discussed in the next chapter. Space has to be rented, the stand has to be designed and built, equipment has to be made ready and transported to the hall, give-away literature has to be designed and printed, certain advertising may be advisable, and much staff time will be occupied in manning the stand. It is so costly that some companies will not exhibit at all while others exhibit only irregularly or in inexpensive Joint Venture schemes abroad. Nevertheless, on the whole, exhibitions such as those held at Olympia and Earls Court, London, are well supported and attended. Throughout the year exhibitions are taking place every week, and the magazine *Exhibitions Bulletin* is packed with dates, venues and details. Exhibitions are, despite the misgivings of some firms, a major marketing medium, which suggests that the costs must be relative to results.

And yet very few exhibitors, and what is worse very few PR practitioners employed by exhibitors, recognise the great opportunities which exist for enhancing the value of an exhibit by the provision of PR support before, during and after an exhibition. The most that many

PRO's and PR consultants seem to do is either to place press material in the press room, or to make a last minute appeal to the press to see some gimmick on the stand on press day. But by then it is practically too late. PR support for exhibitors begins three to six months before the doors open.

But before considering what should be done let us stop to discover whether the special effort and cost is worthwhile. After all, if the vast majority of exhibitors do not bother surely there must be a sound reason for their apathy? The plain truth is that PR in this country is so poorly understood and so imperfectly used that neglect of this sort is not at all surprising at this stage in British PR history. Thus, it rarely occurs to anyone (not even to PR practitioners!) that the press room at an exhibition is the end and not the beginning of PR support.

The effect of PR support is to extend the value of the stand to people who cannot or will not attend so that the impact and cost of the exhibit is spread over an infinitely larger number of potential buyers. In addition, PR support can increase the number of visitors to the stand. These are bonuses not to be ignored!

The cost of providing this support is, relatively, very small. When preparing his estimate of time to be expended in order to arrive at an annual fee the PR consultant is unlikely to need to allocate more than three to five days time, spread over a period, to each client exhibition. Materials and expenses will not add too much to the bill if press releases are kept to a reasonable length, press packs are avoided, and the press room is not flooded with too many big photographs, while the press officer does not waste too much time and money hob-nobbing in the exhibition bars when he would be better occupied doing some work in his office.

Thus we arrive at a time, materials and expenses cost which should not exceed £150–£200 for a London exhibition (unless a private press reception is laid on which may be necessary with a big exhibitor at, say, the Motor Show) but more travelling expenses will be incurred if the exhibition is in the provinces, Scotland or overseas or if a provincial press officer has to travel to London. The bulk of the expenditure can be divided into three categories: (1) advance press relations; (2) supplying the press room; (3) attending the press preview and official opening. In the case of overseas exhibitions a further cost will be the translation of releases.

One of the largest single material costs, which does need to be rigorously controlled, is that of photographic prints, very few of which may be used because of the competition from so many exhibitors and the fact that most journals can print but two or three pictures at the most. Unless a picture has news value it has no place in the press room, and most of the pictures to be found in most exhibition press rooms have no place anywhere.

It is very easy—tragically easy!—to denigrate what is (or is not) done, but what should and can be done by the press officer intent on doing all within his power to enhance the value of his organisation's stand at an exhibition? The following plan, based on the author's own experience, is recommended:

1. *Advance Planning*

When the annual budget is being prepared it is important to know the details of the exhibition programme. This applies whether press relations are handled by a staff man or by a consultant. Time can then be allocated, and preparatory work can begin at once because it is often necessary to work from one annual exhibition to the next if the organisation is a regular participator. The press officer will need to know names of exhibitions with venues, dates and stand numbers. He should have a plan of each exhibition so that he knows the location of the stands which have been booked. Even if there is but a tentative proposal to go in an exhibition, the press officer should know about it. This means that those responsible for exhibitions must work in close collaboration with the press officer, and vice versa. Moreover, they should understand why the press officer wants this information and what he can contribute.

2. *Contacting the Exhibition Organisers*

The press officer should contact the organisers of the exhibition and obtain any available literature and instructions to participants. For example, he should find out who is editing the exhibition catalogue and make sure that he, *and no-one else in his organisation*, is responsible not only for supplying the description of the stand but for supplying it to whoever requires it by the specified copy date. He should also find out what special PR facilities are likely to exist, such as a cinema in which his organisation's film can be shown, or a seminar in which his organisation might be able to take part either on the platform or in the audience.

3. *Contacting the Exhibition Press Officer*

As a result of contacting the organisers, the press officer will have learned the name of the exhibition press officer and he should contact him as early as possible. He can discuss with the exhibition press officer what his organisation will exhibit and supply information which can be used to publicise the exhibition as a whole; he can discover who will officially open the event, and what VIP's are expected to visit and on what days; and he can generally work with the exhibition press officer to their mutual advantage. As a result of this collaboration he may be able to get news about his organisation's exhibit issued in advance stories from the press office, and he may be able to ensure that the official opener and VIP visitors come to his stand, not because of any arm twisting or bribery and corruption but merely because the exhibition organisers know that the stand is worth a visit.

Equally, by knowing on what days VIP visitors will be attending the press officer can bring in his own VIP visitors without any risk of a clash of dates. For example, at the 1965 International Watch and Jewellery Trade Fair at Earls Court, Smiths Industries Ltd brought to their stand the Mayor of Cheltenham in honour of the high-grade watches made in Cheltenham which were shown on the stand. Similarly, when it was discovered that Edward Heath (the President of the Board of Trade) was to be a VIP visitor to the Scottish Industries Exhibition in Glasgow arrangements were made to present him with the 38 millionth alarm clock made in Smiths Industries' Wishaw factory, and the press officer to the exhibition put out a photo call which brought some fifteen press and TV cameramen to the stand. This did not happen by accident: Scientific Public Relations Ltd had been working with the exhibition press officer for months. The same consultants were also responsible for borrowing the first BBC *dalek* to feature on the Advance Electronics stand at the 1964 Instruments Electronic Automation Exhibition.

It is, of course, essential to work closely with exhibition press officers so that one may know exactly what arrangements are being made for a press preview or press day. Some organisers are very lax about press facilities, and some exhibition organisers do not appoint their own press officer until two or three months before the event. But we will deal with these problems in the next section on PR for Exhibitions. The point is made here to emphasise the need for liaison between the press officers on both sides. The author is convinced from his own practical experience that there is a tremendous and largely uncultivated field of new PR endeavour in the realm of exhibitions.

4. *Obtaining Advance Information about the Exhibit*

This is by far the most difficult part of the exercise, and it may be this which deters some PR consultants from doing more for their clients who exhibit. Exhibitors are notoriously indecisive about what they are going to exhibit and although they may be genuinely anxious not to reveal trade secrets about a new product to be launched at the show, quite often there are no secrets and it is just inefficiency which makes information unavailable. Yet the press officer must have some knowledge of his organisation's intentions if he is to gain useful coverage in the journals which are previewing the exhibition or publishing special numbers to coincide with the event.

5. *Press Previews*

Monthly magazines previewing exhibitions usually require copy six weeks before publication, and some like to work even further ahead to avoid special issues being something of a tax on their staffing resources. The exhibitor who does not know what he is exhibiting is likely to be left out, or given a bare mention which is of no consequence. But the press officer can overcome problems like this by making sure that editors are given at least a general description of what the company makes which is certainly better than a mere list of name, address and stand number!

Another problem arises in that editors often obtain lists of exhibitors from the organisers and then write to each exhibitor asking for information. It seldom occurs to these editors to write to the person they normally deal with for press information, and so the letters are vaguely addressed to the company, very often at an address different from the one from which the press officer (or the PR consultant) operates. The letters are thrown away, passed around, filed or eventually passed on to the press officer or PR consultant, so that opportunities of press coverage are lost despite the invitations. A way in which the exhibition press officer can obviate this problem is given in the next section.

Nevertheless, the astute press officer can circumvent the trouble caused by such careless mailings and clumsy handling of correspondence and produce an advance story six to eight weeks in front of the exhibition date. In time, that is, to distribute it to all the magazines and newspapers likely to be interested. In doing this he must be careful to head the story with the name of the exhibition, the date, the venue and the stand number because not every editor will know these details (there are new exhibitions opening every week in London alone), and in the case of weeklies, and more especially with dailies, the story will be received a long time in advance. With this type of release staggered mailings are not so helpful as they might as first seem because by receiving the release a long way ahead the editor of a daily or weekly may have his attention drawn to the exhibition so that he is encouraged to produce a preview he might not otherwise have thought of doing.

At this early stage the press officer may suffer from the disadvantage of having no pictures of the main exhibit, but he can usually supply a picture of a product which he is assured will be on the stand even if it is not the highlight or the secret new product.

From these remarks it must be apparent that the press officer has got to show considerable initiative to overcome the many obstacles to enhancing the value of an exhibit, but it can be done.

Some time prior to the opening of the exhibition the press officer should receive from the organiser's press officer details of press room arrangements such as the location of the press room, the number of releases and pictures recommended, and the date and time of the press preview and official opening. He should not be surprised if he receives nothing or if it is sent to the wrong person or the wrong address. The exhibitor's press officer should take the precaution of telephoning the exhibition press officer a fortnight before the opening date to make sure that he receives final information and tickets to the press preview if these are necessary.

Two different kinds of preview have been mentioned and in case this is confusing it should be explained that magazines will sometimes preview an exhibition in the sense that they will publish a guide to the exhibition (as distinct from reviewing the event afterwards), while some organisers invite the press to attend a preview of the exhibition, either on the day previous to the opening, or an hour or so before the official opening on the morning of the first day. Big exhibitions like the Motor Show have a press day, but the first morning of the Boat Show is given over to the press and the official opening.

6. *The Press Room*

Owing to the physical peculiarities of exhibition halls the offices are mostly placed close to the outer walls so that the middle area is left free for exhibition purposes, and this results in cell-like press rooms often situated in obscure places.

It pays to deliver press room material personally and, if possible, to have some say in how and where it is to be displayed. In well organised press rooms the material is laid out on tables in alphabetical order (racks are a nuisance because the releases will droop forward, losing their identity) while a sample picture is given a number and displayed so that copies may be requested from the stock held by the press room staff. It is essential to visit the press room from time to time to see whether stocks of press releases or pictures require replenishing.

To avoid repetition it is sufficient to say here that the press release supplied should be brief and provide news, not a company history or something equally irrelevant, that pictures must be captioned, and that nothing else is required.

7. *Manning the Stand*

It is rarely necessary for the press officer to be present on the stand after the first day unless the exhibit is very much a PR effort and he has work to do. The major part of PR support for an exhibit should have been completed before the exhibition opened, but a supply of press releases and pictures should be kept in the stand office, in addition to those in the press room, and the stand manager should take charge of them in the absence of the press officer. In practice, a staff press officer is likely to attend the stand more frequently than one employed by a consultant, unless the fee is large enough to cover the time expenditure.

8. *Press Visitors to the Stand*

There are several ways in which the press can be invited as guests of the exhibitor. These will be in addition to the efforts made by the organisers to attract journalists and may be on a different day to the press preview or press day. It depends on the resources of the exhibitor, the size of his stand, and what kind of show it is, indoors or out-of-doors. The latter category includes agricultural shows from the Royal to local county ones, and big events like Farnborough Air Show.

A big exhibitor may throw a press party on his stand, but only a limited number of these can be attended in any one day and it may be unwise to compete. In most exhibition halls private rooms can be hired for press parties, so size of stand is not necessarily a limiting factor. The more modest exhibitor can still invite the press by sending journalists an open invitation to call at any time, when hospitality will be available.

Sometimes, despite a press day, it is a good idea to invite the press to come back on another day for a reception and demonstration on the stand. Kelvin Hughes did this at the 1966 Ship's Gear Exhibition at Olympia in order to demonstrate their automated ship's bridge, and in this way they secured a monopoly of shipping journal interest in their unusual exhibit.

A few years ago Mi-Dox Ltd introduced Danish and other continental orchard and farm equipment at the Royal Show. The stand consisted of no more than a tent with the implements displayed on the grass in front. There was not room for a press reception, but a special invitation card posted to agricultural and horticultural journalists, inviting them to come and take pictures and partake of wine and cheese, was rewardingly successful, and picture stories appeared afterwards in fifteen journals. This only goes to show that one does not need a vast pavilion and an ever-flowing bar to achieve valuable press coverage.

9. *After the Exhibition*

As a result of the event many new press contacts will have been made so that new names and addresses must be added to the addressing plate library. Some of these interested journalists will have asked for more information, additional pictures, opportunities to visit the factory or feature articles, and all these things must be attended to before the interest is allowed to flag.

10. *Clearing the Press Room*

On the final afternoon a last visit should be made to the press room to collect surplus pictures and press releases. Pictures cost money and there is no point in leaving them to the press officer to throw away, while the press room staff will be busy enough without having to dispose of your material too. If the exhibition press officer has been helpful and the press room has been well run, it is only courteous to express one's appreciation. PR is a friendly world, and it is likely that there will be future opportunities for further co-operation.

PR Support for Exhibitions

An exhibition press officer should be appointed to an exhibition as soon as the event has been agreed upon, and with exhibitions which are held at regular yearly or two-yearly intervals press relations activity will be constant. Large exhibition organisers have a staff of press officers and this continuous effort is automatic, but the complaint can be made about smaller sponsors that they appoint press officers far too close to the event with the result that exhibitors do not get the PR support they deserve from the organisers.

During the months leading up to the event the press officer can stimulate knowledge of the exhibition and interest in it by issuing news stories and supplying feature articles. This is, of course, done extremely well by the press officer to the Ideal Homes Exhibition through the associated *Daily Mail* and *Evening News*, and the same steady build-up of news stories heralds the Schoolboys and Schoolgirls Exhibition. Of all exhibitions, the Motor Show at Earls Court must have the most unprecedented publicity build up of all, and throughout the summer months there are even charity draw tickets on sale in seaside resorts, competitors being required to guess the attendance at the next Motor Show!

But the press officer can do very little if he does not know who is going to take part and what they will be showing because his stories will be about the interesting things that people will see. Since we have already said that finding out what is to be exhibited is no mean task for the exhibitor's press officer it is doubly difficult for someone even further removed from those responsible for exhibits. Yet he needs to be constantly filling in the picture of the eventual event so that he can talk and write about it. His job does not start and finish with the press room.

So, collating information about exhibitors is an important part of his job, but first he has to discover who can supply the information. Usually, the person who signs the contract for the stand space, the only name that the organisers have, is useless to the press officer. He needs the name and address of the advertising manager, publicity manager, PRO, press officer or PR consultant. The only way to track down this person is to ask, and this means writing to each exhibitor as his stand booking comes in, asking for the name and address of the person who will be dealing with PR on behalf of the exhibitor.

This request often comes as a surprise to exhibitors, many of whom do not use PR and had not realised that PR had anything to do with exhibitions! Others respond very willingly, and are only too glad to put their PRO or PR consultant in touch with the exhibition press officer. A library of plates or cards can now be assembled so that all communications from the press officer to exhibitors go direct to the person responsible for supplying information. This should be a first essential of any exhibition but it is rarely done. If it is not done much of the correspondence from the exhibition press officer to the exhibitors is liable to go astray, be mislaid, misunderstood or just not answered. And this is a pity because such a breakdown in communication may deprive both sides of valuable PR opportunities.

Ideally, the exhibition press officer should issue numbered bulletins, reporting progress to exhibitors and telling them what else may be required of them and to a greater or lesser extent this is done by organisers of the larger exhibitions. An advantage of such a bulletin is that it does indicate that there is an active press officer and even if one goes astray because the exhibitor has no PR organisation, or fails to act upon a request, succeeding communications must surely evoke a response.

When the press officer knows what the exhibition is going to look like, having been sent artist's impressions of stands and told about special working models and demonstrations, he can issue worthwhile advance stories to arouse the curiosity of potential visitors and encourage them to book the forthcoming event in their diaries. This is clearly of benefit to exhibitors and depends entirely upon their co-operation.

The following questions must be decided: Should there be a press reception, a press lunch, a preview on a previous day, or a preview prior to the official opening at, say, 11 a.m. on the first day? How are the press to be invited and received and what facilities will be provided? Should the official opening be made at a seated assembly, or in the open at the main entrance? All the various factors mentioned above have to be taken into consideration and no hard and fast rule can be laid down, as many matters will be governed by the subject, location, size and news value of the event. It is a fairly general rule, however, that the best press generally results from a preview held before the first day.

Another controlling factor is the day of the week on which an exhibition opens. When an exhibition opens mid-week or at the end of the week (like the Do-It-Yourself Exhibition) an afternoon given over to a press preview is a very good thing, giving the press—especially photographers—ample time to gain interesting material which they can use next day or even at the weekend. But when an exhibition opens on a Monday morning a Sunday press preview will not be popular, and the possibilities of press coverage are more limited.

On these specially organised press previews hospitality is necessary, but the author's own experience shows that a "dry" press room is preferable, especially since there is seldom a lot of space and it can be a very busy place. Most journalists are busy people and the ones who hang about drinking in the press room are mainly correspondents and freelancers who have time to spare. In any case, there are plenty of bars and the exhibitor's club to which the press officer can take a journalist if he wishes to offer him a drink.

An interesting preview arrangement was laid on by the press officer to the International Watch and Jewellery Trade Fair when exhibitors were invited to table a miniature exhibition for the benefit of the press, TV and newsreels in the Café Royal although the exhibition itself was to open at Earls Court. This was a brilliant idea with a mass attendance by the press for a whole morning. It also overcame any possibility that stands might not be completed in time for a preview earlier than opening day, one of the hazards of exhibitions being that some stands are still being completed during the opening ceremony!

But the biggest hazard of the press officer who is seriously concerned with providing the *press* with a service is the material which the exhibitors bring to the press room. Some of it should be banned. In the interests of exhibitors, the exhibition organisers and the press the press officer is entitled to demand that (a) press releases be brief; (b) photographs be captioned and (c) no press packs or wallets be supplied. The conscientious press officer acts as an intermediary between exhibitors and the press and this double duty has to be remembered since it can be crucial to the success of the whole operation.

To achieve the co-operation of exhibitors at the 3rd Export Services Exhibition held at Olympia by Mack-Brooks Exhibitions Ltd in September 1967, the following instructions were issued by the author who was the press officer:

PRESS ROOM INFORMATION

3rd Export Services Exhibition

The following information is supplied so that you may take the fullest possible advantage of the Press Room and PR facilities provided by Mack-Brooks Exhibitions Ltd. Your co-operation will assist in the overall success of the Exhibition. Please ring me, or see me in the Press Office, if I can assist in any way with press relations beneficial to the Exhibition.

Press Preview: Monday September 11th, 10 am—11 am.

Official Opening: by the Rt. Hon. George Woodcock, CBE, PC, General Secretary of the Trades Union Congress, Monday September at 11 am.

Press Room: The Press Room is situated to the right of the main entrance to the National Hall. Room No. 102.

Exhibitor's Material for Press Room: should be supplied to the Press Room on Friday September 8th if possible.

Please note: Press releases and black and white pictures are welcomed, but releases should be as brief as possible, and lavish press packs are not wanted either by us or the press. We do not want house journals, sales literature or picture postcards. Attached are some useful hints.

Highlights of the Exhibition: With your co-operation we shall produce a press release about the unusually interesting things to be seen at the

Exhibition. Please send or 'phone brief details not later than Wednesday September 6th to the address on this letter-heading. Items should include special displays, working models, new products, etc. Please make sure you are included in this official release.

Film Shows: Daily showings of exhibitors' films will be shown in the Exhibition Cinema, and accepted films are required in the Press Office on Friday September 8th.

Special PR Efforts: Exhibitors are encouraged to send press releases and pictures direct to the press, and also in advance of the exhibition. The Press Officer will appreciate a copy of such stories.

If any exhibitor plans to make a special PR effort, is likely to receive VIP visitors, is inviting the press to a reception on the stand, or is in any way seeking to interest press, radio or TV, please keep the Press Officer informed. If he can help in any way, he will be delighted to do so.

News Stories During Exhibition: Please inform the Press Officer of any news which can be distributed about orders taken, VIP visitors, and so on. The Press Officer will also welcome information for the review which he will be distributing to the press at the close of the Exhibition.

With your support we hope to obtain even more press coverage than last year.

Before reproducing the *Press Room Hints* which accompanied the foregoing letter to exhibitors, let us consider the information supplied to exhibitors as the final communication from the press officer. It was posted on August 17th. The Exhibition opened on September 11th. It was sent to the PR addresses as accumulated during the previous months, or direct to the only address known in the case of last-minute bookings of stands. The effort was made to ensure that the right person got the information, and in some cases exhibitors did not appoint PR advisers until the last minute.

Moreover, as stressed in the last sentence of the opening paragraph of the letter, the press officer did not offer to handle PR for individual exhibitors—that was not his job—but he was concerned with *press relations beneficial to the Exhibition.*

First of all, the document was set out as briefly and simply as possible, clearly identifying every item with a bold headline, and setting out all dates and times so that they could be acted upon.

The announcement about Mr. Woodcock opening the exhibition had already been issued as a press release and published, but the time announced for the opening enabled exhibitors to make special arrangements such as making sure that they had their managing director or chairman on the stand to welcome Mr. Woodcock during his tour of the exhibition. Certain exhibitors also arranged floral presentations in the fashion characteristic of the Far East. (Several exhibitors were showing air freight, shipping and banking services connected with the Far East).

Material for the press room was requested *in the press room* by the Friday. This seemed a little early for some PR consultants which tended to indicate that they were working too close up to the event. The instruction aimed to avoid parcels of press releases being sent to any other address (such as that of the exhibition organisers, or the organisers' PR consultants) which could have meant late arrival of material. The press room was the obvious address, and it was best to deliver it in person. Strangely, not every exhibition press officer makes this sort of thing clear, with the result that exhibitors have to ring up and ask when and where the material is required. This is particularly true of exhibitions outside London. Since the heaviest demand upon the press room will be at the press preview and on opening day, it is essential to have the press room stocked and fully set up *before the press arrive*! Posted press releases may arrive at any time. Even if the exhibitor's press officer cannot visit the press room on the specified date there is usually someone connected with the stand who can.

Some exhibition press officers produce numerous lengthy press releases, but beyond an advance copy of the official opening speech and a comprehensive summary of the exhibition, there is no need to produce many releases on behalf of the exhibition itself. Significantly, such collections of official releases are frequently ignored by the press. However, some exhibition press officers do excel themselves by summarising every exhibitor's press release in a collective story.

The instructions also encouraged exhibitors to work closely with the press officer about their own private PR activities, very important because there is nothing more disconcerting to the press officer and his press room staff than to have photographers and reporters asking where they will find some special PR activity or personality about which he has been told nothing although the exhibitor has sent invitations to the press.

Moreover, such instructions can also suggest to exhibitors that they should do something interesting and newsworthy which will attract attention to their stand.

On this occasion two PR consultants organised ingenious and colourful PR "spectaculars" for their clients. Hodgkinson Partners Ltd (on behalf of Trans-Mediterranean Airways' new Tokyo service) brought James Bond's Japanese girl-friend to the exhibition in a rickshaw and had her present George Woodcock with a traditional red carnation. On behalf of McGregor, Gow and Holland, with their Blue Funnel services to the Far East, London Press Exchange Public Relations Ltd had a Japanese girl present a garland of carnations to Mr. Woodcock. Despite the fact that the stand was on the gallery and was not visited until the end of the tour, once told the press photographers waited until 12.30 p.m. and stationed themselves in readiness for some very attractive pictures. Throughout the exhibition girls in the costumes of different countries presented hundreds of red carnations to visitors to the McGregor, Gow and Holland stand, adding to the gaiety of a serious but very colourful businessman's exhibition.

The second document issued to exhibitors on the same date received a number of compliments, but while it succeeded in dissuading exhibitors from wasting money on press packs it failed to make *PR consultants* put captions on their client's pictures! This extraordinary feat of folly is hard to believe unless one is a frequent visitor to exhibition press rooms. And a photograph dangling from a press release by a strip of Sellotape is not captioned either, and can only be counted as a nuisance. This document read:

PRESS ROOM HINTS FOR EXHIBITORS

Who do not Employ Professional PR Services

Press Releases: 1. The release (50 copies for the Press Room please, with spares for your stand) must contain news of interest to the press reviewing the Exhibition. The first paragraph should summarise the complete news story.

2. Releases should be as short as possible, the ideal being a story restricted to one side of one sheet of paper, complete with stand number and the exhibitor's full name and address.

3. In addition to supplying the Press Room, exhibitors are advised to send press releases direct to specialised magazines likely to report the exhibitor's participation in the Exhibition.

Photographs: 1. Please supply 25 half plate glossy black and white prints.

2. Each picture must be fully captioned and bear the address for further information.

3. Pictures must not be stapled to press releases.

4. Colour pictures are not required.

5. The Press do *not* want:

(a) Press packs or wallets (d) Timetables
(b) House Journals (e) Sales literature
(c) Picture postcards (f) Company histories

During the Exhibition the staff of the Press Room will be delighted to receive new stories occurring during the Exhibition.

The title was a courtesy to fellow practitioners, rather tongue-in-cheek perhaps since they were the chief culprits to whom the instructions were addressed! It was, regrettably, far from being a case of telling one's grandmother to suck eggs.

Let us look again at the list of six prohibitions at the end. It may seem unbelievable but the author possesses press packs containing the full range of these items. What possible use or interest these can be to a journalist is something which defies the imagination except of the PR consultants who squander their client's money in producing these bumper collections.

As already said in Chapter 10, "*One of the abominations of all kinds of press event is the over-elaborate so-called press kit*", and in the press room there is even less excuse for its use than at the press reception or on the factory visit which is at least restricted to one organisation. When asked why PRO's put these monstrosities in the press room the excuse is made that this is what the clients want. This is nonsense. When consultants do what clients want they should stop pretending to be consultants. Does a doctor obey his patient? A consultant's job is to advise: he is paid to know better than his client.

The point is surely that at most a journalist has a brief case (and often he does not have even that): to take away all the press packs and bulky press releases found in most press rooms he would need a suitcase. So it is a matter of plain common sense to put in the press room concise information which journalists are likely to want to take away with them.

Some readers may not believe that anyone does actually put elaborate and lavish press kits in exhibition press rooms, and the following six examples are taken from the 2nd Export Services Exhibition, 1966, the Ports and Terminals Exhibition 1967, the International Packaging Exhibition 1967, and the London International Engineering and Marine Exhibition, 1967.

Exhibit A. The material was contained in a three-colour pictorial cardboard wallet with a cut-out inside spread effect to reveal the contents of the two halves of the wallet. The contents included two press releases, one being history and one news; an 8-page letterpress printed pictorial history of the company; a blotter; a picture postcard; and two timetables. A well-known PR consultancy was responsible.

Exhibit B. The wallet was in blue on white and laminated, and the *nine* items of press information were stapled together and indexed. Not one of the nine releases bore a printed heading or any form of identification, not even a name, address or telephone number. A separate press release described the stand, but the only identification was the company name typed at the bottom. The releases were beautifully reproduced. They were also quite well written and informative—except about their origin! Entire stories failed to mention the subject! These mysterious sagas were accompanied by three equally mysterious photo-prints of line drawings except that the company symbol appeared on the sides of vehicles in the pictures which were, nevertheless, uncaptioned and without even so much as an identifying rubber stamp. Finally, there was a photo-print of the company symbol with a flapped caption bearing six words to the effect that it was the company symbol. This must be the most uncommunicative set of information ever put in a press room, yet it came from an exciting new organisation which seemed to take it for granted that editors would know what the stories were all about. Fatal! Actually, the last eight releases relied on the first for identification, but what happened if they became detached in an editorial office?

Exhibit C. Again the wallet was a reversed-colour laminated one, and it contained four press releases, very well produced in themselves but their impact and interest was obscured by the totally unnecessary press pack. Produced by a PR consultant.

Exhibit D. Here at least we had a transparent plastic wallet which helped to quickly identify the contents, but these were incredibly numerous and bulky. They consisted of a printed booklet about the stand and its layout; a copy of the house journal; *nine* press releases, mostly three pages long; *and* 13 *photographs* each 10 × 8 inches! The cost of that totally unnecessary press pack must have been staggering. There was one redeeming feature: like the P. & O photo captions previously praised, the captions had printed headings which is an excellent idea. But who wants nine press releases and 13 photographs!

Exhibit E. This harsh cardboard wallet printed in two dull colours, and overprinted for the particular exhibition, was merely for the purpose of holding two press releases comprising three sheets of paper. Like Exhibit C, it was needless. The press releases, quite nicely headed, would have gained far more attention by themselves.

Exhibit F. Here we had a plastic bootlace file, all very clearly identified with a two-colour title page, an index, and no fewer than 11 *press releases*, virtually a bound book of press releases! When we realise that most journalists writing about the exhibition will probably say no more than 50 words about any individual exhibitor we can only wonder why exhibitors persist in offering these admirably produced but totally useless press kits. This one was issued by the British subsidiary of a European company, and editors (if they ever saw it) must have been highly amused by the request to send a copy of the publication *to the continental address*! On the very last page—*the 21st*!—of this monster press release collection the reader was told that German, French, Italian, Spanish and Portuguese versions were also available. Once again we see how money can be wasted on bad PR.

The only way to put a stop to this sort of nonsense, which only helps to encourage the press in their disrespect for PR, is for exhibition press officers to agree on a form of standard procedure which can be distributed by all press officers prior to all exhibitons. The *Press Room Hints* issued on behalf of the 3rd Export Services Exhibition did have the effect of greatly improving the standard of material in the press room, and the only press pack (complete with uncaptioned pictures) came from a last-minute exhibitor who probably did not receive the *Hints*.

15

Exports and Overseas Press Relations

Peter Bloomfield, former Director of the Institute of Public Relations, in an article called *How Public Relations Can Service the Exporter* which appeared in the *Board of Trade Journal* on April 7th 1967, wrote:

"*Whatever the reasons, the general image of Britain and the British overseas is not working in our industrial favour and there is an urgent need to change this by whatever means are available to us. Such means are readily available and they can be summed up as an intelligently intensified use of public relations and, in particular, full use of Government and commercial* PR *facilities, which are considerable.*

"*The primary objective of public relations in this context is to shape local opinion, although there is much confusion between its product—and service—as opposed to its policy—and prestige-selling job. Getting news coverage of new important installations, new products, new applications, or new services; communicating company policy statements; publicising speeches made abroad by key executives, interviews with executives and overseas visitors, announcements of promotions of key distributor-dealer appointments; covering participation in trade fairs or industry exhibits: contending with unfavourable nationalist attitudes or legislation; creating an image compatible with local preferences but accommodating the global proportions of the corporate structure—these are some of the complex* PR *problems often faced by companies in overseas markets, quite apart from their more direct product or service selling activities.*"

Later in this article which should be in the hands of every press officer (as well as every businessman for whom the article was written), Peter Bloomfield advised use of nationals, and explains how the exporter can work with "*a British or US public relations consultancy* (*or counsellor as they are known in the United States*) *with a wide network of overeseas companies or associates*". While this is the ideal for a big manufacturing company we must not forget the very large number of medium size and even small companies who could very easily expand their business through overseas trade if only they made the effort to do so, and press relations can be a great help to them. Moreover, there is on Britain's doorstep the immense European market which is rapidly being captured under our very noses by the existing members of the Common Market, Italy in particular. When Italian companies like Fiat and Indesit set out to sell to Europe they make their British counterparts look like back-street amateurs and it is in this sort of hard, competitive world that the press officer may soon find himself battling. It is very pertinent, then, to also consider press relations aimed at the European market which is almost comparable in size with that of the United States *domestic* market!

Inevitably in such a chapter as this—which is really the subject for another book—there will be repeated references to the Central Office of Information. The myriad services of the COI are so diverse and so useful that the author finds that on behalf of one or another client he is usually in touch with the COI at least twice a week. In his previous capacity as an industrial PRO he was also constantly dealing with one COI division or another. If there is any criticism to be made of the COI it is that it is so vast with so many people doing so many different things that the newcomer to its services may be bemused by it all. However, there are explanatory booklets.

The COI is indispensable, as a government information service should be on behalf of a nation which lives by its exports, but as Sir Fife Clark, director general of the COI has said, "*Private industry has tended to lag behind the Government and public services in its use of public relations*," and the COI is a PR service ready and willing to assist private industry in export markets.

No doubt the tremendous emphasis placed on export promotion by the Labour administration has given a well deserved pat on the back to Sir Fife Clark and his staff about whose efforts some sections of British industry used to be unkindly sceptical. The success of the COI, like most things in life, owes much to the effort put in by other people and certainly to the appreciative way in which the various services are used. An industrialist has no right to grumble about something he never bothers to use, yet a few years ago there was a tendency to regard the COI as an unwarranted luxury maintained at the taxpayer's expense, and that its budgets should be severely pruned. When such idiocy abounds it is no wonder that, as Peter Bloomfield said in his *BoT Journal* article, "*all investigations overseas show a serious unawareness of British industrial achievement*". When one considers the negligible use made of PR internally within our shores it is not surprising that this is the state of affairs externally.

Without the COI, coupled with the associated efforts of the Export Services Branch of the Board of Trade, Britain's export trade would be in a very poor way, and the British people would be suffering from a bankrupt economy. In this chapter much will be said, therefore, about the beehive in Hercules Road, but it is only one of the many ways in which the ingenious press officer can undertake press relations on behalf of his company's export trade.

Just one instance of how a company can co-operate with the COI to its advantage concerns the Films and Television Division, and the making of a new film by Smiths Industries' Film Unit on behalf of the Clock and Watch Division. The subject of the film was the design and production of a high-quality but competitively priced seven-jewel watch at the Anglo Celtic Watch Company factory at Ystradgynlais near Swansea. Bill Hutton, Divisional Publicity Manager, insisted that this film be made with COI advice and approval right from the beginning with the object of having it eventually accepted by the Film Acquisition department for overseas distribution. Now, this is surely an excellent example of knowing what the COI can do for a company and then going all out from the word go to collaborate in order to achieve the best possible result. The film (which won top-rate reviews) is now doing a job overseas for both Britain and Smiths Industries.

Before examining the various ways in which the press officer can extend his efforts overseas let us first begin with the man whose main task is to do with the home market. Can any of his present activities help to make his organisation better known and understood outside Britain? The chances are that with very little extra effort his present work can be made to gain this valuable additional effect. First of all, however, he must discuss with the sales department whether overseas sales are wanted, or whether because of restricted franchises or because of import restrictions in certain countries it is not desired that effort be squandered where it can do no good. Policies must be clearly understood by the press office.

A few examples of these problems may be helpful to the reader. A company selling chemical products found it wise to avoid the South American markets because home production was encouraged in those countries. Another company, marketing a German-made machine, had to avoid press coverage in the German-speaking parts of Europe. An Australian company manufacturing in Britain was interested only in European markets. A British company, marketing an American-made device for which it had UK rights, was embarrassed when an article in a British food magazine was reprinted in India where it had no franchise to sell. An American oil company, with plant in India, found it policy to run an extensive press relations campaign to show that it was not squandering the country's meagre credit and that it was actually buying and using Indian-made equipment. On the other hand, a British company producing a very specialised machine for the printing industry was faced with the problem that there was only a handful of potential buyers in the UK and that sales could only be made on a world basis. Consequently when a machine was sold to Brazil, and then another to Greece, these sales made ideal stories for overseas distribution, and both the COI and the External Services of the BBC at Bush House made good use of these stories.

An article of special interest to the press officer concerned with export PR appeared in the Spring 1967 issue of the IPR journal *Public Relations*. Called *Writing For Export*, it was contributed by N. H. Alexander of Engineering In Britain Information Services, an organisation which specialises in providing news stories and feature articles to foreign journals. At the time of publication of the article, EIBIS claimed to have had their stories accepted by more than 3,500 journals, actual published items totalling 120,000, which is an impressive record of achievement on behalf of its clients. The following extracts from Mr. Alexander's article are therefore relevant to this chapter:

"*It should be recognised first of all that journals (except those few devoted specifically to news from overseas) are primarily concerned with the activities of their home industries. The amount of space an editor can allocate to industrial information from other countries is limited. In smaller countries, such as Austria or Finland, which are accustomed to looking abroad for technical advances, it may be a quarter of the whole; in the major technical countries, such as Germany or the USA, it will be less.*"

It is the author's experience that one way to meet this snag—and Mr. Alexander gives us one of those glimpses of the obvious that many of us are too blind to see!—is the picture-and-caption story which is not only attractive and concise but has the advantage of explaining the story pictorially and thus helping to overcome many language and dialect problems. Some years ago the author did this very successfully with a picture of a Rentokil operator working from the platform of a mechanical hoist to apply Scarecrow Strip bird repellent to ledges of the Woolwich Equitable Building Society headquarters at Woolwich. This picture was issued with numerous translations including Japanese, and was published the world over. It was a simple, dramatic close-up picture—the photographer was actually on the platform of the hoist with the operator—and the story was kept to a minimum number of words. This was part of a fairly inexpensive PR programme to help make Rentokil known and understood internationally: today, Rentokil is the world's largest pest control servicing organisation.

Next, Mr. Alexander wrote about the "publishable press release" which this book has been at pains to expound:

"*For the common run of industrial news a story that can be used straight away will take precedence over one that requires extensive re-writing. . . . He* (the editor) *is interested in British products and activities only if they are likely to interest his readers. Beating the patriotic drum will not impress him. To take a hypothetical example, the export of pumps from Britain is of no interest to anyone outside Britain: the import of pumps into France may be of some slight interest to French journals; but the use of British pumps by a French refinery to solve a tricky corrosion problem will interest chemical industry journals all over the world. . . . It is simple politeness to anticipiate the editor's difficulties and include brief explanations of geography. This applies also to British firms and institutions—it is not self-evident that Courtaulds is a textile company, or that the General Post Office runs the national telephone system* "

This means that in writing releases for overseas distribution it is even more imperative not to take anything for granted. As with organising a press event, the press officer has to be a pessimist, anticipating trouble which in this case can be misunderstanding or perhaps complete lack of understanding because the story lacks essential if elementary facts. In all press relations work it is fatal to imagine that anyone is as familiar about one's subject or organisation as one is oneself. Names must be spelt out at least the first time before initials may be used; metric measurements and correct foreign currencies must be used; addresses must say *England*—there are Brightons and Croydons and also English counties all over the globe; it is wise to refer to people as Mr. Mrs. or Miss because Christian names are not necessarily revealing of correct sex; and especial care must be taken to use uncomplicated words which are not likely to translate into something absurd!

The following list which takes into consideration even the most casual use of overseas press relations is intended for all press officers who wish to carry out press publicity overseas.

1. *British Journals with Overseas Circulations*

In many industries, trades and professions American and British journals have international circulations, partly because they are accepted as world authorities, partly because it would not be economic to produce similar journals in some countries, but also because it would be uneconomic to produce such journals in America and especially Britain unless there was a circulation beyond that possible in the country of origin. Some of these journals, such as *Machinery Lloyd*, have multi-lingual sections. It follows, then, that one important approach to export press relations is through publications printed in Britain.

2. *Overseas News Agencies*

In addition to Reuters, Belgian, French, West German, Italian, Spanish, Swiss; Bulgarian, Czechoslovakian, Hungarian, Polish, Rumanian, Russian; Canadian, United States; Egyptian, Israeli; Ghanaian; Pakistani, Chinese; and Australian news agencies are located in London, and their addresses will be found in the COI booklet *Overseas Press Correspondents in London* or in the identical list which appears in the *WPN Directory of Newspaper and Magazine Personnel and Data*. Radio and TV representatives are also listed. Subscribers to Universal News Services may also take advantage of UNS overseas wire services.

3. *Overseas Press Correspondents*

The sources given above also list the London representatives of leading foreign and Commonwealth newspapers and magazines, some being full-time staff but others part-time correspondents who probably have a full-time job elsewhere and so are rarely free to attend press receptions. It will be noticed from the lists that in some cases a private address is given, while others are the addresses of British publications where they are employed.

4. *Freelance Writers, Press Services*

According to the country or the topic there are many freelance writers and news services which specialise in supplying certain types of material. Once the press officer begins to send material overseas he is bound to be approached by them, but a number are well known in certain fields, and most of them prepare reports on British exhibitions for overseas journals. Since they operate permanently in Britain and do their own translating they are very useful to know.

5. *Overseas Press Mailing Lists*

Just as a plate library has to be created for UK journals so will it be necessary to create one for appropriate categories of the overseas press.

It is, of course, less easy to maintain these addresses. Many are published in British year books such as *Advertiser's Annual*, the *Newspaper Press Directory* and *Willing's Press Guide*. Press year books are also published in most large countries but it is expensive to buy them all, while the information is naturally given in the language of the country. No one book published in the UK gives a comprehensive list of overseas publications, and it is usually necessary to work from them all.

Generally speaking, it pays to send a story direct to a journal in its own country, preferably by airmail.

One of the best ways to build a reliable press list is to seek the advice of the company's overseas branch managers and agents, asking them for the names and addresses of appropriate journals, and better still asking them to send copies to the press officer so that he may study their contents and see whether they are likely to accept his stories. Yet another method favoured by the agents themselves of British companies which operate entirely through agents is to send them copies of press releases in English which they will translate and send direct to journals in their own countries. Obviously, this has a mixture of advantages and disadvantages, not least being that the press officer relinquishes all control of what is said and where the stories are sent. It is difficult enough letting a local works manager deal direct with the provincial press, but working through overseas agents whom one seldom if ever meets is full of pitfalls. Nevertheless, it is a method used by the smaller industrial companies anxious to support their agents but not having big PR budgets. It is better than nothing! And it certainly shows an appreciation by these companies that overseas press relations are important. The large organisation, however, can employ overseas PR services.

6. *House Journals*

This may be one of the most practical methods of communicating direct with overseas government buyers, importers, agents and so on. In some cases, as when the market is mostly among English-speaking countries, an English language magazine will be adequate, but otherwise it will be necessary to print in at least French, German, Italian, Spanish and Portuguese if the journal is to go to Europe, South America and parts of the Middle East and Africa. The Dutch and the Scandinavians will accept English, but elsewhere other languages may be necessary. It is said that the export languages of the future are likely to be Russian, Chinese and German! One advantage of an international house journal is that the contents can be taken from overseas sources, pictures and articles showing the products in use by different nationalities. The French, German and Italian house journal could be an excellent means to develop good relations in the Common Market. To avoid unnecessary bulk, it is better to print separate language versions.

We are extremely fortunate in having printers who are highly skilled at this type of work, with special design, translation and foreign typesetting facilities. For example, a house journal could have its illustrated areas printed in bulk by offset-litho, the different language versions being overprinted by letterpress.

7. *External Services of the BBC*

Provided the story is up-to-the-minute and is fully documented, the External Services of the BBC at Bush House, Aldwych, London WC2 (*not* Broadcasting House) will be interested in including it in one of their many English and foreign language programmes, most of which are of an industrial or technical nature. If, for instance, the story is about a large export order being despatched from London Docks it is necessary to give full details of the product, the order value, the date of despatch and the name of the ship and the dock. Such a story needs to be supplied several days in advance, not on the day of sailing and certainly not after the goods have left our shores, otherwise the story will be dead and there will not be time to prepare it for the appropriate programmes.

8. *COI Radio Division*

In addition to the programmes produced at Bush House there are many other radio items, including tapes sent abroad, issued by the Radio Division of the COI at Hercules Road, London, SE1. *Radio Newslines*, a COI radio news service, is used in news broadcasts throughout the English-speaking world and may include Ministerial statements, news about inventions, and stories about commercial and industrial achievements.

9. *COI Industrial News Services*

The COI is interested in distributing overseas good news stories which enhance Britain's good name and arouse interest in British exportable goods and services. It therefore pays in the words of the *Board of Trade Export Handbook, Number* 1, 1967, to keep the Overseas Press Services Division informed of any "*newsworthy story that illustrates the inventiveness, ingenuity and progressive character of British industry. It may be that your product is new, or that it is an advance on earlier products. There may be a reduction in price, weight, size or maintenance costs; or an increase in performance or life. It may have been modified to make it operable by unskilled labour, or by fewer operators, or it may be that it is made by some new process, or of some new material. News of British missions to other countries and of British firms participating in overseas fairs is welcomed.*" This and *Handbook, Number* 2, 1967 were widely advertised in the press, indicating that the government has seriously tried to make its resources available to all who will use them.

10. *COI Photographs Division*

Anyone who has had experience of this division will know that supplied with a good, newsy picture with an interesting factual caption this division will ring and ask if a large number of prints can be supplied for overseas distribution for which the COI will be responsible. This is a first-class service because the press officer might not know how most profitably to distribute fifty or a hundred pictures of a technical product to overseas journals likely to accept them, whereas the COI is thoroughly experienced in these specialist operations. This sort of service can be most valuable to the press officer with only an occasional picture story to send overseas who possibly has to start from scratch to build a mailing list of journals with which he is unfamiliar. The COI is extremely well organised to help the organisation whose overseas activities do not yet warrant the appointment of international or overseas PR consultants.

11. *COI Films and Television Division*

A very versatile division, Films and Television makes, acquires and distributes documentary films; invites audiences through British Commercial Officers overseas; produces colour film magazines and newsreels; makes weekly TV programmes of which *Calendar*, and *News Pictorial* are justly famous in many parts of the world including the USA. The author has had many successful experiences of COI assistance in all these fields and cannot speak highly enough of this Division's efforts.

Much depends on how far the press officer is prepared to work with the COI. Mention has already been made of the way in which a Smith's Industries' film was produced on the basis of consultation right from the script and treatment stages. If the organisation itself has any language versions it helps to increase distribution if these can be made available to the COI as well. The COI has to work to its own budget and so any assistance it receives from industry can only help to make the COI's efforts even more effective. Another way in which the owner of an acquired film can help is to send a press release outlining the synopsis of the film to appropriate journals in the various countries. The film can then be borrowed from the local Commercial Officer who can either supply it direct from his film library, or obtain it by air from London by reference to the COI films catalogues. Published in the overseas press, this news about the availability of the film will help to stimulate overseas showings.

Many British products and services are included in the weekly newsreels, a typical example being the making at Cheltenham of General Services watches as part of the major contract obtained by Smiths Industries Ltd from the British Government for HM Armed Forces. This was a wonderful story for British goods because these watches have to be made to extremely stringent specifications, and then have to undergo rigorous tests before being accepted, and the contract had been won in the face of competition from the most famous Swiss watchmakers. It was, in fact, the first time that a substantial contract of this kind had been won by a British watchmaker, and it was the very story which the company needed to overcome the quite undeserved prejudice that a British-made watch was inferior to an imported one.

The COI's overseas newsreel version of the story was made in the Spring of 1967 although the original story broke in the Autumn of 1966, when a press party was taken to the Hydrographer's Department laboratory at Herstmonceux Castle, Sussex, to see the watches actually undergoing their acceptance tests. The COI Photographs Division was represented on this visit, but the Films and Television Division asked to wait until they could film a month's consignment ready to leave the factory. Consequently, they preferred to wait until the watch was actually in production so that they could film a positive story. Again, here was an instance where it paid to keep the COI informed *well in advance*.

12. *COI Publications Division*

COI publications are produced to a very high standard (as can be seen by a visit to one of the HMSO bookshops) and the press officer will be particularly interested in the magazines *Commonwealth Today*, which includes a new products feature, and *Anglia* which is produced for sale in Russia.

13. *COI Tours and Production Services Division*

This division does not wish to be inundated with sales literature but it can make good use in reading rooms and trade fair pavilions of exceptional examples of prestige booklets, international house journals, wall charts and calendars.

14. *Board of Trade Promotions Overseas*

A programme of BoT supported overseas events is published in the March, July and November issues of the *Board of Trade Journal*. They include trade fairs and exhibitions, Joint Ventures, British Weeks, store promotions and other overseas exhibitions to promote British goods. Anyone participating in one of these events should not only undertake press relations support activity as described in Chapter 14 but should collaborate closely with the Board of Trade, especially so that press releases and captioned pictures may be distributed through the exhibition press office.

15. *Overseas TV Services Additional to COI*

As TV viewing grows throughout the world there is naturally an increasing demand for filmed material, and in London there are several film units producing short news and interest features of the *London Diary* type which may be produced specifically for an overseas television service, or which may be syndicated to takers anywhere in the world. Martin Benson Films make films on a part-sponsorship basis for overseas distribution, provided a commercial subject can be used entertainingly as in the example of their Wilkinson Sword film about bullet-proof clothing.

One of the largest organisations in this field is Visnews, the international newsfilm agency jointly owned by the BBC, Reuters, the Rank Organisation, the Canadian Broadcasting Corporation, the Australian Broadcasting Commission and the New Zealand Broadcasting Corporation. It has built up the world's largest TV news gathering service, and employs some 350 people.

16. *Translations*

This is a constant problem and if the press officer wants to see a practical example of how oddly some translations can read he should collect some of the horticultural literature mailed to this country by Dutch firms who sincerely believe they have correctly translated their Dutch into English. For example, instead of saying that a tulip is *short* they will say *low*. It is this difficulty in choosing the correct foreign counterparts of English technical jargon, and even current colloquialisms and slang, that make it essential to use only the best possible translators who have *current* knowledge of the language. The ideal is to use a national living in his or her country, but sometimes time is against this. When British-based translators are used it is necessary to first of all make sure that they are familiar with the subject matter. Overseas embassies and consultates in this country can often recommend good translators and advice can be obtained from the Foreign Languages Section of the COI.

The following final quotation from H. H. Alexander's article makes clear some essential points in preparing the original English version on which translations are to be based:

"*Turning now to style and language, remember that many people who are not naturally English-speaking—in India, Scandinavia and East Europe, for example—may be reading your story in English, and that your own translators also have to comprehend it fully before rendering it into their own language. Keep your sentences simple, therefore, with subject, verb and object in that order wherever possible. Use correct syntax, punctuate meticulously, and be constantly alert for ambiguities: where an English-born reader might stumble and then right himself by instinct, a foreigner is likely to founder completely. Again, avoid attempts at humour or verbal play: they are almost impossible to translate.*

"*The overall effect of this will be a neutral, rather pedantic style—but that is the way people learn a foreign language. Any editor who wants to liven it up (and there won't be many) can easily do so.*"

That is very sound advice from someone who is daily handling releases to the press of the world.

Finally, the press officer is recommended to keep himself up to date with all the available literature which can assist him with overseas press relations, and at the time of writing the following are suggested but new editions and new titles may be issued from time to time:

From the Central Office of Information, Hercules Road, London, SE1. Telephone 01-928 9 2345:—

Publicity For Exports—the role of British Information Services. An excellent 48-page pictorial booklet.

How You Can Use the Government Export Publicity Services.

Let the World See Your Films.

From the UK Executive Section, Information Division, Board of Trade, Broadway Buildings, 1, Victoria Street, London, SW1. Telephone: 01-222 7877:—

Services for British Exporters, Board of Trade Export Handbook, Number 1.

From the *Board of Trade Journal*, 1, Victoria Street, London, SW1. Price 1s. 6d. Issue of April 7, 1967:—

How Public Relations Can Service the Exporter, article by Peter Bloomfield, former Director, Institute of Public Relations.

From *Public Relations*, IPR, 20–26, Lambs Conduit Street, London, WC1. Price 5s. Issue of Spring, 1967:—

Writing For Export, article by N. H. Alexander of Engineering in Britain Information Services, 3, Johnson's Court, London, EC4. Telephone 01-353 5151.

16

Some Problems of Press Relations

The Purpose of Press Relations Practice

What is the purpose of press relations practice? Is this an important and useful activity? Can it be justified as a necessary activity in which a responsible and reputable organisation should engage?

These questions need to be put because the necessity for press relations is doubted in some quarters. Even the integrity of press relations practice is questioned by cynics, sceptics and satirists. They condemn all PR as parasitical. Our classical economists had a similar dislike of advertising.

Press relations are essential as part of the communication system between an organisation and its publics. Press relations are a form of human relations, a liaison with people daily concerned with the media of communication. The purpose of these activities is therefore to establish the best possible two-way communication system with editors, journalists, authors, broadcasters, television producers, scriptwriters, film makers, and all such people responsible for material used in publishing, radio, TV and film making, and to this list we must add other forms of communication such as the spoken word generally and visual aids.

Thus, it is an important and valuable practice because it has to do with the supply of desirable information, carefully checked for accuracy, so that members of the organisation's different publics may become better and more correctly informed. This applies to the name and address of the organisation, its personnel, policy, products, services, activities, premises and installations, history and achievements, research and developments. It has to do with the total organisation: in industry it concerns the finance, production and marketing functions.

It is not a matter of arm-twisting, cocktail-partying, or bar frequenting to get unwilling reporters to print stories advantageous to an organisation but of otherwise doubtful merit or veracity. That may be a description of press agentry and there are people engaged in doing just that, but press relations as a feature of PR has nothing to do with press agentry.

PR can be justified as a facet of making known which is a valid and vital function of any self-respecting organisation. A job cannot be done, whether it be by an elected, a voluntary or a commercial organisation, unless its electorate, supporters or consumers have sound knowledge on which to judge whether votes, allegiance or purchases are warranted. Choice depends on knowledge. These people may be influenced, too, by the persuasiveness of various sales promotion efforts, such as advertising, but sales promotion cannot operate very effectively in a vacuum of imperfect knowledge.

Its job is to instruct public opinion and to publicise what an organisation is and does, but it leaves advocacy and persuasion to advertising which itself uses special skills to attract attention, create interest, arouse desire, inspire conviction and provoke action in the manner required by the advertiser.

Press relations also serve the media of communication by supplying information, pictures and facilities to which editors, staff writers and contributors might otherwise have less or no access. Achieving accessibility of information is therefore a prime responsibility of the press officer, although this is no easy task, and press officers are constantly being accused of failing to do this, even of creating a communication barrier between the press and organisational heads. Newspaperman are apt to say, "*I don't want to speak to the press officer, let me speak to the managing director.*" The press officer should be able to speak for the MD, or be the means of introducing the press to the MD, but he should not be there to protect the MD who fears the press.

Do PRO's Protect Businessmen?

The *Daily Express* City page, as edited by Frederick Ellis and containing the popular "Under The Clock" column, showed how good relations could be developed between the press and business leaders and their PRO's. Frederick Ellis consistently carried out the *Daily Express* policy of humanising reports. To quote from his City page of August 8th 1967, stories opened like this:

"*The most violent attack yet made on Government policies is launched this morning by Colonel William Whitbread—the 66-year-old ex-parachutist chief of one of Britain's largest Brewers Whitbread and Co.*"

While the "Under The Clock" column began:

"*Yesterday I was speaking to Mr. William de Vigier, the Swiss-born boss of Acrow Engineers. He started the Acrow business—which takes in builders' scaffolding, steel tubes and a clutch of engineering firms—under a railway arch in Bow Road on a capital of £150 in the early thirties . . . When I spoke to Mr. de Vigier . . .*"

City editors like Trevor Bass in the *Daily Express*, David Malbert in the *Evening News*, Patrick Sergeant in the *Daily Mail*, William Davis in the *Guardian* and others who have made the romance of industry and popular economics subjects of wide reader interest—no doubt meeting the demands of Britain's millions of small investors and Unit-trust holders—are meticulous in their use of detailed information and personal quotes which indicates their reliance upon PRO's and press officers for facts and upon the willingness of PR-orientated businessmen to co-operate with the press for their own good. The City page in these lively interesting newspapers has become a major section, while of course special business sections have boomed in the newspapers read mainly by businessmen such as *The Times*, *Daily Telegraph*, *Scotsman* and, naturally, the *Sunday Times* which pioneered the supplementary business section.

But according to those vociferous critics of PR this happy state of affairs is a rarity. Many PR practitioners wrote to the editor of the *Financial Times* following a curious article which appeared in the issue of April 13 and written by Geoffrey Owen under the title "*Is the company PR man really necessary?*" The *Financial Times* probably publishes more material from PR sources than any other daily newspaper published in the British Isles, and is an extremely well informed and informative newspaper as a result. Its able editor, Sir Gordon Newton, received the Hannen Swaffer award as Journalist of the Year for the "*remarkable rise in international standing*" achieved by this enterprising newspaper. Moreover, it could not have launched its Technical Page in 1967 but for the ready supply of press releases about new technical products.

Such a disparaging article was surely out of place in a newspaper which had proved for itself the value of the PR man. Owen went so far as to say:

"*To journalists, the PR man is often more of a hindrance than a help . . . 'I think I had better put you through to our public relations man.' How often has that dreary phrase cut short a promising conversation between enquiring journalist and managing director, so that instead of talking to someone who at least knows the answers, even if he may be reluctant to reveal them, the journalist is faced with a blank wall of incomprehension—someone who is unable or unwilling to understand what the questions mean.*"

This strange contradictory article later contained the following admission:

"*Public relations is not a matter of lavish cocktail parties and lengthy lunches; it is a question of communications, and the fewer barriers there are between the two parties, the better for all concerned.*"

Among the more polite rebukes which the *Financial Times* saw fit to publish were ones from John Keyser and P. R. Easton. Said Keyser:

"*Mr. Owen objects to the PR man preventing the journalist from having access to top management. It would be intolerable to permit this freedom to all journalists. Top management, especially the Managing Director, has heavy calls upon its time and cannot be asked to be available to any journalist who chooses to make contact. Many journalists display abysmal ignorance of the industry concerned and often keep on firing questions out of the blue for perhaps half an hour. The supply of information to the Press must be the responsibility of a specialist department. Provided that the chief PRO is (a) competent, (b) ethical, (c) a member of top management, (d) has a knowledge of how the Press works the journalist will get more satisfaction from dealing with him than by trying to deal with other functional heads.*"

This pre-supposes a number of conditions which may not always exist in every organisation, but it is up to management to employ PR people of this calibre.

P. R. Easton, managing director of Peter Roderick Public Relations, made some forceful comments:

"*Surely, Mr. Geoffrey Owen in his rather contradictory article on PR in industry said two things: Firstly that there exist managements with no appreciation of Press relations, or the need for it (true); and secondly that there exist some unqualified PR men who obstruct the passing of information from management to the Press (also true, but surely not very common these days?).*

"*Having made these points, he goes on to establish the clear need for someone to interpret the journalists' foibles . . . So why the totally misleading, negative and harmful headline implying that company PR men are really unnecessary?*"

Is Geoffrey Owen right, is he justified in his lament that the tycoon and the business executive is too willing to call in the PRO rather than deal direct with the press? Was it sensible of him to write:

"*Like industrial relations, public relations is too important to be left to a specialist department; top management has to play an active role. Indeed, in many medium-sized and smaller companies it is questionable whether a public relations man, let alone a department, is needed at all.*"

This peculiar sentence overlooks the role of the PR consultant, and reveals Mr. Owen's naive impression that British industry is lavishly endowed with staff PRO's, which unfortunately it is not.

There are many different answers to the question "*Do PRO's protect businessmen from the press?*" And there is just one basic reason why there are so many different answers. Let's examine some of the answers first.

Two perfectly true examples will help to demonstrate two contrary answers.

Through carelessness, some workmen had caused a fire in property where they were working. Firemen, police and the press were soon on the spot, and the accident happened to occur close enough to head office for the managing director to be quickly informed. An alarmed managing director, fearing bad publicity, telephoned the company PRO for advice, even though the PRO was 300 miles away at the time on an important PR assignment. The PRO could only advise the MD to do nothing since the story could not be denied.

In the second case a factory caught fire, and firemen, police and the press were quickly on the scene. The MD was soon there too. The PRO once again was not available. This MD simply called the press together, gave them all the facts unstintingly and cheerfully, bade them goodnight and soon had them on their way. The story made a small paragraph in one or two nationals next morning.

In both cases the PRO had only a modest department and he could not be everywhere. But in the first case we have the MD who would not act without advice, while in the second we find an MD of a rarer kind who knows exactly what to do when confronted by the press. The two stories are perfectly true, yet they are extremes and in between are many other PR circumstances involving different people, situations and reactions. Let us look at some more examples because this is the sort of world in which the press officer has to work and survive.

A TV news interviewer was provided with facilities to interview the chairman of the organisation in a private room after the press reception. Twice, the chairman was rehearsed by the TV interviewer; then came the actual filmed interview. But this time, the third time, the interviewer slipped in a question which was dynamite. The chairman, caught unawares, fluffed his answer with a "*Yes, but,*" reply. After the shooting had been completed the press officer pointed out that the question and the answer took unfair advantage of the chairman and should be cut.

The TV interviewer was annoyed. The interview never appeared on TV. Without that damning question and answer the interviewer had lost a dramatic if damaging story.

The next is an example of a piece of silliness which is just as typical on the business side as the unscrupulousness which the businessman sometimes suffers at the hands of press and TV interviewers. The company was American owned, and the chairman was liable to fly over from the States, and implement policy in no uncertain manner. On one occasion he descended upon a factory, kept trade union officials and the press hanging about long beyond the appointed hour, announced redundancy sackings, and flew back to America. This naturally received a very bad press, and staff and community relations were reduced to a very low state. Although the company employed PR consultants they were left to read about it in the papers.

The managing director of another company complained to his PR consultants that a certain factory in the provinces never got a good press and that it was ignored when the activities of other factories in the town were freely reported. Moreover, the works manager complained that the local press were only interested in the factory when there were labour disputes, and that on one occasion a local press photographer had walked right into the factory and taken pictures without having the courtesy to ask permission. The PR consultants arranged for the local press to attend an award ceremony, and a luncheon was also arranged so that the works manager and the industrial correspondents could establish good relations and discuss their mutual problems and needs. It was thought that this would lead to a more sympathetic attitude on both sides. It was a fiasco. Because of the earlier incident over the press photographer the gatekeeper was overzealous and kept the press waiting so long that they missed the award ceremony. But worse than that, one of the reporters was tipsy on arrival, shocked the company executives by his abusiveness, and instead of reporting the award ceremony insisted on criticising the company's labour relations in the past. Understandably, that works manager remains as hostile as ever to the press.

Contrast this with a factory in North London whose PRO makes a point of writing specially slanted press releases so that whenever a story goes out nationally a separate version goes to the three local papers. The management of this factory is well known to local reporters, and hardly a week goes by without this company, its personalities or its products being mentioned in the local press. This is a deliberate piece of community relations so that people in the vicinity are familiar with this company, its policies, products and the people who run it. Such an enlightened policy does wonders for staff recruitment. This is, of course, common practice with PR-orientated companies, but in this particular case the exercise is exceptionally successful because the company really sets out to make the newspaper staff share in the exuberance of the company's promotional activity. The result is that these reporters always know where to turn for a story, and they are greeted as friends and treated with frankness.

There are still more sides to this businessman versus the press problem. The journalist may be wise, knowledgeable and capable, but this cannot always be the case. No-one is infallible. Journalists have to deal with so many topics that they are masters of none, and their reportings are no better than they can be. A company chief may well hold the press in awe, and think journalists are oracles until he is asked to address a press conference, and then reads with horror the hash they have made of his technicalities and of his replies to questions. This applies to the popular press and general reporters, not to specialist correspondents or to the trade and technical press where the journalists are generally masters of their subjects, although even then it is surprising how often journalists on technical journals ring up for explanations of elementary technical terms! Many directors and other top people in companies, especially technical staff, become quickly disillusioned and unwilling to talk to pressmen whom they have reason to believe will not understand what they are told. Not surprisingly, they leave it to their press officer to seek publication of material in approved form.

Then there is the problem of the company which is in trouble. A few years ago a highly reputable company was publicly criticised for negligence which led to the banning of a certain substance. Two popular dailies hounded this company, and a typical trick was to seek a contradictory statement by ringing the company's London office, then its out-of-town headquarters, and then the factory where the trouble had occurred, seeking to find a divergent story. In this case the MD decided to sit tight, say nought, and ride out the storm.

The British press, incidentally, has a morbid fear of chemicals, and the more popular the journal the more it seems intent upon furthering misunderstandings about them. One Fleet Street journal ran a scare story about chemical products being indiscriminately burned on a November 5th bonfire. The managing director of that company was so furious that he personally visited the editor and demanded a retraction. The cartons were empties, a lot of harmless throwouts, but the story had arisen from a reporter seeing the dreaded names on the burning packages!

In one case, however, deaths of hospital patients were actually caused by a production mistake. But this company adroitly killed all press speculation by publicly admitting its negligence and accepting full responsibility. That story soon disappeared from the news columns. Presumably an admission of guilt is poor news!

It is very easy to castigate the press, less easy to understand the contradictions of policy even within the same publishing office, but let us be charitable and realistic about press relations problems since the reasons may not always be apparent to the businessman.

Competition is intense. Newspapers fold. A story is a story. It is a business as tough and relentless as any other with vast sums of money at stake. The huge IPC empire is worth millions of pounds. The daily advertisement revenue of national newspapers at £5,000 a page is an income that has to be fought for in competition not only with other newspapers but also with weekly and monthly magazines and, during the past decade, with commercial television. A credit squeeze can be near-disastrous in the newspaper world. The weekly battle between Sunday newspapers like the *People* and the *News of the World* is savage. When magazines fail one after the other as *Picture Post*, *Everybody's*, *Illustrated* and *John Bull* (finally, despite re-naming) did in the fifties it was a bitter blow to British publishing with its large gravure plants set up for printing mass circulation journals. (Yet so great are the swings and roundabouts in this business that when the *Daily Telegraph* first wanted to introduce a weekly colour supplement there was insufficient gravure printing capacity in the country and they had to go to Germany.)

We have also seen the demise of the London *Star*, *News Chronicle*, *Sunday Chronicle*, *Sunday Empire News*, *Sunday Citizen* and that delightful northern daily, the *Daily Dispatch*. Among women's magazines, *Woman and Beauty*, *Woman's Illustrated*, *Woman's Day*, *Woman's Mirror*, *Everywoman*, *Modern Woman*, *Good Taste* and others have vanished. Four big women's weeklies, *Woman*, *Woman's Own*, *Woman's Realm* and *Woman's Weekly* are all that are necessary to carry the possible mass women's market advertising, including colour advertising. *Housewife* has been merged with *Ideal Home*. Humorous magazines, such as *The Passing Show*, have never succeeded, save for *Punch*. News magazines have seldom survived for long, and those now on sale in Britain are of American origin. It is only a matter of time before the number of popular morning newspapers is reduced again. A national advertiser does not really need to take space in more than the *Daily Mirror* and the *Daily Express* to get excellent coverage of the mass consumer market. The advertising agencies work out cold-blooded media schedules by readership survey and computer, and a six-figure advertising campaign may well be distributed between only half-a-dozen publications with the least amount of duplicated readership. A newspaper like the *Sun* is mathematically ignored by most advertising agencies. Even though the *Daily Mail* acquired the *News Chronicle* it was still left behind in the space selling race led by the *Daily Mirror* and the *Daily Express*.

And yet the peculiar resilience of the newspaper and magazine publishing world has been shown by remarkable successes in surprising quarters. First the *Sunday Times* colour supplement was followed by those of the *Observer* and the *Daily Telegraph*, while we have seen the "heavy" Sundays increase in influence, and then the *Financial Times*, *The Times* and the *Daily Telegraph* have won increasing circulations and introduced competitive features such as the Technical Page in the *FT* and the business sections in *The Times* and *DT*. Of these, *The Times*, since its acquisition by Lord Thomson, has shown how interesting a serious newspaper can become. Meanwhile, the *Guardian* has developed from a Manchester daily to a semi-national until it has reached the status of a national, while the *Scotsman* is by no means confined to Scotland and has introduced a financial supplement. But it is war between the various press empires. Don't let us forget that.

In the provinces, the weeklies have dwindled, and the cities that once had four or five morning and evening papers, like Liverpool, Bristol and Manchester, are reduced to a single morning and a single evening paper. Famous dailies in Brighton, Bristol, Birmingham, Edinburgh, Liverpool, Leicester, Manchester, Nottingham and Leeds have folded or been merged with other local papers in recent years. Web-offset has introduced a new economy in local newspaper printing, and national trade weeklies and large house magazines have taken advantage of these new and cheaper printing facilities. The provincial press scene is full of interest, and its constant study is imperative to the proficient press officer. A few provincial Sundays still manage to survive, while the pictorial county magazine and the local glossy magazine has become a publishing phenomenon despite TV and the death of the society and general interest magazine when published nationally.

A lot of cant is uttered about the duties and responsibilities of the press, as if there was something sacred about news. The only reason why anyone publishes a newspaper today (as distinct from the days of small political sheets) is that it is a profitable business. When a publication ceases to earn profits it folds. Newspapers like the *Sun* are rarities, and the *Sun* came about only because the original paper, the *Daily Herald*, was losing money. The *Sun*, with all the prodigious effort that has been put into it, has done little better and may have disappeared before this book is published, just as the Co-operative movement's *Sunday Citizen* had to go.

The press does not have a public duty to publish news. If that were so the newspapers would be state-owned and they would concentrate on publishing news like those in Russia, whereas in fact newspapers are highly organized private enterprises in which entertainment often occupies far greater space than news. Or shall we say that the news is not so much about the happenings of society as about the things—sport, gardening, motoring, fashion and so on—which are of greater interest to readers so that the modern newspaper has much more of a magazine content than it did before the Second World War. This is very true of provincial evening newspapers which have used family interest features as a means of getting papers into the home, instead of being left behind on the home-going bus or train, with the result that it has become possible for them to offer a more valuable advertising medium to local tradesmen.

There is nothing disreputable about this, so long as we admit the truth of the matter. Newspapers are not public institutions or benefactors: they are businesses. It is therefore hypocritical to suggest that salacious Sunday newspapers have anything to do with the freedom of the press: they represent no more than the freedom to make money in a capitalist society. Once this is recognised our managing director need be less astonished if he is reported in an undesirable manner. Such treatment may well contribute to the profitability of the paper!

For no truly valid reason the reading public clings to the sentiment that whatever appears in print must be true. This is one reason why some people seek editorial mentions, believing them to have more credibility than advertisements. While it is true that the editorial expresses independent journalistic views irrespective of the wishes of the organisation or product described, whereas an advertisement is in most cases clearly and understandably biased in favour of the advertiser, the reverse can be equally true. This is worth pondering upon. *The editorial can be critical and biased, the advertisement purely informative and free of comment!*

Two tenets are perhaps bewildering, these being the so-called "right of the public to be told the facts" and "the freedom of the press". The two are quite different things. The public has no right to pry into private affairs through the agency of the press, radio or television. This is a specious claim made by some sections of the press which has required a Press Council to be set up in the public interest. But freedom to express opinion, like free speech and the secret ballot, are incontrovertible democratic rights which we cherish. If anyone takes up a public position, be he politician, author, artist or even a tenant who writes a letter protesting about his rent, he makes himself subject to comment for that is the penalty of fame. The higher we climb the further we may fall.

It is at this point that the public man has to beware of seeking one kind of publicity and getting another, for the press may not agree with the opinion he holds of his organisation, products, services, policy or himself. And this is where we came in with the controversial situation of the journalist who objects to being unable to directly contact the businessman who in turn is wary of speaking direct to a journalist.

If we accept that the press is a business like any other we can also accept that it can afford to publish only material that an astute editor will expect to interest his readers. That is the harsh judgement that will be passed on every press release. Editors do not print press releases as favours to PRO's. Nor are they got at and bribed with money, lunches and drinks. They are unlikely to be "conned" by cunning PRO's. Naturally, it pays to know who writes what feature on which paper but it is truer than most people realise that it is easier to get a story published, without benefit of press contacts, simply because it is worth publishing.

Reverting to this question of bias, is it not historically true of the press that it *is* biased? The early newspapers were small circulation opinion sheets. They grew to be the papers of the political parties. Many of the most influential provincial dailies which have now ceased publication were Liberal newspapers, and as newspapers they enjoyed a great tradition. There is still the Yorkshire Conservative Newspaper Co., Ltd which publishes the famous *Yorkshire Post* every morning, and the *Yorkshire Evening Post* which not long ago absorbed the *Yorkshire Evening News*. While some national newspapers have certain special policies, when it comes to party politics and elections there is no doubt which sides are taken. The British press is predominantly right-wing, and it is an interesting reflection on the power and influence of the press that it could do nothing to prevent Harold Wilson and his first Labour government from coming to power. However, the *Daily Mirror*—so popular with the Forces with its *Jane* cartoon—is reckoned to have contributed to the return of Labour immediately after the

Second World War, although circumstances were favourable to change.

Nevertheless, these political sympathies make it all the more absurd to attribute altruistic motives to news gathering. Few politicians have had a more hostile press than Harold Wilson and George Brown, and while press freedom implies that public figures must expect to occupy the hot seat of press comment, the British press does seem at times to indulge in a heady disrespect for rather than healthy criticism of our Prime Ministers, whatever their Party!

The press officer may have to attempt to understand the difficulties of press relations in the light of this sort of anarchistic outlook by the so-called "gentlemen of the press". Moreover, in Britain where there is such an inexact separation of powers between executive, legislature and judiciary, it may be expected that the press will prove a very unruly fourth estate to the older estates of clergy, lords and commons. And in the midst of this we have to recognise that while advertising made the popular press possible it is now making the less popular newspapers impossible. The British press, admired so much by those in the emergent countries who are astonished that such an outspoken press can survive, is a paper jungle of contradictory beasts.

As we all know, the defects of the press are constantly set before our eyes when the numbers reported killed or injured in wars, disasters and accidents vary from paper to paper. It is a matter of importance that the press officer provides both press and organisation with a means of achieving accuracy. Here lies the essence of good press relations. The press officer must be jealous of his ability to be accurate even when no-one else is. Sometimes it is his desire to be accurate and not his anxiety to be careful which is misunderstood by the press who think him ill-informed or lacking in authority when they telephone him for factual information. A responsible press officer must be sure of his facts because retractions and corrections are always too late to mend the damage caused by erroneous information once it has been published. Far more attention is given to the first account, and the amendment may not be seen by those who read the original story. The press officer has to keep constantly in mind that when, for instance, he issues a story to monthly, weekly and daily publications at home and abroad, and also to news agencies, radio, TV, freelance writers, foreign correspondents, and the Central Office of Information an error in a price or a dimension could be perpetuated to all kinds of media throughout the world for months and possibly years. It can be a chastening responsibility as any press officer will know who has made a mistake and then had to sit back and receive the press cuttings for what seems to be an eternity, especially if it is the sort of story which gets quoted and repeated over the years.

That is why secretaries engaged in PR offices have to be self-starters capable of telling their boss when he has boobed, and that is a quality more important than being able to touch-type. The next two vital qualities are ability to spell and punctuate. Any fool can type, but only one in a thousand secretaries will close a parenthesis. God help PR if our secretaries adopt the letter style using no punctuation: it is bad enough discouraging the secretary who does not indent paragraphs: Imagine trying to read newspapers without paragraphs or punctuation: they would be as uninviting and as unreadable as the average modern advertisement which is destroying the power of the copywriter to persuade. Paragraphs and punctuation give legibility and meaning to the written word. Their absolute necessity is undeniable.

But what makes a story is not always in the interest of the person who is vulnerable to criticism or, worse still, is vulnerable to bias. A PRO himself, and PR itself, is always vulnerable to criticism from satirists and intellectuals. So many practitioners perform their functions badly that our business is made an open target, and it could take us centuries to live this down just as doctors have had to live with the epithet "quack" for very similar reasons. At the present time it would be very difficult indeed to win a sensible and fair-minded appraisal of PR on British radio or TV or in much of the British press. When we sit with our families watching TV, and the typical side-lash is made about PR, we have to endure the troubled looks from wives and children because better people than us have charged that we are charlatans if not crooks.

We have to face a mental brick-wall of unwillingness to understand PR. The press has had its run long enough, and has set pompously on its backside, castigating its former members who have had the temerity, but not always the skill, to seek greener fields. Second-career journalists are not necessarily God's gift to PR, but in the PR business of the future (it *is* much more a business than a profession, and it's certainly not the near-religion of the PR disciples who used to preach the Gospel according to the Institute before it was recognised that marketing and communication were quite respectable bedfellows) PR practitioners, including press officers, have got to refute the professional funsters and get on with the job of communicating what has to be told with purpose and without apology. If PR allows itself to be a mere whipping boy it never will play an important part in business, central government, local government, voluntary organisation, or in any other field.

All this is vital to the press officer who needs to be seen as being as valuable to the press as the press is to him. Then a real situation of good press relations can exist, with goodwill on both sides.

No doubt there will always be a certain amount of wrangling because a journalist in search of a sensational story is warded off, but it is much more to the point that through the services of press officers hundreds of organisations are now easily accessible to the press, that there is an organisation specially set up which can help (not hinder) the press whenever the organisation is newsworthy. This really is a big point, and so it is worth repeating that but for press officers the press, and other communication media, would be truly hindered from obtaining reliable information. There are still far too many organisations which have no form of easy communication with the press, and such organisations are more likely to be unhelpful and to fob off the press than those which appreciate the value of the press when well-informed and the need for a press officer as a press service.

We have scrutinised a great many answers to the question whether the business man is too willing to call in the PRO rather than deal directly with the press. These answers reveal the complexity of the press world, the fact that it is a business and not some lofty pious calling, and indicate both the need for good press relations and their absence in far too many organisations.

The reason, the solitary reason for this muddled state of affairs, is that much of top management in Britain has a fetish about accountancy instead of one about efficiency, and consequently they have an imperfect knowledge of aids to efficiency such as PR. Inevitably this means that such management, with its machine-like mentality that has lost contact with humanity, is incapable of performing the person-to-person function of press relations, whether directly or through a press officer. Too many top businessmen are capable in many capacities but lack the resolute simplicity of the managing director in the second story quoted who knew exactly what to do and did it. The great majority of top businessmen in Britain are in desperate need of skilled press officers, and our potential business leaders of tomorrow should put PR down as a priority subject in their management studies.

It is necessary to demolish some sacred cows, myths and conventions of public relations. There is no mystique about communication, only the need to convey facts, expand knowledge, and create goodwill through understanding. Those are not empty generalisations but potent shibboleths. The task of communicator may fall upon a specialist executive but even where none is employed someone has to deal with the press. This book tries to tell anyone, from managing director down, what is required of a press officer.

But more than that, the modern view is taken in these pages of what must be more properly termed the communication business. Instead of separate professional organisations for advertising, public relations and marketing we need a single Institute of Communication which can amalgamate them all. It is possible that the first step will be a federation of communication institutes and associations. What a blessed relief such a coming together will be for the businessman whose more cogent mind never has understood the water-tight compartments into which the various practitioners have confined themselves. One serious problem remains: *are there enough big enough people who can think in broad communication terms* to fill the future positions of communication manager in industry or communication executive in a comprehensive communication agency which can offer not only the existing complex marketing and advertising service but also the complex public relations service which is not nearly developed as yet?

This may mean that the PR business will first have to develop along the same path taken by advertising during the past thirty to forty years. The Healy Plan for the re-organisation of the IPR provided an interesting forward peep. Then, when PR consultancies are providing services parallel with those of advertising agencies the two will do well to combine forces as communication agencies. And the sooner the better!

The expression "public relations" is likely to be retained by the PR counsellor who, being a person of broad experience in all fields of communication, can given counsel to organisations regarding a pure consultancy service.

It bears repeating throughout this book that the terms "public relations" and "marketing", taken in their broadest sense, are synonymous, meaning communication. In "communication" we have a simple term which everyone understands, and it is free of the unfortunate connotations and undertones of "public relations". Agreed, it is apt to be confused with radio and tele-communications, but they are specialist technicalities and if we refrain from using the final "s" our expression is surely clear enough. Our problem is often that the abbreviation "PR" is frequently taken to mean some ominous or underhanded behaviour. There is even a drug called PR! No doubt people in the communication industry could be dubbed "commies", but the same could be said about other abbreviations such as "Co" and "pro". The simple expression "communication" is not capable of many undesirable abbreviations. We could therefore have a CM and CO (again!) with acceptance as ready as that for O & M and R & D.

Both marketing and public relations are concerned with communication in order to keep an organisation in being, and this is a matter of human relations. Both use similar media, both are deeply involved in human relations. Media may be used differently, and PR may use a greater range of media, but both are so concerned with communication that it is thought by some PR and marketing people that their functions are identical, that they are both in the communication business so that the former distinctive terms are redundant and should be discarded.

The post-war decades in PR have been experimental. The final third of the 20th century must see a rationalisation of our communication techniques, and the Common Market could be the proving ground when language problems will demand simplicity of communication if the nations of Europe are to enjoy the community relations envisaged in the Treaty of Rome.

17

The Image and Marketing

"Image" is a much maligned and generally misunderstood word.

In advertising circles it is understood to be the creation of a clearcut idea or impression of a product or service. Advertising will set out to establish a particular image—a distinctive image—which identifies the product or service as being the cheapest, most lavish, most reliable, most exclusive, most fashionable or whatever may be the most advantageous and sales promoting characteristic. There is a so-called intellectual disinclination to admit the validity of image-making, as if it were immoral, but this attitude is irrational and not particularly intelligent.

If a company wishes to market a product it is essential that prospective purchasers should know what kind of product it is and for whom it is intended. Is it a Rolls-Royce or is it a Mini-Minor? Critics who pretend that it is an abuse of freedom of choice to persuade are really sceptical of the ability of human beings to compare the choices and make up their own minds. People are not so gullible as intellectuals and Left-wing politicians would have us believe. A bad product can seldom be sold twice to the same victim.

A lot of nonsense is talked about the "persuasion business", and expressions such as "hidden persuaders" have been coined to this end. May British press officers never be guilty of "engineering consent", as Edward Bernays so horribly expressed his idea of PR. American PR counsellors direct their efforts towards "persuasion", but we are not concerned with persuasion in British PR.

That does not mean that we are purely informative, full stop. We are informative in the service of proper understanding which is a highly necessary part of any organisation's activity, whether it be a voluntary, trade association, public service or marketing organisation. A hospital may not be thought to be "selling" its services, at least not under the British national health scheme, but it will not function fully unless its specialist services are known in the right quarters—you don't take an accident case to a children's hospital—and this depends upon communication.

Similarly, what is the use of marketing a good which no-one understands, or about which people are sceptical, apathetic, prejudiced or hostile? PR educates: it does not persuade. It presents facts so that people will be made aware: it does not present those facts *in such a way* that those informed are influenced in their preference. But people tend to like the things they know and understand best, and so it is only fair to say that people are more likely to buy the known than the unknown. That is where PR can aid the truly persuasive arts of selling, advertising and merchandising. It can break the barriers of ignorance, but it does not have to boast or advocate or urge any action beyond asking for further information, samples, patterns, price lists, or possibly stockists' names and addresses. This is a subtle difference, but it is all the difference between PR and advertising.

But just as there are advertising people who find it difficult to recognise this subtle difference, and cannot see PR (especially press relations) as anything else but another weapon in the promotional and persuasion armoury, so there are PR people (especially in non-commercial PR) who fear the closer association nowadays being forged between PR and marketing because they think information is likely to be presented less honestly, more persuasively and therefore with greater bias. Perhaps because so many marketing ideas have been imported from the USA, they fear that PR may become Americanised on persuasion lines. There need be no foundation for these fears if we recognise that PR (or communication) is a far greater field of activity than those activities, like selling and advertising, in which persuasion is a necessary part.

But even within advertising some interesting new thoughts are being expressed about persuasion! You cannot really persuade people to do things they do not want to do, buy what they don't want to buy, or believe what is repugnant to them. People are often more cussedly independent than their protectors imagine. Brainwashing does not work, given access to choice. Motivation research, as pioneered by Ernest Dichter, has revealed some home truths about buying motives, often using elaborate techniques to prove the unacceptable obvious!

Conversely, Christians are Christians, Moslems are Moslems, Communists are Communists mostly because the propaganda was inculcated when there was no other choice. Many of us are subject to a form of mental conscription simply as an accident of birth. Get a child young enough and it can be taught to believe anything, but later in life the awkward questions can arise. Not many people do enjoy much choice in their political or religious views unless they have a very liberal education and enlightening personal experiences which invite comparative thought. Very little education anywhere is unbiased and free thought is an exquisite scarcity. Advertising and public relations have to be seen against this background, not picked on as isolated bad influences in an otherwise pure world.

While it is not the function of PR to persuade, PR is concerned with image making if we frankly take this to be the establishment of a correct impression of an organisation, its policy, products or services. This is rather broader than the advertising concept of an image which is usually limited to a brand image rather than that of an entire organisation. Thus, it is the PR task to create clear lines of communication so that our subject is known and understood for what it is.

Note that word "communication". As pointed out in the previous chapter, sooner or later it is going to be more sensible to talk about the communication business, communication officers and communication consultants. We shall be better understood and respected then.

A misguided criticism sometimes levelled at image-making is that it is a means of obscuring the truth and of creating a "favourable" image which we would like people to accept in place of the true image. In other words, we are accused of saying things are better than they really are, of glossing over imperfections, or of downright lying about deficiencies. Malcolm Muggeridge once described PR as "organised lying". How do we reply?

The fact is that everything in life is liable to misuse: murder can be committed with a useful tool such as a hammer, criminals can find loopholes in the law, and parsons may assault choirboys. Some human beings will stoop to anything, given the chance. Without laws, codes and rules there would be utter anarchy and we are one another's keepers. Is it therefore surprising that businessmen with a keen eye to profit and a blind eye to ethics will misuse the ability to communicate ideas and information to the public and have no scruples about presenting a false image which is to their financial advantage?

But the PR practitioner and the press officer must have scruples, and they must be prepared to refuse their services to those who would abuse them. Good press relations depend on this ethical adherence being understood by editors and journalists. But a good many newspapermen are cynical enough to disbelieve that PR people have any scruples whatsoever. Unless press officers recognise their duty to the press and to themselves they cannot properly perform useful duties for their employers.

In an article called "*1,000 Days of Harold*" which Labour MP Brian Walden wrote in the *Evening News* on July 12th 1967 there were some references to PR which have a bearing on this argument. Brian Walden wrote that Wilson dominated contemporary British politics as Gladstone once dominated Victorian politics. Then he went on to say "*Such domination is built upon no such rickety foundations as implied by phrases like 'good public relations'. It is a complete misunderstanding of his talents and programmes to see him as a creation of the admen.*" This is a good example of the false image that PR so often has among politicans—that PR is normally and commonly misused to present false images, to pretend that things or people are what they are not.

The author challenged Brian Walden, pointing out that the article was itself an excellent piece of PR for Harold Wilson in that it set out to create a better understanding of the Prime Minister, his problems and how he was going about them. It was a very interesting article.

Brian Walden was kind enough to reply, admitting his own association with a PR consultancy, stressing that he had no hostility to the practice of public relations, but in more than one point of his letter expressing his doubts about the veracity and impartiality of PRO's. He wrote "*I have had dealings, and I have no doubt that you have too, with public relations men operating on behalf of the South African Government, the Portuguese Government, the Chinese Government, the petroleum companies and numerous other bodies—affable, engaging, informative men, but hardly objective. Therefore I do unashamedly regard any reputation built* solely *on the efforts of public relations agencies as being rickety and in respect to the Prime Minister I said, if you remember, that his domination was* not *built upon such an insubstantial basis.*"

It is easy to understand Mr. Walden's point of view, and he would be absolutely right if reputations, or images, were built "*solely*" on PR efforts. But they are not, as he was at pains to explain in the case of the Prime Minister. You cannot succeed in persistently presenting an image that owes nothing to reality. An image must be earned. It is a matter of gaining credit for achievement. So, once again, we come across this strange misunderstanding that image-making means faking images. To come to Mr. Walden's experiences with the PRO's of foreign governments whose policies he presumably does not admire, he is confronted by a mixture of propaganda, opinion and fact. In this book we are concerned only with the dissemination of facts, and in the case of South Africa the facts, and the image, could concern an accurate impression of South Africa's industrial progress or of its attractiveness as a tourist centre. But in Western democratic eyes nothing is likely to change the image that events have created of South Africa politically, although propaganda may seek our sympathy. It would be proper for a member of the British Institute of Public Relations to engage in an image-making programme about, say, South African wines, but it would be totally improper for such a member to try to pull the wool over our eyes about the country's illiberal internal politics.

Such falsifying may be desired by those lacking a good image, but the only way to create a good image in place of a bad one is to use PR techniques such as opinion research and problem analysis to discover how the causes of the poor impression can be removed. Then, when a good image is deserved it can be made known and established by PR techniques such as press relations.

This principle has to be quite clearly understood and upheld. Expressions such as "image-making" and "creating favourable images" are bandied about as if PR was a form of wizardry or black art.

Sometimes, however, a different situation occurs when it is necessary to change an image or create a new one. Times and products change and what was a household word in mother's day may need a new look in daughter's day. An organisation which began making, say, simple wireless sets may today produce sophisticated electronic equipment; similarly, a shipping company may now be principally engaged in air travel. Calor Gas had a pre-war country cottage image but today the image is greatly changed, and there is an industrial one as well.

It is, of couse, very much a management responsibility to determine what image or character the organisation should have, and this is closely linked with marketing policy, and with the determination of the means of distribution and the type or class of buyer to whom the products or services are aimed.

Public Relations in Relation to Marketing

Assuming, therefore, that we are not dealing with just an information service but with an organisation, commercial or otherwise, which has something to sell let us now look at public relations in relation to marketing. We shall then see the part that can be played by press relations in what is called "the marketing mix".

There are many definitions of marketing, and it can be said that marketing includes everything from the conception of a product to its final consumption including after sales service. Or, as David Malbert, City Editor of the *Evening News*, succinctly put it on June 14th 1967, marketing is "*producing and selling at a profit goods that satisfy the customers*".

Marketing comprises a vast kaleidoscope of activity, but what is extremely interesting to the PR practitioner is that whereas selling used to seek markets for products marketing seeks products for markets. This implies social responsibility as well as economic efficiency. It brings human relations into selling at the very time when the supermarket appears to be destroying the human element in selling. The marketing man recognises that markets are publics which is very similar to the PR man's concern with publics. Nowadays, the marketing man will prefer to sell to a particular public, and not to all and sundry with haphazard hopefulness. This feeling for what people want, this rational desire to satisfy human wants, is sensible economics coupled with acceptance that what people want matters and that business and its management is a good deal more than buying cheap and selling dear. The old philosophy of the Lancashire cotton spinner that many a mickle makes a muckle is only true today provided effort is made to deserve the mickles.

Because marketing is based on human relations there is a very distinct affinity between public relations and marketing. There needs to be a much greater appreciation of this affinity by both marketing and PR people, and given that affinity there is less likely to be misunderstandings about image-making. There will be many occasions in the future when it will be futile if the marketing man does not have complete understanding of PR, and vice versa. And this means that the press officer is going to become a very important member of the marketing team.

But this does not imply bending PR techniques to handle below-the-line promotional stunts which advertising agents now find unprofitable to provide.

The marketing man can benefit tremendously from the sympathetic activities of a press officer who understands the marketing process, that is, how goods come about and are sold. At present marketing is just as much a mystery to many press officers as public relations is to many marketing men. The press officer can help as a communication or intelligence agent, feeding back market information through monitoring, press cutting services and personal contacts, while also performing his outward function of disseminating information about the organisation, its products or services through communication media to the channels of distribution, opinion leaders, and consumers.

Press relations, even though only a part of PR, can be a marketing aid of real practical value. Can this be measured, the methodical marketing manager is bound to ask. It can, but not in inches of press space multiplied by advertisement space rates. This is a fallacy because there is no comparable money value between editorial and advertisement space or, indeed, any similarity of impact or readership. The two are utterly different. But it is reasonable to contend that press relations can be measured in physical effect, and the difference made by press relations effort can be seen to be apparent. Let us take some examples.

A new product is to be launched on the market. No-one has heard of it, and the claims made for it may appear to be unbelievable. It is possible to conduct an advertising campaign of sufficient weight to force home the message, to make known the product and convert disbelief into acceptance. But this would require a prodigious expenditure on all forms of promotion—press, TV and other advertising, point-of-purchase display, exhibitions, dealer campaigns, merchandising schemes and so on—and only a very large company with a big sales force and good outlet relations could expect to combat the very genuine resistance of trade and customers. Even among very big companies with first-class promotional and distributive resources, there have been some resounding flops. Whatever happened to instant tea? With mass consumer goods such as foods, beverages, toiletries and detergents which have small unit repeat sales, and large numbers of outlets, a large advertising budget can be justified. Moreover, without it the economies of mass production and the resultant necessary turnover would not be possible.

But it is often the case with something more specialised that at the initial stage of placing a new product or service on the market any expenditure on advertising is a waste of money because, frankly, there is no justification in spending the sort of money necessary to achieve the impact which would make it sufficiently well known and at the same time convince enough potential buyers of its merits. The trade and technical press is heavily endowed with advertising but some of the smaller or newer advertisers are advertising so seldom that a similar, or even a smaller, sum spent on various PR techniques (not only press relations) would be more beneficial in lifting sales up to the point when display advertising would be essential to the maintenance and expansion of sales. The "various PR techniques" might include house journals, films, technical seminars, private demonstrations and exhibitions, dealer conferences, and works visits, according to the nature of the product.

Brian Cox, PRO of the Midland Bank, has gone so far as to claim that in the long term £20,000 spent on film can do more than £20,000 spent on advertising media, meaning conventional press advertising. He was reported by Gloria Tessler in *World's Press News* of September 29th 1967, as saying this in answer to questions at the first Film In Action Conference co-sponsored by the British Industrial and Scientific Film Association and the Industrial Film Correspondents Group. Referring to the Midland Bank's film *Why Not Uncle Willy?*, Mr. Cox said "*We take the view that in this particular instance, making a will concerned with your family is very much more effective if put over on film than it is purely on a plain piece of paper.*" He added that the film had already been seen by more than 2,000 audiences.

Such forthright retorts are not likely to make Mr. Cox very popular with advertising agents, but the author's plea is that there can be many instances where a lot less than £20,000 is at stake—£5,000 even—and at the initial selling stage when the return may be in some doubt, when PR rather than advertising may be the better buy, when, in fact, much can be done less expensively through PR techniques.

It is here that PR, and to a very considerable extent press relations, can do a measurable job in educating the market as a preliminary step to an advertising campaign. This is where press relations really come into their own so that an astute marketing manager can use press relations purposefully and with appreciable result.

He might need to precede advertising by a PR programme of twelve months duration, doing so at a time when from a press relations point of view his new product has all the advantages of possessing genuine news value. In this way, the forces at the disposal of the marketing manager are marshalled strategically and there is no question of PR being a luxury, or something whose results are uncertain and incapable of assessment. Either potential buyers are interested or they are not.

A press relations campaign may take a little time to get under way and to snowball if only that a story issued in January may not appear in a monthly journal before March at the earliest, and later still if the journal is printed by gravure, but enquiries and reactions will provide a test of market interest and will give a guide to the appropriate time for the advertising launch. It could even work the other way and warn that a launch costing thousands of pounds was unthinkable, or that a product should be modified.

An instance of PR techniques being used for a pre-launch (although without benefit of press relations) has occurred with Standard-Triumph cars which have been tested out on a number of "guinea pig" drivers before being made available to dealers for public sale. Press relations techniques were used in the original introductions of Rentokil's damp-proofing and timber pre-treatment systems. These PR methods are not used often enough, and too many companies blunder into needless and wasteful initial expense, possibly because they go to advertising agencies which want to get on with the advertising and lack the patience or expert knowledge to recommend pre-launch PR tactics.

The real answer to this problem is for companies to engage a PR or communication counsellor who specialises in PR allied to marketing, and that does not mean PR in the guise of publicity stunts. Advertising agencies, on the whole, tend to offer very meagre PR services unless they have a very well organised PR department or, better still, an independent subsidiary PR consultancy.

18

Research and the Recording of Results—Comparisons with Advertising

Because similar techniques may be involved, and also because research may be used before and after a PR programme, this chapter will endeavour to deal with research generally as it is applied to PR, and the recording of results which may or may not refer specifically to press relations.

"Results" is something of a dirty word in PR. We have the purist information officer, more often than not engaged in the government service, who disclaims any responsibility for results as if that puts him in the Queer Street of salesmanship. Then there is the professional consultancy attitude that service is being sold, and just as the lawyer cannot guarantee success nor can the PR practitioner promise results.

To some extent this is supported by the tenth paragraph of the IPR Code of Professional Conduct which reads:

"*A member shall not propose to a prospective client or employer that his fee or other compensation be contingent on the achievement of certain results; nor shall he enter into any fee agreement to the same effect.*"

This principle tends to suffer from its interpretation differing from its intention. Doubtless its intention (there is no published explanation of what some of the vaguer principles of the IPR Code are meant to mean!) is that a PR practitioner must not guarantee to obtain, say, a hundred press cuttings for £100 because, obviously, such a guarantee is impossible to honour. But if a PR consultant or a staff PRO did not achieve satisfactory results, that is, results which satisfied his client or employer, he would expect to be dismissed. Results, whatever the IPR Code may attempt to say in its protective ambiguity, are just as vital in PR as they are in selling, advertising or anything else when the spender wants to know what he is getting for his money. This was emphasised by Professor Thain at the first Harvard-style marketing course held by the IPR at Jesus College, Oxford, in July 1966.

From the preceding two paragraphs two conflicting concepts should be noted. First, a professional service is charged on a basis of hours expended to the best of the practitioner's ability, no more, no less. Second, that ability is bound to be judged by the observed or proved effectiveness of performance. This surely means that in order to stay in business the practitioner has to operate competitively and, like, the barrister, the more successful he is, the more famous he becomes. The resultant extra demand upon his services creates a scarcity value which means he is able to charge higher fees. In other words, a PR practitioner will tend to be paid what he is worth *on the basis of results*, and the incompetent practitioner will tend to go to the wall. In certain safe and protected jobs he may merely fail to gain promotion, but he will still be judged by his ability to succeed in doing whatever he is employed to do. This elementary economic law applies to all callings, even to the likelihood of vicars becoming bishops.

Having said that certain other things need to be said and considered before we can define the areas in which research and the recording of results are either feasible or capable of reliability. One of the difficulties about judging PR activity is not that its results are intangible (that is an old hare!) but that a PR programme may be so diversified and diffused that it is not always possible to know which of many actions occurring at different times have contributed at all (or least or most of all) to the overall result.

An advertising campaign can be so devised, by computer even, so that a campaign can be limited to entirely measurable action—as with keyed advertisements. But a PR programme can be scattered over many media aimed at far more different publics than is usual in an advertising campaign which generally has a particular buying public in mind.

This is one of our problems: marketing people are apt to expect that PR can be subjected to checks as precise as, say, dealer audit research which, by recording invoices and stocks of branded goods in retail outlets, can determine the shares of the market held by competing brands and, thereby, reveal the effect of advertising on selling out. However,

PR can probably make better use of opinion polls than can advertising, and this form of research has been shown, especially in the field of politics, to be astoundingly accurate. And since so much of PR is to do with earning the good opinion of various publics PR is fortunate in being served by such an excellent form of research.

Not much has been published in this country on the question of assessing results. There is a chapter on this subject in James Derriman's book, *Public Relations in Business Management*,* and in the many case histories quoted in the author's previous book, *Public Relations In World Marketing*† the results are given in the physical although not the financial sense. These previous writings show, for example, the improvement in staff recruitment or the extent to which a company succeeded in transferring staff from one area to another, as a result of good staff relations techniques. But since PR is seldom *directly* concerned with influencing sales it is less easy to reconcile expenditure on PR with financial results.

On the whole, press relations work is inexpensive by comparison with advertising. There are times when it is distinctly better value for money. One has only to compare the turnover of advertising agencies with that of PR consultancies to realise how very little money, by comparison, is spent on PR. It is not an absolutely true comparison because the two functions are not identical, but a fallacy does exist that with advertising you have a better chance of seeing what you get for your money than you do with PR. This is a fallacy—despite what has been said above about the diversity and diffusion of PR activity—because with advertising all you can initially see for your money is the purchase of media facilities and materials for engaging these facilities, and as with PR we are still concerned with the results following our use of media and materials. But since the PR usage costs far less the results are equally less costly to achieve. This fact should be remembered when PR is criticised on the grounds that the results are intangible.

Very little money need be spent on press relations to obtain excellent results that can be seen, calculated and evaluated which certainly suggests that the so-called intangibility of PR is a myth. Mention has been made of staff moves, like that of Creed from Croydon to Brighton. Had the PR effort failed to obtain the desired numbers the company would have been faced with the extra cost of recruiting and training more replacement staff than was actually the case. Such a cost can be measured as a saving to be attributed to PR.

* University of London Press, 1964.
† Crosby Lockwood, 1966.

Or to take another example, one has only to compare the results from £5,000 spent on product publicity press relations for, say, scientific instruments with a similar sum spent on advertising in the technical press. There is no comparison. The same results as those gained by this advertising could be obtained for a much smaller sum spent on press relations. One reason for this is that product publicity stories will appear in far more journals over a longer period than advertisements can be placed and produced for that sort of money. This is a special case where a trivial amount spent on press advertising can be a waste but a smaller amount spent on PR can be most profitable.

This should not be taken to be true of PR versus large-scale consumer advertising, but it can be all too true of PR versus small-scale industrial advertising where the advertising budget is too small to be worthwhile. Thus it does not apply with the majority of consumer goods that depend on regular repeat sales which can be stimulated and maintained only by means of regular, powerful and controlled advertising. Nor does it apply when the sum of money which either is or can be spent on PR cannot produce the volume of response required to promote a profitable volume of sales. The first sentence applies to small unit items such as beer, soft drinks, foodstuffs, toiletries, cosmetics, cigarettes, petrol and proprietary medicines, while the second sentence applies to consumer durables such as domestic appliances and motor cars. There are other products and services which can be included to mention only insurance, building societies, holidays and travel. The argument is not, therefore, that PR is a substitute for all advertising, but it does apply to specialities and particularly to components which may be specified by engineers or architects, and also to a good deal of industrial equipment bought by managers, executives and purchasing officers.

Publishers will not like this but it is high time we asked ourselves whether much of technical advertising is really no more than an industrial subsidy to the technical press? Some of it should not be regarded as viable advertising in strictly economic terms. But product publicity is undoubtedly inexpensive, and since news about products can be a major reason why people read a magazine, whether is has a subscribed or controlled circulation, the publishers need the support of press officers. Whether the technical press can suffer a reduction in revenue from uneconomic advertisements and survive is a matter of publishing policy rather like farm subsidies, and it might be better all round if there was less uneconomical advertising and an end to uneconomical cover charges of technical journals. (Already, there is evidence that many specialist interest journals are relating their selling prices to real costs because, unlike popular newspapers whose selling prices are largely a means of paying for distribution, the selling price of the specialist interest magazine cannot be offset by advertisement revenue). A technical magazine should be worth buying, and perhaps it has been a criticism of the traditional subscription magazines that it has taken the lively controlled circulation magazines to reach sufficient coverage of available readerships to make advertising attractive!

Would it therefore be fairer if the blocks illustrating product publicity stories were paid for out of PR funds—bringing the cost of economical press relations towards a compromise cost with less economical advertising—provided this did not restrict publication to only those stories which were illustrated at the manufacturer's expense? Unfortunately this proposal is restricted to letterpress-printed journals, and leaves out those printed by web-offset unless they, too, could evolve a special method of making a nominal charge. But continental technical journals, presumably forced to do so by their small circulations, do make a charge for product publicity, and so does a series of well-known magazines published in the Midlands by McShane and Co. who charge for blocks, while others afterwards offer the blocks at cost.

This may well be a solution, technical journals presenting much more informative editorial and fewer unnecessarily large but comparatively uninformative display advertisements, and the contributors assisting with production costs when their material was either invited or accepted. The marketing man could object to the inability to control what was said and when it should be said, but is this really any hardship when the existing practice is reviewed and it is realised that practically all new products are covered editorially and the resultant enquiries tend to rival those received from display advertisements? There are, of course, innumerable objections from all sides, but the clear-cut divisions between advertising and editorial are not likely to survive for long. All this will have a bearing on the recording of results.

This is the hard lesson which many industrial companies are learning. PR pays dividends. It works, as well as or even better than advertising, in those special areas where buyers want the facts, not the selling points. Quite apart from press relations there are PR activities such as private exhibitions, documentary films, house journals, and technical seminars which can be far better value for money than a similar sum spent on display advertisements in the trade and technical press. For the past ten years or so Rentokil have found it more profitable to talk to architects than to advertise to them. Personal confrontation with technical or professional clients and buyers is the modern technique which pays off when the market is virtually one of known, named people. These PR techniques are also proving more effective than direct mail advertising which is traditionally the selective form of advertising. It looks as if PR has a very big future in the industrial field.

These remarks on possible changes in industrial marketing are important to a discussion of research and the recording of results because, let's face it, the amount of money frequently spent on PR, as distinct from that allocated to advertising, is negligible, so negligible in fact that it is cheeseparing to quibble about the results. When companies cheerfully spend a minimum of £100,000 a year on PR as they do on advertising they will be entitled to demand a detailed analysis of results. Moreover, it will be worth spending, say, £3,000 on opinion research to determine these results. At present, however, it would often cost more than the total PR expenditure for a year to find out to what extent, shall we say, opinion has changed or a correct image is understood as a result of the application of PR techniques. But when companies like those selling famous central heating systems, road transport vehicles, communications systems, or electronic components stretch their budgets unwillingly to spend between £2,000 and £4,000 a year on PR one really wonders whether British industry has yet heard about PR, and it is certainly not yet in a position to spend similar additional sums on research into the effectiveness or otherwise of PR. So far as these countless British industrial firms are concerned, PR is something they do on the cheap and any results obtained are practically a bonus! Apart from the combines—and not all of those!—the only people in this country who seem to take PR seriously are those of American parentage. If Britain ever gets into the Common Market PR is going to be needed on a continental scale. Then, the average PR consultancy fee will have to soar to the £10,000 a year *minimum*.

Moreover, while some of the views expressed here may seem heretical—although they are intended to stimulate thought rather than prophesy revolutions—it does seem reasonable to expect that some adjustment in the PR-publisher-advertiser triangle will be inevitable because of the changes taking place and still to take place in the economics of all three activities. More money will be spent on PR, more research will be justified, less money will be spent on advertising, and media will have to adjust itself to the situation or find alternative sources of income. If advertising support is withdrawn (and in 1968 even the

Daily Express looked nearly as slim as in newsprint rationing days just after the war) the media owners will need to seek financial resources from the two remaining sources, PR and subscribers.

There are two further possibilities not to be overlooked in our constantly changing industrial and political society, and these are subsidies from either industry or government. This, in turn, could lead to unprofitable trade and technical journals being sponsored by trade associations and state publishing houses. All this presupposes a shift from industrial advertising to industrial PR which the 1966–8 "Squeeze" indicated could happen. But it is certain that one effect of the Wilson 60's has been to show that while advertising is an essential tool of marketing, not all of it shows as good a return pound for pound as PR, of which press relations forms a major part in the estimation of those industrialists who cut their advertising budgets but retained PR. They suddenly found that not only were they spending very little on PR but that *they could not afford to spend less!*

If and when enough advertising expenditure is diverted to PR to enable organisations to mount PR programmes of a magnitude which justifies investment in the services of Mass-Observation, National Opinion Polls and Gallup Poll some really serious research can be undertaken to test the effectiveness of PR media and activities as distinct from the present use of opinion research as the initial stage in one of the more realistic and ambitious PR programmes.

This argument therefore makes possible the assertion that too much of press relations work is currently undertaken so cheaply with such remarkably good results that it is almost insulting to suggest that results should be recorded for the sake of justifying the expenditure. After all, what does it cost to have an exclusive signed feature article published in a magazine? If it produced only one convertible enquiry, or dismissed misunderstandings from the minds of a few influential people, or aroused new interest among some otherwise apathetic specifiers, it would be cheap at the price which would probably be no more than the cost of a single column inch of space in a mass circulation newspaper.

The author has written numerous articles literally "off the cuff" in a fraction of the time needed by a highly paid advertising agency copywriter to produce an advertisement which has yet to bear art, production and space charges. For eight years the author was himself a copywriter and his book, *Copywriting and its Presentation** was the first post-war British text-book on the subject. Of course, many articles do

* Crosby Lockwood, 1958.

require time and travel to secure the material but even then the cost is infinitesimal when compared with the cost of producing advertisements. And the cost of producing and distributing a press release is but a matter of a few pounds. Given the facts, a skilled press officer can dictate a press release as fluently as a good businessman will dictate a detailed letter. He does not have to seek selling ideas, polish his phrases for telling effect, nor apply the art of alliteration and other devices as the copywriter must do. He does not even have to invent slogans and headlines to catch the eye and dazzle the mind! He does not have to make his press release more dramatic or original than anyone else's. The press officer has to be the Simenon to the copywriter's Shakespeare.

However, there are certain simple ways of recording what has been achieved and the collation of press cuttings and monitored scripts form a very necessary part of the press officer's day-to-day administrative work.

A number of press-cutting services offer to supply cuttings at relatively low charges which are probably too low to permit these agencies to do the job properly. If the subject is fairly broad—furniture or cage birds, for instance—they will produce a reasonable quantity of cuttings, but when restricted to supplying cuttings about a company or its products the best press-cutting agency can give but a partial service. The author's estimate is that at best cutting agencies discover only about half of the possible cuttings. They seem to read very few provincial newspapers, and it is often quite difficult to obtain overseas cuttings.

It is therefore extremely difficult to obtain an accurate check on press coverage unless one's efforts are augmented by members of the organisation who spot and supply cuttings to the press officer. Consultants often find that their clients obtain from their provincial branch and factory managers cuttings which are never produced by London press-cutting agencies. One can send press lists to agencies, or complain, or change to another agency but the results are invariably disappointing. Many consultants would gladly pay double the fees to get the cuttings which evade the existing agency methods.

The collation and evaluation of cuttings is a laborious and tedious task, and those clumsy, old-fashioned giant guard-books heavily bound like ledgers should be discarded in favour of covers containing plastic film sleeves which protect cuttings mounted on sheets.

It is unrealistic to count inches and show total coverages in this way because half an inch in a women's weekly magazine or in a national newspaper feature may well be infinitely more valuable than a whole column in a small circulation weekly newspaper. The quantity of inches is therefore of less consequence than the status of the various media. A London PR consultancy once issued a brochure in which it described some of its clients and the campaigns conducted for them, listing the publications in which stories had appeared. What was most significant to the author was that most of the publications listed were of very slight value to the clients! Cuttings for cuttings sake, you might say. Similarly, at a business exhibition held in London in 1966 the exhibition press officer organised a group of children in national costume who attended the official opening ceremony, thus providing attractive picture material. One of the exhibitors organised a counter attraction on one of the stands of a bosomy model in fishnet stockings. Both attracted the cameramen, but while the girlie pictures appeared in the *Daily Mirror* and other popular papers, the official opening pictures appeared in *The Times*, *Financial Times* and the *Daily Telegraph* which were the newspapers read by potential visitors to the exhibition. Cuttings of this sort must be evaluated not on inches but on readership value.

The quantity of inches is therefore of less consequence than the status of the media carrying the reports. Nor is there any sense in trying to assess an advertisement rate-card value on editorial coverage, saying that these inches would have cost so much if the space had been paid for, for the elementary reason that no-one would use the same space, the same quantity of space, of perhaps even the same media for advertising purposes. There is no logical basis for financial evaluation, although it is true that a count of inches does indicate that there was a substantial coverage of a story, and circulation figures—and readership figures, too—could be totalled to show the possible number of subscribers or readers who had an opportunity to read the report or see the pictures. (Circulation means number of copies sold, readership means number of copies read. The first may be an Audited Bureau of Circulations figure, while the second may be derived from the IPA National Readership Survey.)

To put the point about financial evaluation more plainly still, there are certain products which are never advertised in the women's press although the women's press frequently features them in editorials. And to take this a step further, a good deal of product publicity would never be published in the journals which carry advertising for these products whereas the press releases are accepted and published in numerous journals which would never appear on the advertising schedule. This interesting paradox has been remarked upon in an earlier chapter, and it may be that a special value may be given to press cuttings of this nature because the press relations aspect of a marketing operation is able to spread communication to a wider audience.

The most realistic method of recording results from editorials is by counting (a) the number of enquiries received and (b) the conversion rate of enquiries into sales or contracts. Controlled circulation and some other journals which run reader service systems greatly assist the recording of results because they receive and pass on enquiries. A single item in a publication such as *Building Equipment News* or the *Architect's Journal* will produce around 400 enquiries. Whether or not the reader enquiry system stimulates frivolous enquiries is open to speculation, but this depends very largely on the way in which readers are invited to take advantage of the reader service. If a list is published of those offering literature or samples, and readers may tick the items which interest them, they may tend to go on a spree and their enquiries will be of doubtful value, although on the other hand readers interested in a particular kind of product might not write for information on all of them unless they were listed. The more selective reader service which uses reply cards is likely to be preferable to the list. It is hard to be categorical about reader services because those who apply for literature are already sufficiently interested to read the journal in the first place, and so the manufacturer may be pleased to get further information into the hands of these pre-selected applicants.

There is yet another side to this subject of recording results which is worth examination, and that is to ask if, in a total marketing operation, it is feasible to attempt to measure the effectiveness of *a single isolated facet*?

By this is meant that while the whole may be as strong as its weakest link—or is it?—when a product, a service or even an idea is launched by any organisation from a government department to a manufacturer a variety of things contribute to its success or failure. PR will be but *one* segment of a complete campaign which begins with the original concept and ends with the satisfying of complaints, provision of after-sales service or even the acceptance of praise and testimonials. To extract an element of this complex programme, and subject it to test, is to ignore the accumulative effects of all the other associated elements upon its success or failure. Consequently, a fair test is really possible only when PR techniques are conducted in isolation, and that could be an unusual circumstance.

This argument may be doubted on the grounds that the scientist will analyse the parts of any whole, and test each in turn. But is it so easy in a marketing operation to test every element, the brand name, packaging, sales force, distribution, point-of-sale material, trade advertising, consumer advertising and PR *individually*? Some of these elements can be tested for comparison within their own medium, e.g. the pulling power of individual newspapers can be tested, but it is less easy to compare the pulling power of posters versus direct mail because even within the sphere of advertising they are not doing identical jobs for one is reminding and the other is stimulating immediate action.

For example, before Rentokil took advice from Ernest Dichter and stopped their practice of illustrating their advertisements with pictures of rodents and insects, the PR effort was somewhat nullified by advertisements which made readers hurriedly turn the page! It is all very well having a magnificent PR campaign but it is hardly fair to fault PR if it has to contend with the damaging effects of unfortunate advertising, old-fashioned looking packs, inadequate representation, uncompetitive trade terms, or poor servicing facilities. For example, a PR consultant mounted a very fine PR campaign for a client who made domestic appliances only to find that there was such a muddle over handling orders and making deliveries that the trade was becoming reluctant to stock the product. The product happened to be the best of its kind on the market and was deserving of all the credit the PR consultant could muster for it. This was a case of two-way PR communication, whereby the consultant was able to give very frank advice to his client, but it is very difficult to measure results in such circumstances.

Again, the apparent failure of a PR programme could be derived from the original policy or product, not how the policy or product was communicated. This means that the PR man must have some responsibility for the policy or product if he is to be held responsible for its communication. That is why he needs to rank high in any organisation.

Tempting though it may seem to conclude that the recording of PR results, or even of press relations results alone, is unsatisfactory the opposite view can be tendered that it is far more sensible to plan a total operation, using PR as one of many essential tactics, and to judge the success or failure of the entire scheme rather than of its parts. Analysis may otherwise be imperfect, or rather misleading. What is so important is that PR should be recognised and used at all, not that we should argue about its effectiveness. We cannot do without PR because relations with the public already exist, and press relations must be an integral part of conscious and responsible relations with an organisation's publics. The true problem is that so many people try to ignore PR, and consequently try to avoid any systematic application of PR techniques. Therefore, the test could be made of a year's marketing operation without PR support and then of a year with PR support, and the sales figures could be compared. But it would not be an accurate test because the two separate years could never be the same in every other respect. Nevertheless, it could indicate something, and actual differences in the two years, such as trading conditions, could be allowed for in the calculations.

Can we quote any examples which show that PR has paid off? We did so in Chapter 4 when it was pointed out that new products and services had been launched wholly by PR methods. We say, too, in that chapter how demand can be tested by introducing a new product editorially. It is not difficult to count enquiries or evaluate conversions and they provide a more tangible measurement of success than column inches.

It is possible from the author's own knowledge to quote the example of an electronic component manufacturer who, apart from a catalogue and some direct mail, had never advertised but was making very profitable use of product publicity undertaken by a PR consultant. His products were technically newsworthy, and they produced through the technical press a volume of enquiries out of all proportion to his PR costs which were less than £1,500 a year, fee, materials and expenses included. On one occasion an enthusiastic advertisement manager confronted the company's sales manager with the remarkable number of reader enquiries resulting from a product story published in his journal, using these enquiries as evidence of the pulling power of the journal as an advertising medium. What the advertisement manager could not understand was that the results undoubtedly proved the value of PR but hardly encouraged the sales manager to spend a far larger sum on advertising to obtain perhaps no better than a similar result! In such cases the results of PR are extremely easy to record.

Results can be shown in many ways as when a certain consumer durable company complained that its goods were ignored by the monthlies and weeklies devoted to home interests. They claimed that they manufactured goods superior to many others, and that they were well recommended by authoritative bodies. When a PR consultant undertook the task of setting up a press information centre for this company he found to his dismay that the press were hostile to his client because journalists had never been able to obtain information from the company. Letters from editors were left unanswered, telephone messages were never passed on and generally there was a complete unwillingness on the part of the company to indulge in any kind of communication with the press. Despite this absolute breakdown in press relations the company could not understand why their goods were never mentioned in the press! Once the PR consultant got to work, and established a communication system between himself and the press on behalf of the client, the press cuttings began to pour in for they were very good products which the press did want to know about. The company found itself and its products written up as freely as its rivals.

Now, at the point in time when this example ends (because it is current at the time of writing) the company's trading figures had not been announced, but certain other results were very apparent. Company directors were delighted that their products were at last recognised by the press; dealer-relations were also improved; local press relations in the vicinity of factories were much better; and the press coverage had given the company's field sales force a psychological stimulus. Such results can be seen but they are not capable of immediate monetary evaluation, although in the long run they must contribute to a company's overall success. The modern mathematically minded marketing expert may not be content with such a woolly evaluation: he will cry: "*But show me what I am getting for my money! How does £3,000 spent on PR compare with the appointment of an extra field salesman? Or a series of trade press ads? Or this or that?*"

Isn't this where the skill and judgement of managment comes in, rather like a military commander disposing of his forces? By the time the decision is made, and the expenditure is agreed, the die is cast and the choice must be right or wrong. Some actions will be good, others bad, but taken by and large the venture will succeed or fail and a stalemate is unlikely. There is, therefore, a very strong argument *against* trying to prove the results of PR on the grounds that it reveals the lack of knowledge that management has in PR, leading to doubts about its value. In other words, PR is put in the dock when management is the culprit! After all, management is confident enough to expend money on those aspects of business with which it is familiar. It is a lack of faith in a little understood management function which leads to demands for proof. Presumably there was a time when merchants doubted whether any results were likely to accrue from sending a trading ship to unknown places across the sea!

The important thing is to use PR in the best possible way because, on the basis of expert knowledge or advice, it is *believed* to be the right and proper technique to use. Sometimes it seems to be a very negative form of management to indulge in uncertain tactics and seek to check their effectiveness *afterwards*. A doctor carries out his diagnosis *before* treatment: he does not wait for an autopsy to find out how he should have treated the patient.

This suggests then that the most practical research of value in PR is that—like readership surveys and copy pre-testing in advertising—which helps us to plan successfully, not holds an inquest on results. In advertising it is possible to use some form of research to test almost everything from the product itself to the actual impact of advertising and its effect on retail sales. In PR we are less fortunate, although the research facilities are bound to improve as the demand develops and the finance is made available. PR is still thirty years behind advertising in many respects.

One of the most practical forms of research available to us is opinion or attitude research which can reveal the shift from one standpoint to another during a test period when there has been planned PR activity to overcome a problem defined by original research. There is one hazard here which does not exist in advertising and that is that PR activities are less precise in their performance. An advertisement will appear tomorrow, for sure, but a press story may appear at any time at the editor's discretion over a matter of months. A PR campaign is therefore spread over a much longer and more indefinite period, while PR is also and inevitably more slowly effective than advertising since it has to work more rationally and less emotionally than advertising.

Let us take an example. A long-established national youth organisation is faced with dwindling membership, reduced funds, fading support from adult leaders, and lack of sympathy from parents, teachers, clergy and other essential supporters. A PR consultant is engaged to help solve this problem. What is he to do? An enterprising PR campaign could be mounted, and despite the widespread coverage won by demonstrations, exhibitions, displays, TV interviews, links with famous people who were willing to admit boyhood membership and so on a final check on results—say, on the total number of new recruits—might well be disappointing, and no wonder. It is, after all, a marketing problem using PR techniques, and to try to sell the same old product to a disillusioned and apathetic market is suicidal if not downright criminal.

The first step before spending a penny on PR would be to undertake a field survey (and a quota rather than the more expensive random survey would be quite satisfactory) among the relevant groups or publics whose opinions mattered. The findings could then be studied, and while they may tell us a few things we had guessed or assumed anyway the tendencies revealed would indicate the necessary PR action. We might learn that boys imagine the movement to be old-fashioned, too much concerned with woodcraft and patriotism, too wedded to imperialism, whereas the need is for an organisation more liberal in its internationalism, more nearly adult in its activities, more concerned with the physical sciences than natural history.

Parents may take a similar view but (together with teachers) be worried about the youth movement being a distraction in these days of one examination after another, while some parents may complain of lack of time to give voluntary support to the movement, perhaps because so many of them are involved in do-it-yourself attentions to their homes.

Many, many findings of this sort will be presented for interpretation, consideration, understanding and only when radical solutions have been resolved and a new policy has been agreed will the PR consultant have anything concrete on which to base a sincere and workable PR programme. Given such material as a new name, uniform, objectives, activities, meeting places, leadership structure and a more sympathetic phasing in of the movement's role with that of modern living, the PR consultant (or he could be a full-time PRO, of course) can set about "changing the image". Now this can be a slow job, and it would be wise to adopt a three-year plan of carefully phased change and PR activity.

So, we have had our initial survey. We have a three-stage programme. And we shall need opinion surveys as progress checks at the end of each year, making four surveys in all. It is unlikely that such a joint research and PR undertaking could cost less than between £50,000 and £65,000 over the full period. But this is the sort of money which has to be spent to achieve a campaign planned on the basis of research and checked by regular surveys.

Now let us list the available methods of recording results:

Summary of Methods

1. *Opinion research* surveys in the field to test shift of opinion since the commencement of a PR programme.

2. *Postal questionnaires* (where the public(s) are known by name) to define shift of opinion since PR work began.

3. *Dealer Interviews* to check the effect of PR activity on their attitude to the supplier, or the attitude of consumers to the product or the manufacturer.

4. *Desk research*, checking official statistics, to see what changes have occurred as a likely result of PR activity, e.g. have more dog licences been taken out; do more people protect their food by refrigeration; how many homes now have television sets; how many more people took their holidays in Ireland? Sometimes desk research can provide answers from existing published material, official or independent, which may make expensive field surveys unnecessary.

5. *Quiz competitions* inviting answers which reveal the state of competitor's knowledge about the organisation. This is rather like an intelligence test, has weaknesses of lack of control but has the merit of making what is virtually a questionnaire seem attractive to answer. It must, of course, be limited to single entries to avoid useless permutations.

6. *Press cuttings*. These can be analysed to supply the following specific information:

(a) Number of inches obtained about the organisation.

(b) Names of publications which covered the story—revealing those interested and those who should be approached more directly because they have printed nothing.

(c) Coverage secured by competitors—or indicating their press relations activity.

(d) Activities of competitors in various promotional, financial, production and staff recruitment ways.

(e) Evaluation of improvement of editorial knowledge, understanding and accuracy as a result of press relations work.

(f) Extent to which pictures have been published,

and various other details peculiar to the subject matter, such as whether the timing of despatch of material was right, which section of the journal accepted the story and so on.

7. *Monitored scripts*. By working with a radio and TV monitoring service it is possible to obtain scripts of broadcast and telecast material which can be very important when a controversial topic is being discussed and it is necessary to know what was said as well as the amount of time devoted to it. The BBC and the External Services of the BBC are very co-operative in supplying scripts of broadcasts which have been made.

8. *Readership, viewership*. It is possible to calculate the number of people likely to have bought, read, heard or seen the medium which presented the story, this on the basis of statistics published by media owners, and by media research organisations.

But at the present time there is no research available to show, for instance, whether a documentary film is better value than a house magazine, and even if there were it could be a little specious because in both cases distribution lies in the hands of the sponsor, and it is his efficiency rather than the medium itself which needs to be tested. We have to be careful not to undertake research for the sake of research; we also have to know how to learn from what research tells us. As an example of this, the sales director of an engineering company insisted on producing a house journal for clients which looked like a colossal broadsheet mailing shot from a big publishing house. Moreover, it was printed on heavyweight paper so that it was not only unwieldy but bulky. One reason for the size was to present large pictures, but the effect was to produce a piece of garish advertising material which lacked all the intimacy and character of a journal. A questionnaire was sent to recipients, but so few were returned that it was decided to abandon the journal. The company did not, however, accept the uncomplimentary result of this survey which was that no-one was interested in the journal in that particular form but might have appreciated a journal produced more professionally and journalistically. This may have been a case of a person wanting to do something his way, and not being prepared to do it any other way.

In conclusion it may be that PR research is a much more simple affair than is marketing and advertising research where the problem is more complex. In this field a whole chain of things can be tested: discovering buying preferences, which technique or theme should be applied, how to buy the most economical and effective of a wide choice of competitive media, and what effect this has on the market. In PR we are largely concerned with creating and maintaining understanding and goodwill. Unless people know and like they will not respond favourably to the persuasion of salesmen and advertisers. It is practicable to test the degree of shift in people's attitudes, and it is practicable to measure the coverage obtained in different communication media. The final result of all this can only be seen in the annual results of the organisation. But it may be essential to begin with research to understand what has to be done by the PR practitioner, and that includes the press officer, in the first place.

Appendix 1: The Institute of Public Relations Code of Professional Conduct

This code defines and implements paragraph 3 (A) (ii) of the Memorandum of The Institute of Public Relations under the heading "Objects", namely "to encourage and foster the observance of high professional standards by its members and to establish and prescribe such standards". Public relations is concerned with the effect of conduct on reputation. The following principles have been laid down to embody this concept and enhance relations between the Institute's members and the public to whom they are directly or indirectly responsible in the performance of their duties

1 A member shall conduct his professional activities with respect for the public interest.
2 A member shall at all times deal fairly and honestly with his client or employers, past and present, with his fellow members and with the general public.
3 A member shall not intentionally disseminate false or misleading information, and shall use proper care to avoid doing so. He has a positive duty to maintain truth, accuracy and good taste.
4 A member shall not engage in any practice which tends to corrupt the integrity of channels of public communication.
5 A member shall not create or make use of any organisation purporting to serve some announced cause but actually promoting a special or private interest of a member or his client or his employer which is not apparent.
6 A member shall safeguard the confidences of both present and former clients or employers. He shall not disclose except upon the order of a court of competent jurisdiction any confidential information which he may have obtained in his official capacity without securing and making known the consent of the said client or employer.
7 A member shall not represent conflicting or competing interests without the express consent of those concerned given after full disclosure of the facts.
8 A member in performing services for a client or employer shall not accept fees, commissions or any other valuable consideration in connection with those services from any one other than his client or employer unless such practice is acceptable to the client or employer.

9 A member shall not cause or allow to be done anything for the purpose of touting or advertising calculated to attract business unfairly.

10 A member shall not propose to a prospective client or employer that his fee or other compensation be contingent on the achievement of certain results; nor shall he enter into any fee agreement to the same effect.

11 A member shall not intentionally injure the professional reputation or practice of another member, but if such a member has evidence that another member has been guilty of unethical, illegal or unfair practices it shall be his duty to inform the Institute in accordance with the Memorandum and Articles.

12 A member shall not engage in or be connected with any occupation or business which, in the opinion of the Council, is not consistent with membership of the Institute.

13 A member shall not seek to supplant another member with his employer or client, nor shall he encroach upon the professional employment of another member unless both parties are assured that there is no conflict of interest involved, and are kept advised of the negotiations.

14 A member shall co-operate with fellow members in upholding and enforcing this Code.

This Code is enforceable on all members of the Institute in accordance with the Constitution adopted at the Special General Meeting held on November 29th 1963

Appendix 2: A Short Bibliography

Practical Public Relations (2nd Edition) by Sam Black (Pitman)
Public Relations in Business Management by James Derriman (University of London Press)
The Handbook of Public Relations edited by Nigel Ellis and Pat Bowman (Harrap)
Teach Yourself Public Relations by Herbert Lloyd (English University Press)
Public Relations in World Marketing by Frank Jefkins (Crosby Lockwood)
Industrial Editing by Bernard Smith (Pitman)
House Journals by John Hazzlewood (Vista Books)
The Newspaper Press Directory (Benn Brothers Ltd)
World's Press News Directory of Newspaper and Magazine Personnel and Data (World's Press News)
Advertiser's Annual (Business Publications Ltd)
Willing's Press Guide (James Willing)

Index

Academia Cultura, Caracas, 84
Acrow Engineers, 196
Acuna, Captain J. A., 73
Addressing plates, 19–20
Adeney and Associates, Norman, 76
Advance Electronics Ltd., 79–80, 167
Advertiser's Annual, 20, 187
Advertiser's Weekly, 136
Advertising, 1, 13, 25, 30, 160–3, 201, 203, 210, 216, 224, 229
Advertising Association, The, 144
Advice & Action Ltd, 70, 72
Aerojet General Corporation, 75
Aircraft, charter, 126, 128
Air Ministry, 55, 60
Alexander, N. H., 184, 185, 192
Alitalia, 74
Anglo Celtic Watch Company, 183
Archers, The, 106
Architect and Building News, 33
Architect's Journal, 228
Argentine Navy, 17
Ascot, 16
Associated Container Transportation Ltd., 62
Associated Press, 54
ATV, 107
Attitude research, 232
Audit Bureau of Circulations, 227
Australian Broadcasting Commission, 191
Avdel Ltd., 82–3

Babcock & Wilcox (Materials Handling) Ltd., 62
Bailey, Adrian, 75
Banda duplicator, 92
Bank of England, 66
Bass, Trevor, 196
Bateman, Peter, 41
Beatles, The, 150
Benson Films, Martin, 191
Bernays, Edward, 210
Birmingham Sketch, 103
Black, Sam, 157
Blanch Development Co., Ltd., Alvan, 72
Bloomfield, Peter, 181, 182, 193
Blue Funnel, 177
Board, W. B., 60
Board of Trade, 20, 137, 164, 181, 182, 183, 188, 191, 192, 193
Board of Trade Journal, 181, 182, 193
Bond, James, 81, 177
Boots the Chemist, 34
Boston Teapot Trophy, 73
Bristol Aerojet Ltd., 75
Bristol Aeroplane Company, 75
British Association of Industrial Editors, 131
BBC, 34, 92, 96, 106, 191, 234
BBC External Services, 11, 188, 234
BBC TV, 106, 149
British Industrial and Scientific Film Association, 217
BOAC, 47, 56, 59, 60, 61, 72–3, 74–5, 77, 78
BP films, 104
British Rate and Data, 19, 136
British Weeks, 164
Brooke Bond & Co., Ltd., 73
Brown, George, 205
Buckingham Palace, 149, 153
Building Equipment News, 228

Café Royal, 173
Canadian Broadcasting Corporation, 191
Calor gas, 214
Captions, 91–4, 177, 178–80
Carlyle, 142
Catering, 123, 126, 127
Central heating, 80–1, 112, 159–60
Central Office of Information, 11, 20, 103–5 137, 138, 182, 183, 184, 186, 188–92 205
Chamber of Commerce journals, 159
Chelsea FC, 66
Cheltenham, Mayor of, 167
Chemist and Druggist, 102
Chemical Products, 102
Chemical Trade Journal, 102
Chemical Worker, 102
Chichester, Sir Francis, 110

Church of England, 153
Citrine, Sir Walter, 59
Clark, Sir Fife, 182
Coach transport, 127–8
Coates cider 76, 77
Code of Professional Conduct, IPR, 7, 135, 147, 219–20, Appendix 1
Colville, Commander Sir Richard, 12
Common Market, 182, 209
Communication, 103
Concrete Formwork Ltd., 80
Conservative Party, 138
Contacts, 146
Cooper, H. S., 68
Co-operative movement, 203
Copyright, 88
Copywriting and its Presentation, 225
Cortina, Ford, 148
Costs, 29, 122, 129, 165, 217, 219–35
Council of Industrial Design, 36
Country Life, 101
Courtaulds, 185
Cow gum, 92
Cox, Brian, 217
Crane, 68
Crane Ltd., 80–1
Crawfie, 16
Creed, 221

Daily Dispatch, 201
Daily Express, 148, 195, 196, 202, 225
Daily Herald, 98, 203
Daily Mail, 66, 171, 196, 202
Daily Mirror, 202, 204, 227
Daily Telegraph, 196, 201, 202, 225
Daily Telegraph Information Bureau, 114
Dalek, 167
Davall Teaching Machines Ltd., 84
Davis, William, 196
Deakin, A., 60
Decca Radar Ltd., 75, 78
d'Erlanger, Sir Gerard, 73
de Havilland Comet, 4, 61, 73
de Manio, Jack, 105
Department of Education and Science, 138
Derriman, James, 221
de Vigier, William, 196
Dichter, Ernest, 211, 229
Docherty, Tommy, 66
Do-It-Yourself, 100
Do-It-Yourself Exhibition, 173
Dunlop Dracones Consortium, 69–70, 77

Earl's Court, 69, 73, 76, 116, 164, 167, 172
Eastern Airlines, 2
Easton, P. R., 197
Electrical Development Association division of Electricity Council, 112, 127
Elliot, Cass, 66
Ellis, Frederick, 195
Elvaco central heating, 112
Elvin, René, 157
Engineering consent, 210
Engineering and Marine Exhibition, London International, 69, 73
Engineering in Britain Information Services, 184
Epple-Buxbaum, 72
Evans, Sir Harold, 153
Evans, Peter, 152
Evening News, London, 31, 146–7, 149, 171, 196, 213, 215
Events, organising of press, 109–33
Everybody's, 201
Everywoman, 201
Exhibition Press Officer, Room, 169, 171–80
Exhibitions, 164–80
Exhibitions Bulletin, 114, 164
Exhibitors, 164–71
Export Services Exhibition, 2nd., 72, 178
Export Services Exhibition, 3rd., 174–8, 180

Facility visits, 109, 112–13, 125–33
Farnborough Air Show, 104, 170
Feather, V, 59
Feature articles, 154–63
Fiat, 182
Field, The, 101
Films at press receptions, 111
Financial PR, 195–6
Financial Times, 33, 114, 152, 196–8, 202, 227
Financial Times Index, 45
Flies, 159
Football Association, 66
Ford Motor Company Ltd., 59, 148
Formula, Seven-point, 57, 64–5
Front organisations, 135
Furnishing Review, 152–3

Gallup Poll, 225
Gamages, 32
Gardeners' Question Time, 106
General Post Office, 185
Gestetner duplicator, 49
Gifts and mementoes, 123
Gigi, 64
Gillman, Freddie, 56, 61
Gipsy Moth IV, 110
Giuseppina, 104
Gladstone, 213
Glossies, 101
Godwin Ltd., H. J., 72
Good Taste, 201

Gospels, The, 137
Government and Business Training School, Washington, 84
Granada, 106
Guardian, The, 196, 202
Guernsey Life, 103
Guernsey Tomato Marketing Board, 106
Greater London Council, 138–9

Hangers Paints Ltd., 71, 77
Harrison, H. N., 60
Healy Plan, 208
Heath, Edward, 167
Herstmonceux Castle, 190
Hess, Alan, 157
Highways Engineer, 35
Hodgkinson Partners Ltd., 176
Hospitals, 161
Hospital, The, 161
Hospital Engineer, 161
House and Garden, 100
House Beautiful, 100
House Journals, 187
Hovermarine, Ltd., 71, 77
Hutton, Bill, 183
Hydrographer's Department, 190

Ideal Home, 100, 201
Ideal Home Exhibition, 112, 171
Ilford Manual of Photography, 59
Illustrated, 101, 201
Illustrated Bristol News, 103
Illustrated County Magazines Group, 101, 103
Illustrated London News, 101
Image, 2, 210–14, 233
Imperial Chemical Industries Ltd., 70–1
Imperial Metal Industries Ltd., 71
Indesit, 182
Independent Television News, 106
Industrial Film Correspondents Group, 217
Information services, 134–41
Industrial Marketing Association, 54
Institute of Communication, 208
IPA National Readership Survey, 227
Institute of Public Relations, 7, 8, 56, 91, 135, 147, 181, 193, 208, 214, 219–20
Instruments Electronic Automation Exhibition, 76, 178
International Distillers and Vintners, 59
International Packaging Exhibition, 76, 178
IPC, 201
International Watch and Jewellery Trade Fair, 167, 173
Intruders, The, 104
Invitation cards, letters, 117–21, 130
Invitation list, 116–17

James (Industrial) Group, John, 72
Jane cartoon, 204
Jesus College, Oxford, 220
John Bull, 101, 201
Joint Ventures Schemes, 164, 191

Kelvin Hughes, 170
Kenrick and Jefferson Ltd., 81, 83
Kent and Sussex Courier, 99
Kent Messenger, 99, 103
Keyser, John, 197
Kidd Ltd., Archie, 72
Klein, Rudolf, 138
KLM, 74
Kynoch International Print, 70, 77

Laing John, 104
Lancashire Life, 103
Lancer Boss Group, 63
Lawson Ltd., Edgar, 80
Lee, Ivy, 4
Leedex Ltd., 106
Lewis's, 32
Libertad ARA, 73
Lister and Company, R.A., 63
Local Government Act, 1948, 139
London Fire Brigade, 63
London International Engineering and Marine Exhibition, 69, 73, 178
London Press Exchange Public Relations Ltd., 177
Look and Learn, 102
Look at Life, 96, 104
Louvre windows, 159

Machinery Lloyd, 186
Mack-Brooks Exhibitions Ltd., 174
Macmillan, Harold, 153
Madden, Admiral Sir Charles, 73
Magazines, 100–1
Mailing lists, 19–20, 116–17, 135, 186
Malbert, David, 196, 215
Mamas and Papas, 66
Marketing, 24–5, 32–6, 208, 214–18
Marlene, Lili, 137
Mass-Observation, 138, 225
McGregor, Gow and Holland, 177
McShane and Co., 223
Mementoes, 123
Merryweather and Sons Ltd., 63
Metal Sections Ltd., 63
Metropole, Hotel, 62
Midland Bank, 217
Mi-Dox Ltd., 170
Millichap, Captain R. E., 73
Mini-Minor, 210
Ministry of Information, 137

Ministry of Health, 138
Ministry of Public Building and Works, 70
Ministry of Transport, 138
Modern Woman, 201
Money Matters, 106
Montague, John, 59
Motivation Research, 211
Motor Show, The, 148, 165, 172
Muggeridge, Malcolm, 212
Municipal Engineer, 35
Municipal Journal, 35
Municipal Review, 35
Municipal Year Book, 35

NALGO, 139
NALGO *Directory* 139
Name badges, 121
National Opinion Polls, 225
National Research and Development Corporation, 70
National Rose Society, 61
New Holland Machine Company, 72
News agencies, 47, 54, 151, 186
News Chronicle, 201, 202
News of Industry Ltd., 74
News of the World, 201
Newspapers, 97–8, 201–2
News sense, 10
New Zealand Broadcasting Corporation, 191
Newton, Sir Gordon, 196
Noble, Mary, 64
North Eastern Gas Board, 71

O'Brien, Sir Leslie, 66
Observer, The, 66, 138, 202
Odhams Press, 101
Olympia, 116, 164, 170, 174
Opinion Research, 214, 233
Overseas correspondents, 186
Owen, Geoffrey, 196–8

Packaging Exhibition, International, 76, 178
Pakex '67, 75
Parliament, Houses of, 100
Passing Show, The, 201
Pathe, 104
P & O, 93–4, 179
People, The, 201
Persuasion, 210–12
Photographs, colour, 95, 177
Photographs, quality, 90–1
Photographs, size, 90
Picture Post, 101, 201
Piëst, Hank, 72
Piggott, Lester, 150
Plastics and Rubber Weekly, 39, 54, 85–6
Port of London Authority, 116
Ports and Terminals, 62
Ports and Terminals Exhibition, 1967, 178
Post Office preferred size, 51
Potter and Moore, 64
Practical Householder, 100
Press Association, 47, 54
Press Conference, 109–25
Press Council, 214
Press cuttings, 219, 226–7, 234
Press kits, packs, 121–3, 131, 165, 174, 177, 178–80
Press reception, 109–25
Product publicity, 142–53, 222
Prince Philip, H.R.H., 12
Problem analysis, 214
Propaganda, 137, 214
Public libraries, 140
PRADS, 23
Public Relations in Business Management, 221
Public Relations in World Marketing, 221
PR/Planner, 136
PR/Systems, 23
Puffery, 26, 142–3
Pulman's Weekly News, 99
Punch, 101, 201

Queen, H.M. The, 12, 16

Radio Brighton, 106
Radio Merseyside, 106
Radio Times, 106
Rail transport, 128
Rank Organisation, The, 104, 191
Ransley, Peter, 39, 54, 85–6
Regent Street Polytechnic, 59
Rentokil Fiji Ltd., 72
Rentokil Laboratories Ltd., 70, 72, 77, 103, 104, 149, 184, 185, 218, 224, 229
Rentokil Review, 103
Reproduction fees, 88
Resort PR, 134, 139–40, 142–3
Results from PR, 219–20
Reuters, 47, 186
Revere, Paul, 73
Rigg, J, 59
Rival World, The, 104
Robens, Lord, 150
Rockware Glass Ltd., 75
Roderick Public Relations, Peter, 63, 64, 197
Rolls-Royce, 210
Roneo duplicator, 49
Rouge Baiser lipstick, 64
Royal Pavilion, Brighton, 116
Royal Show, The, 170
RoSPA, 103

Sail Training Association, 73, 78
St. Katherine, 116
Scarecrow Strip, 149, 184
Schoolboys and Schoolgirls Exhibition, 172
Scientific Public Relations Ltd., 83, 167
Scotland Yard, 153
Scotsman, The, 196, 202
Scottish Industries Exhibition, 167
Scottish Public Services, 35
Sergeant, Patrick, 196
SASCO charts, 73, 78
Self-Adhesive Systems Co., Ltd., 74, 78
Selfridges, 32
Sellotape, 93, 177
Shakespeare, 226
Shell films, 116
Ship's Gear Exhibition, 170
Ships Inertial Navigation System, 147
Showerings Vine Products and Whiteways, 59
Simenon, 226
Slides, 35 mm colour, 95, 160
Smallpiece, Basil, 73
Smithells, Roger, 19, 135
Smiths Industries Ltd., 79, 105, 167, 183, 190
Sortrac III, 74, 78
South Africa, 214
South African Government, 213
Sphere, 103
Standard-Triumph, 218
Star, The, 201
Stockey and Schmitz, 72
Stonehenge, 70
Stoney, Captain T. B., 73
Storey, Joan, 19, 31, 135
Storry Smithson Group, 71
Stuart Associates, Denzil, 63, 71
Sun, 98, 202, 203
Sunday Chronicle, 201
Sunday Citizen, 201, 203
Sunday Empire News, 201
Sunday Times, 196, 202
Swaffer Award, Hannen, 196

Tallon Ltd., 59
Tatler and Bystander, 101, 103
Tessler, Gloria, 217
Thain, Professor, 220
Thomson, Lord, 202
Time of Change, 104
Timing, 132–3
Today, 105
Tokyo Rose, 137
Tradabroad Ltd., 72, 77
Translations, 191–2
Trans-Mediterranean Airways, 176
Treasure, 102
Tube Investments, 63
Twiggy, 150

United Dairies Ltd., 75
Universal News Services, 47, 153, 186

Valiant, 147
Venues, choice of, 114–16
Visnews, 103, 191

Walden, M.P., Brian, 213–14
Waldorf, 114
Warrington Guardian Series, 99
Watch and Jewellery Trade Fair, International, 167, 173
Web-offset, 95
Welding Construction Ltd., 74–5
West Sussex Gazette, 99
Whitbread and Co., 196
Whitbread, Colonel William, 196
Whitethorn Press, 103
Why Not Ask Uncle Willy? 217
Willings Press Guide, 20, 187
Wilson, Harold, 161, 204, 205, 213
Woman, 100, 201
Woman's Day, 201
Woman's Hour, 106
Woman's Illustrated, 201
Woman's Journal, 100
Woman's Mirror, 201
Woman's Own, 16, 100, 201
Woman's Realm, 100, 201
Woman's Weekly, 100, 201
Woodcock, George, 174, 175, 176, 177
Woolwich Equitable Building Society, 184
World's Press News, 135, 217
World's Press News Directory of Newspaper and Magazine Personnel and Data, 3, 20, 104, 135, 186

Yorkshire Conservative Newspaper Co., Ltd., 204
Yorkshire Evening News, 204
Yorkshire Evening Post, 204
Yorkshire Life, 103
Yorkshire Post, 204

Zeltex Ltd., 79